Blessed Are
the Peacemakers

Blessed Are
the Peacemakers

Small Histories during
World War II, Letter Writing,
and Family History Methodology

Suzanne Kesler Rumsey

THE UNIVERSITY OF ALABAMA PRESS
Tuscaloosa

The University of Alabama Press
Tuscaloosa, Alabama 35487-0380
uapress.ua.edu

Inquiries about reproducing material from this work should be
addressed to the University of Alabama Press.

Typeface: Adobe Garamond

Cover images: Photograph and postcard from the family
of Ben and Miriam Kesler; courtesy of the author
Cover design: Lori Lynch

Cataloging-in-Publication data is available from the Library of Congress.
ISBN: 978-0-8173-2090-4
E-ISBN: 978-0-8173-9348-9

To the Tribe of Benjamin: brothers, sisters, uncles, aunts, grandkids, great-grandkids, great-great-grandkids, first cousins, second cousins, and I think we're approaching third cousins. This is for all of us.

Contents

Figures

Acknowledgments

FIRST OFF, I THANK GOD AND MY SAVIOR, JESUS CHRIST. YOU GIVE MY life purpose. I pray that this book, my career, and my daily actions are a testimony of Your goodness, faithfulness, and redemptive power.

Thank you, Grandpa and Grandma, Ben and Miriam, for being who you were, for loving and living and being faithful to our Lord and to each other. Grandpa, I still have the stuffed bumblebee you gave me for my fourth birthday and the glass-front bookcase you made. Grandma, I have that china set you kept in the back of one of your cabinets, the crochet blanket, and the memories of you driving me every Wednesday to children's church and youth group. I am who I am because of you both. Sure, I am your offspring (thanks to Miriam's dad, Great-Grandpa Kenneth, for the red hair and blue eyes—my branch of our family tree looks like we are adopted), and I crack the same bad puns and jokes at sometimes-inappropriate times. But more significantly, out of your loving, Godly example, my own life, career, marriage, and faith journey have been framed. I hope that this book honors you and your story. I have been changed by it, and maybe others will be too. I love you both, and I cannot wait to see you again very soon!

Thank you, Mom and Dad. I honestly don't feel like I can put into words how amazing you both are. You raised me to be honest, hardworking, joyful, generous, silly, and faithful, and to persevere. You have supported me without hesitation through academic challenges and a career that makes little sense sometimes. You have walked some hard roads with me and Dave. Every time we are together, it is a party, even if it is another hospital visit. Dad, thanks for continually giving me tours of the refrigerator, for doing the dishes, and for snowflakes. Mom, thanks for folding my laundry, cooking with me, yapping with me, knowing what I am thinking just by looking at me, and having the strength to quickly look away before we both snort-laugh. You both are my first thought when I think of Godly, Spirit-filled people, and I want to be just like you when I grow up.

Dave, you are my best friend and love of my life. You are super awesome. I remember Grandma Miriam looking at my engagement ring almost twenty years ago, patting my hand, and saying, "That's a real sparkler." You are my sparkler, even when you leave your socks in the living room, wear sandals in December out in public, or grow your beard into lumberjack territory. You drove me to archives in the middle of nowhere. You made copies of documents while I dug through archival files. You laughed with me and at me. You forced me to take breaks, and sometimes, you encouraged me to keep pushing. I would not be me without you, and there certainly would not be a book without you.

And finally, thank you to the numerous colleagues and friends who invested time and energy into this project. Meghann Bassett, thank you for transcribing the lion's share of the letters, for editing, and for investing your time and energy into this project. Your friendship, support, and prayer were vital to me and this project. Hannah Wendel, great-granddaughter of Ben and Miriam, my first cousin once removed, and my BFF—thank you for transcribing letters and listening to me talk about the book and just being you. Dr. Sarah Sandman and Dr. Kate White—you read and encouraged and commiserated and applauded me through this whole mess. I puffy heart you both. Shari Benyouski, I could not have done this without you. Thank you for your generosity and friendship; you read every word of this text and helped me push it to the finish line. Dr. Stevens Amidon and Dr. Bill Hart-Davidson, thank you for good conversations and being certain before I was that this project was worth pursuing. Thank you to the anonymous book reviewer. And thank you to Dr. Wendy Sharer, the previously anonymous reviewer of the book (and my latest promotion case). You invested a lot of time and energy into my work and my career, and the weird world of academics is a better place because you are in it.

Introduction

IN THE SUMMER OF 2013, AT THE AGE OF EIGHTY-EIGHT, MY PATERNAL grandmother, Miriam, passed away. After the funeral I was given a lumpy cardboard box filled with letters, papers, odds and ends, and a fair amount of dust and grime. I was excited about the contents of the letters, and my immediate family and I read through a few on the top layer. I assumed that there were some love letters in the box, which would be fun and funny to read. I also assumed that there was a lot of junk in the box, given that my grandmother tended toward the Depression-era habit of saving absolutely everything. I then closed the box, put it on a shelf in my hall closet so that the cats could not get into it, and promptly forgot about it in the press of the academic cycle. As happens over and over in such stories, personal archives get stored and forgotten in attics and hall closets for indeterminate amounts of time.

Thankfully, I remembered the letters only a year later. In the fall of 2014, I sat down with that lumpy cardboard box and began to gently unpack its contents in layers. First was a pile of letters loose on the top. Next, a packet of letters tied with string, a stationery box filled mostly with dust, some buttons and lace, tiny journals with one or two entries, and birthday cards. The next layer was . . . letters and more letters, hundreds of them. Some were tied in bundles, some not. I selected two or three to see what was inside. Each one was three to six pages of handwritten text, both front and back of the paper carefully filled. There were letters from Miriam to my grandfather Ben. There were letters from Ben to Miriam. And there were letters from people I did not know. Some came from my hometown, Goshen, in northern Indiana. Others came from Pennsylvania, Ohio, and, oddly, Rhode Island. Why on earth were there letters from Rhode Island? I wondered. Why were there so many letters? Was this before they were married?

I was terribly confused, given my knowledge of my grandparents. My grandfather passed away quite suddenly when I was four years old. He was only sixty-one. I have only vague brushes of memory of his smiling, bearded face with the handlebar mustache. I remember only hazy recollections of the large white farmhouse out on County Road 42 with the shuffleboard court, swings, Concord grape arbor, and swinging rope hanging off the front porch. I remember

Grandpa Benji, as he was known to us grandkids, holding me on his lap and giving me a stuffed bumble bee. I remember an elaborate Easter egg hunt when I needed help reaching an egg balanced high on a door jamb. He was crafty and enjoyed woodcraft, so my home and the homes of my family members are filled with pieces of furniture, knickknacks, clocks, and other items he crafted. I knew he was a kind man, a jovial man who was given to jokes and laughter. I knew he was musical and enjoyed learning. But that was the extent of what I knew about him or his life.

My knowledge of my grandmother was much more solidified. I was still very young when Miriam remarried a man named Art and moved to New Mexico. They moved back to my hometown when I was in late elementary school. I was about eleven. My knowledge of my grandmother was limited to the woman who had been widowed and remarried, to the person she was in her second marriage to Art. She was kind and teased and joked. But I always felt that there was a deep sadness about her, a subtle bitterness, for lack of a better word, that seemed incongruous with a life filled with family, food, and faith. She was a tiny woman who seemed to get shorter as she aged. She loved to cook and feed people. She sent each of us—every one of her seven kids, their spouses, the gaggle of us grandkids, and likely extended family members and friends as well—a card for every single holiday—Valentines, St. Patrick's Day, Easter, Independence Day, Halloween, Thanksgiving, Christmas, and our birthdays. I even got an occasional one for Memorial Day, Labor Day, Sweetest Day, New Year's, or the first day of school. And each card was carefully marked on the back with the date, should any of us inherit her predilection for saving everything. She loved to crochet, knit, and craft. I spent time at their home playing and crafting. I knew them as the grandparents with the motorhome that I stayed in when we went to church camp in the summer. I remember playing tiddlywinks with her. I remember her telling me stories of when my dad was a kid. But I do not remember her saying much about Grandpa Benji. Oh, there were stories every now and again, but, thinking back, I learned very little about him from my parents and even less from my grandmother.

So, in 2014, as I began to read the hundreds of letters my grandparents had exchanged, I was shocked to discover what their lives were like in the early 1940s and in the midst of World War II. These letters, like one might expect of war-era letters, were filled with love and longing, anguish at being apart, uncertainty and anxiety about the war and the country's future, as well as attempts at humor to keep their spirits up. The most unusual thing about this collection, and unlike most WWII-era letters, was that my grandfather Ben was not in Europe or in the Asian Pacific region fighting the Good Fight. Instead, Ben, a member of the Dunkard Brethren Church (an "old order" sect of Brethren), was a conscientious objector (CO) to the war. The Brethren Church was one of three recognized "historic peace churches," along with Mennonites and the Religious Society of Friends (Quakers). As an active member of one of the historic peace churches, Ben had long renounced any participation in the military, and so he and approximately twelve thousand other men opted to join Civilian Public Service (CPS). Through CPS they performed "work of national importance" at 218 CPS camps across the country. Instead of going to war, or even opting to perform noncombative military service, CPSers served their country by working on a variety of agricultural, forestry, medical, and conservation programs throughout the United States.[1] Ben's first assignment sent him to a work camp in Pennsylvania, where he planted greenery on the newly opened turnpike. Later, he took a transfer to be a ward attendant at a mental hospital in Rhode Island so Miriam could join him.

While my grandfather was drafted and served his country—unpaid and without medical or life insurance—by doing what the government called "work of national importance," my grandmother Miriam stayed home and worked as a day laborer, as a live-in maid, as a farmhand, and in the family butcher shop in order to earn enough money to support them both. At the young age of just seventeen, she handled the sale of their home and all their financial interests. She later joined Ben in Rhode Island to work as a mental hospital ward attendant and in the kitchens. Because of the faith she and Ben shared and their adherence to a principle called "nonresistance," she was unwilling and unable to work in any of the well-paying jobs supporting the military-industrial complex.

Nonresistance is not, as the term implies, compliance or the opposite of resistance. Certainly, Ben and Miriam practiced a type of resistance as academics have come to understand it; they saw war as wrong and quietly and firmly resisted the draft to war and the societal expectations of supporting the war effort. But they would never have seen their actions as *resistant*. Instead, nonresistance might better be understood as "nonresistant pacifism." People of many faiths and creeds practice pacifism, or opposition to war and all forms of violence. It is the belief that all disputes should be settled peacefully. But pacifism is actually an "active" stance; it is not uncommon for a pacifist to actively, and with varying degrees of enthusiasm, stand against or push back against the cultural imperatives of war and violence. Nonresistance, or nonresistant pacifism, takes pacifism a step further by removing that action. If the war was a river, a pacifist would build a dam to try and stop it. A nonresistant person would settle in like a rock and let the river flow over the top of them. Nonresistance interprets and embodies Jesus's call to love your enemies, do good to those who hate you, to bless those who curse you, and to turn the other cheek.[2]

The idea for this book became a reality after I read more of their letters and learned more about CPS and nonresistance as a whole. I realized that Ben and Miriam had a unique story; it was all so terribly *interesting*, you see, and *romantic* to find this dusty box of letters. But interest and romance are not necessarily the foundations of solid academic inquiry. Who would want to read four hundred letters between two nameless, very much not famous people and their extraordinarily ordinary lives? Sinor defines ordinary writing "as a text that is not literary, is not noticed, and one that should have been discarded but that instead somehow remains."[3] Love letters are both within this definition and without it, and she notes that the "ordinary disappears as soon as we approach it."[4] Would writing Ben and Miriam's story for others to read destroy some inherent value it had held in secret? What could something so personal as this archive offer to someone outside my own family? Since I am not the sort of writer who could turn such letters into a novel or beautifully crafted piece of creative nonfiction, I debated how I could position these letters in a larger context to make them readable to outsiders. Would academics see value in something so personal that even family members might not take the time to read the hundreds of pages of text? *I* could see their value, but how could I help *others* see their value as well?

The answer to these questions came in three parts. First, rhetoric and writing studies have taken an "archival turn" in the last decade. Charles Morris writes that "the disciplinary relationship with the archive has deepened recently, and as such one impetus . . . is to engage in reflection on some of the important topoi related to archival research on rhetorical history, particularly questions of method and their relation to scholarly production and professional success"[5] Further, scholars such as David Gold and Jessica Enoch point out that the discipline of rhetoric and writing continues to revise notions of historiography by seeking to offer points of view other than those of the dominant academic traditions.

Within this archival turn, it occurred to me that in the face of large-scale histories of wars, political movements, and public figures what can sometimes be lost are the "small-h" histories, stories of individuals, no-name people from all walks of life who lived, breathed, loved, and died during significant political and historical moments. Consider the breadth and depth of the "large-H" histories surrounding World War II. Innumerable books have been written and are yet to be written about this time period. Public stories of armies and countries, of presidents, of soldiers, of men, and of women certainly exist, and more are being written through the thoughtful, archival research of historians, journalists, and fiction and nonfiction writers. In contrast to these public, or made-public, large-H histories, are countless small-h histories, personal stories, and archival collections of a grandfather or great-aunt or neighbor who experienced the war. In basements, attics, and hall closets all over the world are small stories that have literally not seen the light of day or another's eyes in decades. These private histories rarely make it beyond one interested family member's perusal.

That "family genealogist" will regale often less-than-interested listeners at family reunions, but beyond that, the stories go largely untold. I believe there is great value in these small histories, in the low, the humble stories of people from the middle of nowhere, Indiana. Sinor notes that when the "garbage" of ordinary writing is "taken back for reconsideration," we can recognize that "the dumpster is as compelling a place for the investigation of cultural work as is the art museum."[6]

But how does one portray a small-h history in a way that makes it relevant and readable to a broader audience? The archival turn in rhetoric and composition is reflected in broader public discourse. Today "finding one's roots" has popularized genealogical research through the website ancestry.com and DNA lineage testing services like 23andMe and AncestryDNA. How have we as academics responded to this public discourse? Minimally. Sometimes sneeringly. Genealogy is academic history's red-headed, second cousin once removed. The assumption is that it is performed by bespectacled Googling hobbyists or retirees with no training in the discipline, no understanding of context, data triangulation, verifiability, methodology, or peer review. How could something unearthed by amateur, "armchair" historians be of any use to academics?

The reality is that the lives and literacies of ordinary people *matter*. Your story *matters*. Ben and Miriam's story *matters*. Small histories matter because they allow us a glimpse of the impact large historical moments have on individual people. Paying attention to small histories enables scholars of rhetoric and writing to engage with historical research in a more self-aware and reflective way. The impact of war on an entire nation is made up of its impact on each individual person. We can know, cognitively and historically, that the war caused food shortages, but that history is made real when we hold seventy-five-year-old ration books with some of the coupons torn out or when we read of Ben lamenting another "Howard special" of institutional cafeteria food at a mental hospital in Rhode Island. Without these small histories, their contexts and reflective moments, what good are the larger histories? Without the context of the individual, can we really understand historical significance?

Second, in response to the popularity of finding one's roots, and as an extension of my ongoing research interest in family and intergenerational literacies, I have crafted a methodology I call "family history writing" (FHW) over the past decade. Just as small-h histories *matter*, the research practices of amateurs and everyday people *matter*. In previous work I have defined FHW as a particular form of life writing, which is, as Catherine Hobbs puts it, "a general term for writing about lives in various disciplines and modes."[7] It is the complex mix of researched materials and stories that distinguish family history writing from both genealogy and history writing. In essence, FHW looks at the very fabric of a family's life through storytelling. "If one thinks of family history writing as a complex weaving of research threads, its purposes and the story it tells are made clearer. The warp represents those 'factual' or 'official' research pieces, such as census records, birth certificates, or obituaries. The weft is represented by family lore, oral stories handed down, interview data from elders, and personal memories."[8]

Interestingly, an archive of love letters as extensive as Ben and Miriam's represents factual or official warp threads as they are primary documents, yet the contents of those letters might also be considered weft threads of family lore. In order to contextualize the personal contents of the letters, I offer historical context from other primary sources found in archives and secondary sources of published work. The combination of these threads produces a rich and textured story that is greater than the sum of its parts. FHW stands as a bridge between academic history and small-h histories. It positions personal narratives as central to historiography, rather than tangential, and understands uses of reading and writing in context. Wendy Sharer notes that "what gets preserved in archival repositories is often that which is already deemed significant. The materials hidden under the beds and in the attics . . . might not seem appropriate for these collections. Yet these records—products contained within the lived experiences of our friends and family—are valid, and potentially enormously influential, sources for historical and archival scholarship."[9]

FHW pushes at methodological boundaries as it challenges the emic and etic perspective of the researcher within and without the larger narrative, the verification and triangulation of data, and understandings of reciprocity between the researcher and participants. When studying family history, the positionality of the researcher is simultaneously emic and etic—both insider and outsider. As a researcher, I am distanced from my subject matter in order to analyze it, but I am also very much a part of the research as a member of the family. When research participants have passed away, but the researcher is still a member of the larger family created by those participants, FHW challenges our understanding of how research does (or, we assume, ought to) function.

In addition to not just allowing but expecting and assuming fluidity between research positions, FHW methodology is fluid in how it understands data triangulation and the verification of "facts." The available information, those disparate strands of data, are woven together to make a perfectly imperfect whole. What one is able to find about the family in public records may be precious little, or maybe an estrangement from what the wider family tells, making the retelling of family stories a complicated consideration. One cannot always verify the truth about a family story, but that does not make the story worthless. Rather, what gets told, and, more significantly, *what remains silent* in FHW impacts not just our academic discipline but our families and ourselves.

The third answer to the questions I posed earlier came in examining letter writing itself, a less-studied genre of writing. Examining the letters themselves as artifacts means the text can be situated within *ars dictaminis*, the art of letter writing, stemming from medieval rhetoric traditions and then again in nineteenth-century America. By situating the style and content of Ben and Miriam's letters within this tradition, we are afforded new insights into the genre of letter writing through the concepts of *conduit* through which two people communicate and *platform* upon which a relationship might be built. Developing and theorizing *conduit* and *platform* enables us to see that Ben and Miriam's letters served as a way of "giving meaning to events, rather than a simple record of what happened, [and] we can eavesdrop on a dialogue that lies at the heart of our fragmentary and evolving cultural history."[10]

For Ben and Miriam letter writing was much more than words on a page, more than an example of ars dictaminis. Montgomerie notes that while "big picture" histories of whole conflicts, military strategy, and the fates of entire nations are vital, "the everydayness of war and the intimacy of individual lives can get lost in histories written on a grand scale."[11] Ordinary writing like letters "becomes a highly productive site for investigating how both writing and culture get made *every day*."[12] Even a history of CPS, a little-known "experiment in tolerance," is in many ways a "big picture" perspective. *Blessed Are the Peacemakers* follows the footsteps of Montgomerie in that it "places letter writing, one of the day-to-day routines of war, in the foreground, to highlight the challenges of maintaining family intimacy. . . . It also makes the uncertainties of war its starting point."[13]

Barton and Hall write that the "most revealing way of investigating letter writing is to view it as a social practice, examining the texts, the participants, the activities and the artefacts in their social contexts."[14] Because war and working in CPS are experienced in "profoundly personal ways[,] . . . a letter-based view of war reveals a more equivocal collection of stories about separation, personal challenges (some inconsequential, some profound), hope, sorrow, and (for the lucky) reunion."[15] *Blessed Are the Peacemakers* offers the sometimes inconsequential and sometimes profound experiences, fears, hopes, and challenges of Ben and Miriam's life as expressed in their letters. "Centering the study on letters isolates and highlights the 'letterly-ness' or 'epistolarity' of wartime correspondence, including its physical forms and social conventions."[16]

So the book ahead of you retells Ben and Miriam's story through their eyes and the letters they wrote. As I tell their story, I develop these three salient themes: the value of small histories, the methodology of FHW, and the study of conduit and platform within letter writing. I believe in the inherent value of small histories, personal narratives, and the ordinary life writing of ordinary people. I believe, also, that such small histories are worth sharing with others and that they can have significant impact as authentic research. When we pay attention to the low, the humble, the quiet, we see a very different side of history, and we pay attention differently to historical writing.

CHAPTER 1

Conduit and Platform

I'll see you Tomorrow nite thru my letters and in my Dreams.

BEN, NOVEMBER 13, 1942

*Write as often as you can spare the time I live for your letters . . . about our love.
. . . But isn't that such a poor Substitute?*

BEN, NOVEMBER 14, 1942

Every one is another Token of Love. I'm keeping every one.

BEN, NOVEMBER 17, 1942

*Please write & tell me every thing as I am always so anxious to hear every little
thing that happens to you. And your letters are about all the pleasure I have in this
world since you are so far away.*

MIRIAM, DECEMBER 2, 1942

BEN AND MIRIAM'S SMALL HISTORY, TOLD THROUGH THEIR LETTERS, IS the heart of this book. The daily practice of writing letters and of receiving letters was the foundation of their relationship from the very beginning, and it blossomed into a lifeline—a bracing, essential support system—that sustained them through the months of separation and the difficult terrain of being conscientious objectors (COs) in a world at war. To understand and learn from their story, and to get to know them as real people who lived and loved and experienced the world around them, a place to start is in understanding the letters themselves. I note in the introduction a quote from Barton and Hall's *Letter Writing as Social Practice* that "the most revealing way of investigating letter writing is to view it as a social practice, examining the texts, the participants, the activities and the artefacts in their social contexts." They go on to say that "the aim is to understand more about the phenomenon of letter writing and, more broadly, about the role of literate activity in society."[1] The following chapter examines the characteristics of Ben and Miriam's letters in order to understand their social contexts, their social practices, and how this particular literate activity functioned in their daily lives. Aside from what the contents of the letters reveal about their lived experiences, we can learn a lot about who they were as people through an investigation of the mode of letter

---

Transcriptions of all letters are true to the original spellings, strikethroughs, postscripts, and additions as much as possible. If Ben or Miriam added text within a sentence, I used ^ and wrote the inserted text in superscript.

writing itself. That is, if we look at the way they wrote, that is, the repetitive characteristics of their letters and the "dailiness" of their writing,[2] how they appeared on the page, and other conventions we can also look at the ways literacy shaped their relationship. From such an analysis we can also immerse ourselves more deeply in Ben and Miriam's small history.

The study of letter writing as a genre is simply not as prolific as the study of other written genres such as the book, poetry, the novel, and, more recently, digital texts. In spite of the fact that letter writing is a ubiquitous mode of written communication in business, law, medicine, education, and the home lives of people, we do not often pay attention to the activity of letter writing. Letter writing is a chore, a necessity, a pragmatic and sensible *task*. Our knowledge of letters and letter writing tends to be tacit; we do it without a lot of thinking, but much more takes place when we write or read correspondence. Bazerman notes that "interpreting even the most ordinary junk mail solicitation for a credit card requires an understanding among other things of the postal system, folded paper envelopes, advertising and direct mailing, promised inducements, the modern bank and credit card system, modern application forms, store credit card transactions, monthly statements, internal record-keeping, check payments, and competition among various credit providers."[3] Our knowledge of the conventions of letters, tacit though it may be, enables us to "navigate the complex worlds of written communication and symbolic activity, because in recognizing a text type we recognize many things about the institutional and social setting, the activities being proposed, the roles available to writer and reader, the motives, ideas, ideology, and expected content of the document, and where this all might fit in our life."[4]

Historically, letters are one of the earliest forms of writing. "Examining the earliest cuneiform writing on clay tablets in Mesopotania [*sic*] reveals that although the very first writing which remains was administrative records, by two thousand years BC personal family letters were common, as was official diplomatic correspondence."[5] Bazerman notes that "in the ancient Near East (White 1982) and Greece, early written commands along with other military, administrative, or political business of the state were cast in the form of letters."[6] He notes, too, that "the richness and multiplicity of ancient letter writing practices made letters a powerful communicative force within the early Christian church. Almost all of the books of the New Testament outside the Gospels are in the form of letters, originally between specific parties or small groups and then made available for all who share in the community of the messages."[7]

It was not until medieval times that letter writing became a more formalized rhetorical practice. The medieval description of writing letters, *ars dictaminis*, has been defined as "a rare example of applied rhetoric in the history of discourse."[8] Western rhetoric concerned itself with the rules of composing letters and other prose documents. Originating in the late eleventh century because of declining literacy, it essentially created a formula or a homogenous "standardized statement capable of being depicted in various circumstances."[9] Ars dictaminis "operated within rigid parameters and was taught through equally rigid modeling."[10] The rigid rules of letter writing in ars dictaminis were useful and practical rhetoric. Letters "performed" and "brought into existence the reality of property ownership, legal boundaries, trade, and treaties. Seeing combined with speaking so that seeing became believing."[11] Letters carried the ethos of the writer and, with an increasing focus on etiquette, demonstrated to the viewer/reader behaviors that carried social and political value.

In 1135 an anonymous treatise *Rationes dictandi* (Principles of letter writing) conveyed that "there are, in fact, five parts of a letter: The Salutation, the Securing of Good-will, the Narration, the Petition, and the Conclusion."[12] The salutation was "an expression of greeting conveying a friendly sentiment not inconsistent with the social rank of the persons involved."[13] The securing of good will "is a certain fit ordering of words effectively influencing the mind of the recipient."[14] The narration is "the orderly account of the matter under discussion."[15] The petition is when writers "endeavor to call for something."[16] And the conclusion "of course, is the passage with which a letter is terminated."[17]

This formula for a letter remains today, centuries later. Formal letters begin with "Dear So-and-so" and end with "Sincerely yours." The contents follow a "how are you" to a "here's why I'm writing" to a "could you please" pattern. Lucille Schultz writes, "Visible in the earliest part of the century were a few model letters for children in all-purpose letter-writers; at the same time, a few full-length letter-writers prepared exclusively for children also appeared. In a number of composition textbooks, letter-writing appeared as a topic for instruction by the third decade of the century, and by the end of the century, letter-writing instruction was a predictable part of the composition textbooks used in the schools."[18] Thus, while other rhetorical forms (which were studied at the university level in the United States from the colonial period) have altered, evolved, and changed over time, letter writing became a model that was taught in the schools and has remained largely unchanged, even in the face of advancements in technologies. Evidence of this unchanging format is easily seen in emails, which are a merging of formats for internal correspondence memorandums and external correspondence letters but are largely indistinguishable in form and content from written letters. Their visual structure is set in place, prescribed by visual boxes; one only has to fill in the blanks: to, from, regarding, date, and so on. We write the body of our emails, or at least we probably ought to, beginning with a salutation and ending with a polite closing. And for those of us who teach writing, many of us are encouraged to include instruction on appropriate email etiquette in our composition classrooms because email, like the formulaic and unchanging letter, has become such a ubiquitous part of the education and business world. Letter writing, and pedagogy of letter writing, has not changed in centuries.

So it comes as no surprise that Ben and Miriam's letters generally fit the basic, centuries-old model of letter writing. Their salutation was informal, with only the occasional usage of a more formal "Dear Wife," usually said in jest. More typically Ben said "Sweetheart" or "My little darling," and Miriam said most often "Hi Honey!" and occasionally said things like "My precious darling" or "Dearest hubby." They would ask how the other was doing, then narrate the events of the day. They would ask questions of the other's daily life, ask after friends or relatives, or ask for updates on situations or finances. And they would conclude with elaborate expressions of love and commitment, often including small drawings of hearts, Xs and Os, drawings of lips or a circled spot that said, "our kiss."

But Ben and Miriam's letters offer us more than just representations of the traditional ars dictaminis formula, or rather, their particular formula demonstrates a capacity of letter writing that a study of ars dictaminis would not necessarily reveal. Their letters are both a *conduit* through which two people communicate and a *platform* upon which their relationship was built. They offer both the intangible conveyed *through* a letter and the tangible *foundation* that the materiality of letters affords. In a study of war-era love letters, Montgomerie notes that "letters were a conduit for the exchange of information, and a way of keeping relationships going during periods of extended separation. . . . Writing and receiving letters help them through some hard days. Letters became important symbols, tokens of remembrance and hope."[19] The transmission of a message across distance is an ancient practice. But love letters transmit more than a message. They embody love, affection, support, and hope—intangible reality conveyed in the tangible, tactile letter.

In discussing ars dictaminis, Fleckenstein notes that spectacle or display was important in the civic engagement of thirteenth-century Europe. "The success of a rhetorical performance [of a letter] was linked to the effectiveness of the rhetor's material appearance, including his delivery, for that outer appearance and those external actions served as a 'mirror' to the rhetor's inner virtue."[20] While Ben and Miriam did not generally read or perform their letters aloud, at least to my knowledge seventy-five years later, the contents of the letter, the conduit pattern of expressing emotions and hope, *mirror* one another. It was as if they, by repetitively stating their love for one another and laboring to say it in just the right way, could be assured of that love returning. They put into the letters what they saw of themselves, and that message reflected on the receiver as well.

Montgomerie says, "Certainly letters had their limits. It was hard to find the right words to express the mixed feelings created by separation and new experiences. The tedium of Army life was perhaps as difficult to convey as its novelty. It was hard, too, to write about the normality of civilian life without causing offense."[21] Similarly, it was challenging for Ben to find ways of making the tedious work of digging holes for bushes interesting when conveyed to Miriam every day for months, and Miriam found it difficult to tell of the realities of her underpaid manual labor as well as the goings-on in a hometown that was drastically different from the home they had created before he left. Finding the right words to convey love, sending love *through* the letter was of paramount importance to both Ben and Miriam. This can best be seen in the patterns they followed for closing letters.

Ben's conclusions typically were filled with descriptions of how much he loved Miriam, how much he missed her, how much he longed for them to be together, how he was sexually faithful to her. Only ten days into their time apart, Ben ended his letter with what serves as a good example of how he closed his letters throughout the months ahead:

November 14, 1942

Darling my arms ache for you, and my heart is hungry for your love. Honey It's so hard to Keep on top sometimes, But I try to keep doing something so I don't have time to get home sick But I'm oh so lonely when I go to an empty bed Darling it's then I miss you most. And when the lights are all out I crawl down under the covers and there I can talk to you and no one hears and no one can see me when I break and have to let a few tears wet my Pillow. I've loved my Pillow a few times but since I've held you in my arms The Pillow is such a Poor Substitute I better quit talking like this or I'll be crying out loud. Oh Honey I love you from the Bottom of my heart clear to the top and want you and only <u>you</u> Oh! so much. Goodnite now darling and I'll be in Bed by 10:00 o'clock. . . .

Well Nity Nite Sweetheart

As Ever and always,
Your Sweet "Hubby"
Ben

Write as often as you can spare the time I live for your letters. The one I got today you wrote Thurs. and Darling it was sure a swell one. I love for you to tell me about "our" love. And in that way we can share it thru our letters. But isn't that such a poor Substitute.

Nite Darling
Ben

I can't hardly stop. But I'll write again tomorrow. Bye Darling for now.

xoxoxo

xoxoxo

I LOVE <u>YOU</u>

There is a winding down of his time with her and a slowing of the passage through the conduit. He did not want to stop writing, to stop the sending of his love to her, to halt the conduit, but he must to make it to bed on time and to get the letter actually in the mail and sent to her. His letters at the end formed a triangle, an arrow almost, pointing toward home. He visually and verbally lingered over them, drawing out the experience. In other letters he added multiple postscripts, doodles of hearts and lips in the margins, decoratively written words of affection and any last-minute thoughts. Like a later twentieth-century love affair over the phone, it is as if he was saying "no you hang up first" or a twenty-first century attempt to be the last text of the night.

Miriam's letters are not as visually indicative of the conduit, but they still demonstrate the same principles. In general, Ben's letters are more systematic in their pattern than Miriam's. Miriam, instead, wrote in clusters or thematically, so her closing often began midway through a letter and then finished at the end. In the following example most of her conclusion is at the end of the letter:

November 17, 1942

Honey I can't seem to think of anything but you & me and how much we love one an other and want each other. Oh honey. I want you so much my heart aches and my arms seem so empty. I'm trying to be brave but it's so hard to be; cause I love you so much. Honey never forget that I love you and always will no matter what. Oh how I miss you darling Well darling I must close and go to bed. I'm so—tired. And then I'll dream about you and me and ^then we'll be together even though we aren't when I wake up; so darling take care of your self and ^please don't take any more risks than you have to honey. I'll try and not worry about you & you'll have to promise to do the same. God will take care of us. Oh honey I love you, love you, love you and I miss you so much it is almost unbearable to get along without you near. Honey remember me in your prayers and I'm doing the best I can.

So night honey and I'll be with you again to-morrow night. Your Mimmie & little sweetheart

I love you darling & oh how I miss the peace and quiet of our own home.

Like Ben's letters, there was an outpouring of emotion in the conclusion. But visually the ending of Miriam's letter was blunted. Often Miriam wrote in the dark hours of midnight, after working herself to exhaustion during the day as she tried to financially support them both. Her life was not ordered with military precision, and there was always plenty of work left to do. She did not suffer from boredom the same way Ben did at camp. So, her letters wound down but ended quickly as she either fell asleep over them or rushed to get them into the mailbox and moved on with the myriad tasks of the day. Additionally, because she often included such sentiments throughout the body of a letter, the ending was more utilitarian, as if she had simply turned off the faucet to stop the conduit flow.

And when they each received a letter from the other, it was like a drink of cool water in the desert. At the receiving end of the conduit, it is as if they pulled in the emotions sent by the other. They absorbed the love, the affection, the connection to what was most important. I can imagine them first reading quickly to absorb the love sent over the miles, then rereading more slowly to capture every detail of the letter. They wanted to see the emotion they sent through the conduit mirrored from the other; they read and reread the letter, often kept on their person the entire time, until the next arrived. And when they did not receive a letter, the letdown was tremendous. For example, on November 20, Miriam wrote,

> I was so pleased and relieved when I got home from work and found your dear letter waiting for me. . . . I know just how you felt when you didn't get any letter from me cause I feel the same way when I don't get any from you. And when I have only gone on working because I think I'll hear from you & then there isn't anything it just makes me feel all empty and lost. I write every evening although I am tired and have only gotten to bed 2 or 3 times (since you left) before twelve. It about gets me down to work from 8 to 8 and not get too much sleep but darling I can't talk to you so I must do the next best thing.

Thus, the conduit is an explanation of the emotion sent *through* letters. Letters were, essentially, a vehicle or a means by which they could transport the intangible. As Miriam put it, "*I can't talk to you so I must do the next best thing.*" As a conduit, their letters functioned as an "open ended transactional space."[22]

In addition to functioning as a conduit through which they might share their love, Ben and Miriam's letters functioned as a platform upon which they built their relationship. At first it might seem that conduit and platform are similar. The distinction comes in that conduit refers to the intangible expression *through* the letters, whereas platform refers to the physical, tangible *materiality of* the letters. By describing their surroundings, the physical layout of the room they were in at the time—Ben's bunkhouse or Miriam's parents' kitchen—they created a pattern, beginning that immaterial representation of the material space that was just for them. Early on, Ben established the practice of writing about his day's work at the end of it, usually in the dining hall or the rec room. He was often surrounded by other men following the same practice. Miriam, in contrast, wrote whenever she had a moment, often working on the letter at different points and places throughout the day.

The further importance of platform is that when holding a letter, Ben held a thing that Miriam had held just a few days ago or Miriam held a letter onto which

Ben had pressed a kiss in the corner, just for her. The "thinginess" of a letter gave reality and physicality to an emotional existence that may have seemed transient without being able to see or touch one another regularly. As such, this physicality was more than symbolic and more than just the paper the words were written on. Ben and Miriam engaged in practices that developed and enhanced the materiality of the letters by creating a sense of place and space, by sending news clippings or cartoons, pictures, string or yarn or fabric swatches, or even the Thanksgiving wishbone. John Shlereth's take on material culture suggests "a strong interrelation between physical objects and human behavior. Despite its cumbersomeness, the phrase continually presses the researcher to consider the complex interactions that take place between creators and their culture. In other words, the assumption is that there is always a culture behind the material. Moreover, the name has one other asset: it simultaneously refers to both the subject of the study, material, and to its principal purpose, the understanding of culture."[23]

To establish a sense of place or space, they each began their letters by greeting the other as if they simply sat at the kitchen table after working all day or as if one had knocked and the other opened the door. For example, Miriam's letter on December 7, 1942, began:

> Hi! Honey! And I can just hear you say Lo! Honey and then come in the door and encircle me with your arms and give me such a sweet kiss and then we'd tease one another a little bit and then go & eat supper.

Ben included phrases like:

> It's just me knocking. May I come in?
>
> I'm back again this eve. and well talk a little while together.
>
> I'll bet you can't guess who's here: right, It's me again, glad? I'm glad you are.

Miriam wrote things like:

> Come, let's sit on the davenport together. I wish that we could. I'd give you such a thorough loving you'd never forget!
>
> Here's your little pest again! Mad? No! Well I'm glad.
>
> Here I am again for our evening chat. How I wish you were here on the davenport beside me. I'll bet we wouldn't talk—much! ha.
>
> Here I come! To bother you again. Do you mind? I know you're delighted and I'm glad.

By referencing physical things like the kitchen table or the sitting room davenport, Ben and Miriam invoked a sense of sitting down together to talk. By inviting each other into the shared space, they effectively shut out the outside world, closing the door on everything but the other person. Letter writing was almost a sacred space that they shared and that reinforced their relationship by both referring to the space and by developing physical representations of that shared space. In essence, the letters provided a physical platform to replace the much-preferred physical connection to one another, and Ben and Miriam developed that platform as they developed their relationship.

From the very beginning, Ben especially included descriptions of what he ate. For example, on November 8, 1942, he wrote, "We had a swell dinner again. Boiled Beef, Noodles, Potatoes, Gravy, Vegetable soup, celery, Bread & Butter Then for Desert we had peaches and cake." But more than that, he sent letters that included artifacts or items from his camp life. These material elements of his new life contributed to the sense of place and space he and Miriam were developing. Not only did they write about their nesting process, he showed her elements of the actual composition of his new nest. In a letter dated November 8, 1942, Ben included a smudged paper napkin from dinner. He wrote on it "Sideling Hill Camp Wells Tannery Pa.," and at the bottom, "we have these napkins every meal." Artifacts ranged from copies of the camps newsletter, programs from special church or music programs, photos, and even a chicken wishbone saved from his Thanksgiving dinner (which, I admit, was a rather gruesome discovery when sorting through the letter archive the first time).

While they invoked a private space and place in their letters, relationships do not develop in a vacuum. Thus, an aspect of Miriam's letters that reinforced the creation of place and space was that her letters often included notes from each of the family members to Ben, references to the entire family sitting down to write him, and descriptions of the general silliness exhibited by the family as they collectively wrote. Beginning in her first letter, Miriam noted that little Charles, her youngest brother who was only about three at the time, was trying to write a letter to Ben. "Charles is writing 'Benny' a letter & he scribbled awhile & then you should have seen him he has to dot an I (i) about every so often with a great big punch." Later she wrote, "Charles has written you a letter. He took great 'pains' in writing so when you answer why say something to him about it. We don't know what he said but your guess is as good as mine. Well honey I must sign off for tonight." So young that he does not fully understand print literacy, even Charles "wrote a letter" to Ben and dotted his i's. While this is pretty standard literacy development practice, it is noteworthy that Charles took on the genre of letter writing to Ben so early. He mirrored the writing that his parents and older siblings did. A few days later, Miriam wrote, "Charles has just got some notebook paper is gonna write 'Ben' a letter. He has a great big yellow pencil in his chubby little hand and is patiently toiling to write you a letter. With his tongue between his teeth and his chin resting on the table."

It is typical for Miriam's letters to describe the family and what was going on around her as she wrote, though just as often she finished her letters at midnight in bed. In a letter only dated as November 1942, Miriam's mother Maureen wrote,

> Charles has been playing doctor rubbing on water for the hurt. Now he is singing Deep in the heart of Texas. Dail is reading a library book (The Call of the Wild) Barbara has been working Arithmetic and Verda is reading a story book. Granny and Ethel are just sitting and commenting once in a while.

Such descriptions of the goings-on in the Carpenter household at the kitchen table helped Ben to imagine himself there as well. While living with her family just after Ben left for service, they were such an embedded part of life that in some letters Miriam's family members just picked up a pen or pencil and wrote notes in the middle of Miriam's letters if she left them sitting out while writing them.

Miriam's father, Kenneth, is the only family member who rarely wrote to Ben. Instead, he contributed cartoons and other things he found. Miriam wrote, "The pictures that are with this is daddy's weekly contribution. If he finds something he thinks would tickle you he cuts it out and I send it in the next issue of the 'Kesler Times!' He cut those out of last night's paper before he had even finished reading it." They included cartoons, newspaper clippings, programs from church, hymns, and other literacy artifacts from their daily lives, again creating a sense of place and space. "Kesler Times" was their version of a newsletter, which is a break of the letter-writing genre and a slight shift over to the newspaper/newsletter genre. Certainly, letters contained news of events at home, but to call them "times" meant they saw the nature of letter writing to be more fluid than textbooks would dictate.

While family is part of the platform, the focal point was Ben and Miriam's personal relationship. Miriam's family continually teased her that she did not read her entire letters to them. Understandably, Ben and Miriam shared very personal information within the letters, things that Miriam did not want to share with her family. Early on, Grany [sic] wrote a note that Miriam included in one of her letters. At the end she wrote, "Here's hoping we will hear from you tomorrow [even] if Miriam don't read it all to us. Ha. Heaps of Love—Grany." A few days later, Miriam wrote, "Dad said the other day. Why don't he (you) write a letter that you can read all of it to us? You see I just read the parts I want to. Some of the words are too precious for others to read or hear. They mean so much to me. And I read & reread your 'swell' letters and I am so glad that I know you mean every word you say."

But the platform of their letters is not a perfect system for developing a relationship, as anyone in a long-distance relationship can confirm. Additionally, the platform, physical letters included a dependence upon the postal system for delivery. As Montgomerie notes, "how important it was to maintain an imaginative and physical connection with absent loved ones, even when there was no realistic expectation that a letter would get through."[24] One of the challenges of their relationship was that they were constrained and reliant upon the postal service. Similar to those in military service, "waiting for mail was an emotional roller coaster, the highs and lows even more torturous when shared. Sometimes there would be mail for one . . . and not the other."[25]

Though they wrote each other every single day, they often would not get any letters for many days in between. The first instance of this occurred very early in Ben's time in service. Only a few days after Ben left, Miriam wrote,

> I have wondered about you all day. What you were doing? Where you doing it and who you were with? My curiosity is nearly getting the better of me. You see I haven't heard a scratch from you except the card. Was awful glad to know that you got that far safely. And I'll be expecting big fat letters from you in the near future.

She was worried that she had not heard from him except a postcard sent while he was on the road to Pennsylvania. Here is the first instance where they were subject to the postal system for their correspondence and, more importantly, their relationship and connection to one another. Miriam wrote later in November, "The letters I got to-day were the ones you wrote last Sat. and Sun. Don't you think it takes a long time to get mail back and forth. I do."

In wartime correspondence between family members, they often numbered the letters because of the unpredictability of the postal service. A wife might number hers in the upper corner of each letter so that her husband could put them in order more easily when he received them, and he would know whether he was missing one,[26] which is an interesting additional marker for the letters to stay in sequence. For Ben and Miriam, usually a date sufficed. However, Miriam had a habit of only putting the day of the week at the top, so now with the dates on the postal stamp faded, sometimes it was a little bit difficult to put things in order. I think, too, about how numbers at the top of a letter would also show a level of faithfulness by the letter writer to the soldier and vice versa. A soldier would know, even if he had not heard news in some time, that letters were being sent just not reaching him if he were to receive letter number five and then letter number eleven.

Another factor of platform and the materiality of letters is that once Miriam found work as a hired girl in Goshen, there were two Mrs. Benjamin Keslers in the same town. Miriam instructed Ben about how to address letters to her when she started work for the Holdermans. "You can address my mail c/o . . . Holderman . . . Be sure & put the Jr. on the end or I might not get it." They both knew that should his letters accidentally go to his mother (Mrs. Benjamin Kesler Sr.) she would open them and read them and maybe not even give them to Miriam for some length of time.

So letters served as a conduit through which Ben and Miriam transmitted their love over the miles. They functioned as a means of sending the intangible. They also served as a platform upon which they built their relationship by recreating the physicality of their relationship. The effort they put into maintaining their relationship through their letters was successful, and yet, that effort was larger than may be evident from the excerpts above. Miriam and Ben wrote very long letters to one another, which is a bit of an understatement. Miriam referred to them as "books" frequently. At one point in November 1942, she wrote that she "then cleaned out my stationary box (the one you gave me a long time ago) and sorted my writing paper. It's mostly envelopes as there was 1 envelope for each sheet of paper & think how many letters I have sent and how many pages of writing all in one envelope so that paper and envelopes aren't coming out even." Stationery sets came with equal numbers of pages and envelopes, as if each letter should be only one page. Her letters were far longer.

If the level of their commitment to remain connected were to be measured by the length of their letters, certainly it is evident how much they cared for one another. In the five months of correspondence while Ben was at Sideling Hill Camp, they wrote more than 245,000 words to one another. In total, during the twenty months represented in the letter collection, throughout the four years while they served in CPS, they wrote more than 380,000 words. In trying to wrap my head around just how lengthy the letters were, I looked up the length of famous novels as comparison. *Gone with the Wind* by Margaret Mitchell is 418,053 words, *The Brothers Karamazov* by Fyodor Dostoyevsky is 364,154, and *Anna Karenina* by Leo Tolstoy is 349,736. If we assume about 400 words per manuscript page, their letter book would be 862 pages.

The sheer size of the text they wrote together demonstrates that the platform created within the letters had far-reaching, long-standing impact. The product of their letter writing was a relationship that lasted forty years until Ben's sudden death in 1981. They raised seven children together, who in turn raised sixteen grandkids (including me), who in turn are raising thirty great-grandkids, and the first great-great-grandchild arrived just this last year. We all laugh at the same puns, we refer to sexual intimacy with a wink and an eyebrow waggle, and we end our letters with hearts and Xs and Os. We are the materiality of the letter platform continued forward.

CHAPTER 2

Beginnings (Early Life)

Benjamin Elias Kesler Jr. was born Friday, August 13, 1920, to Benjamin Elias Kesler Sr. and Lulu Matilda Thurman Kesler. At the time of Ben's birth, Benjamin Sr. was sixty years old and Lulu was thirty-five. Benjamin Sr. had twelve children from his first marriage to a woman who was Native American, so the story goes.

Miriam Elizabeth Carpenter was born to Kenneth Carpenter and Maude Maurine Holman Carpenter on Sunday, April 5, 1925. The Carpenters owned a butcher shop in LaGrange County, Indiana, and Miriam's childhood diary notes that she worked there. "Butchered 6 hogs. . . . Boy am I tired. Didn't get lard cut. Started cutting them up at 2:30. Stayed 10 below most of afternoon. Water froze on my hands."

Having established the nature of their letter writing, and to immerse ourselves in Ben and Miriam's small-h history, we must start at the very beginning. (It is a very good place to start.) In the above anecdotes and in this chapter, I employ family history writing (FHW) methodology for the first time. As I note in the introduction, FWH weaves together sometimes disparate threads: the content of the letters, family stories passed down orally, data from external archives, historical context, and more. This chapter presents a means for understanding the methodology as differentiated from "mere" genealogy. Like genealogy, I begin with their birth information, which is easily found on ancestry.com. In fact, using ancestry.com, the giant among family history databases, I can trace the Carpenter or Kesler lineage back several more generations with minimal time and effort. Doing so would be amusing, perhaps, but only to me or to my immediate family. (Many of us have that one uncle, bless him, who sends out the occasional email with some obscure lineage connection or gravesite visited.)

But the amassing of names and dates does little to make the information interesting or relevant beyond the family (and, to be honest, may not be that interesting even within the family). FHW methodology expands the knowledge base beyond just a family tree of names and dates. It views Ben and Miriam as individuals, as people, with specific stories and lives lived. It contextualizes their names and dates into something more vibrant, real, and impactful. Then by sharing that knowledge base, we can know them as people and learn from their example. FHW thus provides both clarity and a deeper valuing of their lives.

In some ways, classic genealogy could be seen as somewhat selfish. The thinking might go, "*I* want to learn where *I* come from, who *I* come from, and about *my* ancestors." Christine Sleeter notes that "most family historians focus much more on the family itself than on the social context in which the family lived."[1] Critics of family lineage research often note that in addition to being selfish, the practice is steeped in privilege, racism, nationalism, colonialism, and sexism; records are kept for those deemed worthy of remembering (e.g., white, male, affluent). Those seeking the information are often white and affluent, and the topics of racism and sexism are not generally discussed. Sleeter coined the phrase "critical family history" to account for how critical theory can help researchers illuminate the social contexts of family lives.

FHW methodology, like critical family history, seeks to position the family history within a larger social context. Instead of focusing exclusively on the amassing of names and dates within a familial line, it is outwardly focused. Researchers focus on finding information and making it thought provoking—contextualized in larger social histories—and usable or relevant to a much broader audience. We dig into archives not just for selfish reasons but to share the information beyond ourselves. FHW is outward focused from the start.

So the following chapter begins at Ben's and Miriam's beginnings. It provides their birth information and their parents and even grandparents. But it also incorporates more detail than the family tree. We hear directly from them through early letters and saved artifacts from their childhoods. We also see the beginnings of their relationship through letters saved while they were dating, family stories, and other outside archival information. In this "weaving" of information, we begin to truly *know* them and understand them as people. It also helps to understand their literate lives, providing more context for the use of letter writing later in their lives.

Ben's story begins with his parents' marriage in 1918. After the death of his first wife, Benjamin Sr. remarried spinster and faithful churchgoer Lulu on October 17. Their marriage certificate hangs in my home, and the archive I inherited has letters shared between them while they were courting. Ben was the only child of Benjamin Sr. and Lulu and was considerably younger than his half-siblings. The family tells me he was proud of being "lucky thirteen" born on Friday the thirteenth and being the thirteenth Kesler offspring. Because of the death of one of his older half-siblings, Ben was raised alongside two of his nephews, Joda (Joe) and Frank, who were close in age with him.

Ben was born into somewhat turbulent times for the Kesler family, as Benjamin Sr. was in the process of founding the Dunkard Brethren Church after breaking away from the larger Brethren in Christ denomination. Benjamin Sr. felt that the wider church was moving toward being too secular and wanted to preserve certain aspects of their long-standing faith tradition. So the Dunkards broke away from the wider church in the 1920s. Benjamin Sr. traveled a great deal from Missouri to Indiana to Ohio and parts in between at various church plants.* The Keslers moved from Missouri to Goshen, Indiana, in the late 1930s after Ben had completed high school.

To understand Ben's literate life, it helps to understand that my great-grandfather Benjamin Sr. was not only a preacher but also the school teacher wherever they lived. The story goes that he was late to almost everything because he was always in charge. Church, school, and meetings could not start until he got there. Ben carried on this habit, so to this day my father loathes being late because of it. Benjamin Sr. was, at the time of Ben's conscription, eighty years old. He was still preaching weekly. He wrote extensively for the Dunkard Brethren newsletter the *Bible Monitor*. He traveled extensively to his various church plants throughout the Midwest and is credited as the elder who founded the Dunkard Brethren Church at the turn of the century as a separate entity from the Brethren in Christ.[2]

Reflective of his father's literacy, Ben was highly articulate in his letters. He had finished high school and clearly built relationships based upon his literacy, as will be apparent later in this chapter. As an adult, he was regarded as well spoken, had strong musical abilities, and wrote both songs and poetry for publication. This adept use of literacy in his adult life had a much less auspicious beginning. The archive contains a few records from Ben's childhood, including report cards from eighth grade through his senior year of high school. The eighth grade report card shows grades that ranged from mostly "I" (below average) to "M" (average). In fact, aside from P.E. in which Ben routinely scored ratings of "E" (excellent), grades ranging from below average to average were Ben's norm. The first instance of an "S" (superior) or "E" (excellent) in regard to an academic content area is found his senior year in both English and public speaking.

Also included in the archive are two poems he wrote at some point in his youth. "The Misssippi [sic] Flood" is comprised of twelve handwritten, rhyming stanzas describing the disastrous 1927 flood of the Mississippi River, which has been called the most destructive river flood in the history of the United States. The second poem, titled "Stay in the Book," is a typed and mimeographed copy of four stanzas admonishing the reader to return to biblical scripture as the basis for decisions and life in general.

Miriam was Maureen and Kenneth's oldest of five, with Dail, Barbara, Verda, and Charles following. In addition to the butcher shop, the Carpenters owned a farm on postal Rural Route #2, in Shipshewana. Like Ben, Miriam also had a print rich childhood. Inside her early childhood diary, shortly after her thirteenth birthday, Miriam wrote on a scrap of paper,

---

* A "church plant" occurs when an existing church sends people and/or funds to another location for the creation of a new church. The existing church "plants" people and funds, what they might call "seeds," for new growth at the new location.

Believing that tobacco and alcoholic drinks are of no benefit to us, we hereby enter
into an agreement with our teacher that we shall not habitually use either tobacco
or alcoholic beverages for the next ten years. Signed this 25 day of April, 1938.

—Miriam Carpenter

Seeing as my own father, at age sixty-five, still does not use tobacco or drink alcohol, I would say the covenant extended much longer than the promised ten years.
Even I was raised to believe tobacco and alcohol were wrong, wrong, wrong, and
I did not have my first drink until I was twenty-two and graduated from college. I
like to say that my Presbyterian-raised husband corrupted me, but I think I was
well on my way to understanding "all things in moderation" before I met him.

The Carpenter family were members of the Dunkard Brethren Church over
which Benjamin Sr. was pastor. Near as I can tell, this is how Ben and Miriam
met, though they may have also attended young people's functions in the area. I
do not think they knew each other from school, since they lived in different counties and Ben had already graduated.

Miriam's letter writing is also coherent and readable. Her handwriting is superior to Ben's in both form and spelling. At the time they met she was a sophomore
in high school, and her writing style is highly articulate. But Miriam did not graduate from high school. I am told that Miriam's high school teachers apparently
tried to persuade her to finish school because she was well on her way to becoming
the valedictorian. Based on family discussions and the timeline of the letters, because of the war Ben and Miriam opted to get married before she could graduate.
If they had waited for her graduation, they may not have been able to get married
before Ben left for service.

Letter writing was an established practice of Ben and Miriam's long before
they were married and long before they were separated by the war. The earliest
dated letter between Ben and Miriam is January 14, 1941, more than a year before
they were married and nearly a year before Pearl Harbor was bombed on December 7, 1941. This first letter from Miriam was to her "friend" Ben.

Topeka, Indiana
January 14, 1941
Hello! May I come in?

I take it for grated I may. I certainly hope everyone at your house feels better
than they do at ours. It seems there has to be some of us on the "hummer" all
the time. . . .

I'll send your ten commandments since I forgot to give them to you. Daddy
says another ∧(of his I should say) definition of love is "two divided by nothing." Well I
can't say as I'd all know what to write as a fittin' one. I might make a stab at it and
I don't believe that would be such a terrible one. But I shan't so don't worry. . . .

Do you and Galen and the rest of the boys get together very often? I think it's nice if you can. I wish there was someone I could be with here. I get so lonesome and feel so deserted sometimes. The girls at school are friendly (I mean some of them) but they act like birds; they all flock together and you can go elsewhere. I would appreciate hearing from you once in a while too or even seeing you during the week ~~are~~ or do you always have plans for the evenings? . . .

This morning I had a few minutes spare time so I did a little snopping. We brought everything down from the attic the other day and it's scattered all over the upstairs. There's a great big box in my room that has a whole bunch of little ones on top of it. And mother had told me that in one there were the letters that daddy had sent to here and in another the ones which she had sent to him. So I opened up the one which she had sent to him. The edges were frayed and it was very worn and finger printed. Anyhow I read it and I began to think mine sounds very frigid compared to hers. I guess I was afraid it would ~~be~~ sound too fresh to say some things and anyhow I didn't want to. I hope it doesn't fell like tinkling ice to read it. Does it?

If it does I'm sorry because I didn't intend that it should.

Miriam's letter indicated that letter writing between friends who were becoming more than friends was a practice that her own parents passed down—and as noted above, this was a practice of Ben's parents as well. Also, the fact that her mother kept those letters had to have made an impression on the "snooping" Miriam. It is also interesting that letter writing at this point in Ben and Miriam's relationship was still a family affair, as Miriam went on to explain:

Daddy said last night that he read all in coming and out going mail. So before he went to bed I said, "Say aren't you going to read this before I send it." And he said, "Oh, hmm! I'm so sleepy I couldn't see the words." The old tease. Well that's a man for you. Oops. I mean don't that sound just like some people? Ha!

I hope your nephews have quite recovered from the shock of seeing me Sunday evening. You could honestly say you found me on Main Street of Carpenterville if you had been here yesterday. There were twenty cars and trucks and one buggy here. How's that for traffic.

Say if I'm not careful I'll have a book to send to you. This is about enough idle chatter (and clatter mostly) for once don't you think? Anyhow I better sign off because it's about time for the bell to ring.

Please overlook this horrible scribbling.

By the way unless some of us are sick we'll be to church Sunday (I hope!) So I'll be seein' you!

Vāle amo amicitia!

Your friend,
Miriam

(If you can translate what I wrote before I closed ok. If not ok.) It might make a big difference if you could but not too big a one.

Much like a chaperon would monitor young people on a date, her father customarily would read her letters. The fact that he forwent doing so here shows both his good humor and his trust that Ben and Miriam were being appropriate. But from what my family tells me, Miriam was extremely sheltered, especially considering she grew up on a farm. My mother recalls a conversation she had with Miriam just after my parents were married. "While [Ben and Miriam] were dating she thought she could get pregnant if she sat on a chair after a boy sat on the chair! I remember her laughing with me about that. . . . She spent quite a few sleepless nights before she was married worrying about it." Clearly Kenneth, Miriam's father, had nothing to worry about in their early letters.

Ben responded a week later, which shows that even these early letters were sent through the mail. Though they attended the same church, they lived in different counties. His letter was openly flirtatious, and he both lamented "having to" write a response to her and being excited about getting to know her better:

Goshen, Indiana
R.R. #3
Jan. 21, 1941
Well: cookie, wookie;

I see you took my dare, so I'll have To live up to my half of the Bargain and answer won't I? I was expecting to see you at church Sunday and perhaps get out of this but it didn't work. . . .

You wouldn't needed to have bothered to send the "Ten Comandments" in your letter You could have waited till you saw me. But maybe you thought I needed them. (I wonder) And Oh say while we're on this subject I have another definition of LOVE. LOVE is an itching sensation around the heart that you can't get to, to scratch. How do you like that. Maybe you don't know a whole lot about it yet, But ask your dad if it isn't right. he seems to be posted along that line. . . .

No I don't always have plans for the evenings, and I may take you up on your suggestion sometime if you really want me to. Anyway thanks for the hint.

Your Mother probably doesn't care if you read the letters she sent to your father now but I'll bet at the time she wrote them she was very particular who got a hold of these letters untill they were sent. tease her a little about it and see. It may be though she could give you a few lessons in writing letters. If you get what I mean.

Ben flirted with Miriam in a courtly and conservative manner, which was appropriate to the time and to their faith tradition. His letter involved references to both her parents with the expectation that they would read the contents, and he also teased her and alluded to meeting up with her some evening. Meeting up with her at a social function or at church would have been typical courting practices, as he indicated later in the letter:

> As you probably already heard, some of the young folks from Pleasant Ridge were planning on coming out soon. . . . I'll tell you all about it sun. if you come to church. If not may I come over Wed. and take you to Prayer Meeting, then I can tell you everything?
>
> You wern't here Sunday so I had to do the second best and sit with Ruth. . . . If you come sun. I'll be with you if I may.
>
> I can't translate that ending on your letter I just hope you weren't raking me over the coals or giving me a bawling out. If it would make such a great difference to me if I could read it don't you think I should know what it says? Maybe you will tell me sometime will you?
>
> I think I'll close for it's time I was in bed 'cause I got to get up before breakfast in the morning.
>
> See if you can read this.
>
> 25 15 21 – 1 18 5 – 13 25 – 19 21 14 19 8 9 14 5
> 13 25 – 14 15 12 25
> 19 21 14 19 8 9 14 5.
>
> A friend always
Ben

Ben
<u>Please</u> write again
I am enclosing a revised 23rd Psalm.

In my family, I grew up hearing that Ben was a bit of a ladies' man. His letter was typed. Apparently, he would keep track of up to fifty different girls by writing a single form letter that he would mimeograph and mail to keep up with his game. It is unclear whether the above was such a form letter, given that many parts of it responded directly to questions Miriam asked of him. Perhaps some spots are part of the form letter, and others not. His practice of stringing along so many girls meant that there was some anxiety and frustration from Miriam over the next few months. Yet, it is clear that he wanted to continue to correspond with her. Miriam responded promptly:

Topeka, Indiana
R.R. #2
Jan. 23, 1941
Dear Ben;

I hope you'll forgive me for writing so soon. But if I don't you won't get this letter this week. . . .

I must say I envy Ruth's position last Sun. To think she had you all to her own little self. My I bet she was tickled tea-kettle pink.

As for last Sun. I'll tell you exactly why I was home. Mother and Charles were both ill and the rest of the family were nearly so. . . . The doctor told mother she couldn't do any work for two weeks ~~so~~ but he didn't tell me that. ha! I am now chief cook and bottle washer at the slaughter house. My I love that! Ahem! Or do I. Everything is so greasy. The knives were so sharp that I was afraid I'd cut my self. But I didn't and then I wasn't particularly watching what I was doin' and I sawed my finger with the meat saw. Whew did that hurt! . . .

I hope this scribblin' is readible if you would see how I'm writing it you wouldn't wonder why it's so bad. Here I sit in the living-room with the stationary box turned upside down and this paper on it. To top this off I'm sitting in a rocking chair and every few minutes I get in a couple of rocks'. . .

I hope there wasn't paste smeared all over that other letter. I didn't have a stamp so I slipped the money in the envelope and took it to school where I finished the letter. I ^had addressed the letter and sealed it when it suddenly occurred to me that I had left the money in the envelope. So I jerked open the flaps and got it out and then of course all the stickum goo was off the flap and it wouldn't stick so I dashed over to the Home Ec. Room and got some paste and stuck it on. I hope I won't be so thoughtless with this one.

Miriam, even at this early stage in their relationship, established a platform for their potential relationship by describing in detail the physical details of her letter writing practice. I find it fascinating the details she chose to include in a letter to him so early in their relationship. She portrayed humor and spunk, but like any girl early in a romance, she was still uncertain and timid of where things stood. She flirted but also showed caution when expressing her feelings:

You'll probably think I didn't appreciate your letter but I did. Gran said that ever since I got it I've been in an entirely different world. I was though beginning to wonder if you were going to be like the rest of the boys. Not keep your word. I'll hope you'll forgive me for even thinking such a thing when there was absolutely no grounds for such thoughts. . . .

I hope when you get this message it will be as ^a ray of sunshine. Since I am yours. Yes I figured out the code. And what I wrote in Latin doesn't matter. It was far from bawling you out or raking you over the coals. I'll tell you that much. . . .

I am hoping to remain your friend.

Miriam

There is a break in the archive with at least one letter from Ben missing. Several weeks pass between the letters, though clearly the relationship had continued. It seems that Ben and Miriam had seen each other at social functions, and while at these functions, they were observed as being an item. Yet, their courtship was still cautious and conservative, involving the entire family:

February 6, 1941
Topeka, Indiana
Dear Ben,

I hope this letter makes sense. You wouldn't wonder why it wouldn't make sense if you were here.

Charles is bouncing an apple on the table. (Imagine that) Well anyhow he's dropping it on the table and daddy has the paper spread all over the table and he's trying to read. Mother and Gran are talking a blue streak. The girls are ready for bed and are sitting here munching apples. Guess I'll get me one maybe it'll help me think. Dail is visiting the Boss's son to-night so he wasn't home. . . .

Did I have questions fired at me or did I last night? I'll tell the world I did! Every body wanted to know where you were. Oh yes and you know "Pantywaist Yoder" was sick last night and couldn't be there to strut his stuff. Bless his dear Soul how I miss his sweet face. Not much! If he hadn't pestered me so much I'd like him a little better. Maybe.

You ought to see Charles he has the dominoes on the table and has one turned on it's side and a valentine propping up on that for a song book and he was just singing "That little boy of mine" to his heart's desire and at the top of his voice. By the way it was Charles whom you heard singing Sun. Mother said he didn't have the tune at all and he had his song book upside down. But it's all the same difference to him. He's ready for bed now and Gran asked him if he wasn't her little man. He said he was and then I said You're Mimmie's what—He didn't say anything and I said "Sweetheart" He said No, Ben's sweetheart. Geepers! Out of the mouth of babes. . . .

Hoping to remain forever your friend. Good night. S.W.A.K.

Miriam

Aside from the amusing discussion of "Pantywaist Yoder" and the antics of her youngest brother Charles and her family members, there is one other significant thing to note in this letter. Miriam signs off with "S.W.A.K," an acronym that will be repeated hundreds of times over the coming years. "Sealed with a kiss," she said. One has to wonder if they had shared a kiss at that point or if Miriam was being a bit forward. I suspect the former.

After this letter, a few in the series indicate that Ben's "ladies' man" practices were finally getting to Miriam. In the following letter she showed some confusion by first calling Ben "Dearest" but also noting that "I'm still not convinced I'm the only girl in the picture."

February 12, 1941
Topeka, Indiana
Good Evening My <u>Dearest</u>

When I came home to night from school I was both surprised and delighted. In fact I can hardly express how pleased I am with your lovely gift. And do you know that when I am in the room where your picture is your eyes follow me every where. That is ~~another of~~ the strange thing about it. Did you ever notice the fact? Just try it once and see. I think you must have posed just a certain way as it is very seldom that the photographers can produce that effect. No matter in what position I'm in you seem to be looking directly at me.

I too hope that our friendship shall last throughout a lifetime. I hope it shall never be shattered as others have been before and I shall do all in my power to see that it doesn't no matter <u>what</u> happens.

I got my valentine greeting for you last week. . . .

I think all of the verse applies except the last three lines which are a little far-fetched. Because I'm still not convinced I'm the only girl in the picture. . . .

I do amo ti. So good night.

Miriam

Her confusion over the status of their relationship came to a head in March when Miriam had finally had enough of the guessing game. She became assertive and direct in asking where things stood. Like the beginning of many relationships, they had to have "the talk." In a letter we are able to clearly see her angst and longing, even more than seventy-five years later.

Shipshewana, Indiana
March 12, 1941
Dear friend Ben,

. . . I have been wondering if I unconsciously said ^something to ^you which ^hurt your feelings or that I shouldn't have in my last letter. I didn't mean to but never-the-less something seems to have spoiled everything. I guess when I wrote it my feelings ran away with the pen. But I did appreciate your picture so much and I thought that you must care a little bit or you wouldn't have sent it.

You know as I do that up to this point we have always been very frank with one another. I didn't beat around the bush and pretend to you to be something I wasn't and I'm sure you didn't either. So will you please tell me by an early reply by mail or by telling me <u>directly</u>, <u>truly</u> and <u>honestly</u>, the answer to a few questions, please?

Clearly, Miriam was done with the wondering and the in-between space of their romance. The conduit of their letters had been a steady, growing flow, but things had clogged a bit, so to speak. The letters served as a means to see how their conduit developed and the hiccups along the way as Miriam, like anyone new to a relationship, both blamed herself for some unknown infraction and questioned him and his loyalty to her.

> Have I said or done something to hurt your feelings? You seem to be so distant since the Pleasant Ridge young people were here. I still can't understand why you did not wish to have me included in the bunch on Sat. night when you refused to come after me when they asked you to. . . .
>
> I suppose you realize about what everyone would think after we had just been seen together the Sun. before and then to see you with Audrey the very next Sun. And I had to be alone even without Ruth. Has Audrey or some other girl come between you and I? If so that is your privilege. But I should like to know ^as someone is sure to be hurt. Do you think I'm too young? Am I too cool? Do the girls now-a-days always tell the boys when to come back? Do your parents dislike me and object to our being together? As I believe you respect their wishes as much as I do mine. Or has Bill's coming back filled in the vacancy so that you don't care for a girl <u>friend</u>? Has someone been gossiping about me so that you have been turned against me? Was there anything wrong with my conduct at Ruth's party? I tried to be a good sport in spite of Rosa's affections.
>
> In these past six weeks I have lived in wonderment not knowing what to think or expect. So won't you <u>please</u> relieve me of these burdensome questions?
>
> It has been my policy to not let any one come between you and I but now I'm on the spot. I received a letter today asking me for a date. So what am I to do since I don't know what your answers will be to my questions? For it will mean a lot to me either way they are answered as I figure these answers will be for my own benefit. . . .
>
> If you don't think that I deserve an answer I shall not bother you any more.
>
> Hoping to remain forever your friend, Miriam.

I have to admire her candor. Miriam described herself as frank and open, and this letter certainly evidences that. She ended with the statement "if you don't think I deserve an answer I shall not bother you any more." She was blunt, anxious about ending the relationship but self-possessed and confident of her worth as a person. Her ability to convey these things in a letter speaks both to her aptitude as a writer and also to the importance of the topic.

I can only assume that Ben made things right between them. The next letter in the series was several months later. Miriam began it with "My Dearest Ben," and closed with "Your Miriam." Ben wrote a series of letters to Miriam that summer while he was away on vacation and church "camp meeting." He called her "Darling" and "Sweetheart" and closed with,

[May 30, 1941]
Well Sweetheart, I've told you about all that has happened and of course driving this far I am naturally a little tired. But I had to spend a little time talking with you before retiring. You see Darling, I <u>love</u> you with all my heart and I miss you already till it nearly hurts. so if you don't mind I'll spend each evening with you before I go to bed. May I? No, don't take me wrong I won't spend the rest of the time with someone else you know that, for I'll be thinking of you <u>always</u>. But each evening I can sit down and think about you, Plan for an talk with you, then when I go to bed I can dream about <u>you</u>. Oh! My Beautiful Dream <u>I love you, love you, love you</u>, and wish you were here with me. I'll close now Little Darling it's 9:30 and we've got to go to Gettisburg in the morn. it's about 35 miles, I'll tell you all about it. Sending all my love I'll always be your <u>true sweetheart. I LOVE YOU.</u> Ben.

Based upon the letters, they were engaged before he left for the vacation. Miriam unknowingly forecasted both their marriage and their future during the war when she wrote her response:

Shipshewana, Indiana
June 3, 1941
My dearest hubby,
Oh! O! I mean sweetheart. Say isn't it queer how easy it is to make mistakes. Gee but I was glad to hear that you got there ok. Only one thing and that is that I wish I were with you. Oh Ben, you can't imagine how I've missed you. To think you've been away <u>seven</u> whole days! It seems like seven years. But darling you sound as though you don't think I trust you. I do with all my heart. You don't think I would have stayed here if I didn't do you?
Oh darling I love you so much I can hardly endure having you so far away.

There is a break in the archive of about a year. The next items in the chronology are cards saved from their wedding on April 5, 1942, four months after Pearl Harbor, on Miriam's seventeenth birthday. The archive contains perhaps twenty greeting cards. Cards ranged in size from a standard 4" x 6" down to a teeny tiny 1" x 2.5" note and envelope that made me squeal at its cuteness. Most cards contain only the name of the guest such as "Aunt Ellen and Uncle Will" or "Mr. and Mrs. Mervin Kaufman." Others included short messages like,

I am wishing you a Long and Happy Married Life.

Just a school mate

Millie Borntrager

Write me a letter sometime Miriam.

A card that was received a few weeks after the wedding is striking in that it reveals that even as Ben and Mimmie celebrate, men were being shipped to war; here, specifically, a friend was shipped to Australia to fight in the South Pacific.

> Dear Ben & Miriam:
> You've heard that old adage, "Better Late than Never," haven't you?
> John, Jr. has been sent to Australia to fight for Uncle Sam. We have hesitated writing to you, hoping to hear from him to know that he arrived there safely.
> But, wherever he is, we know he shares our joy over your marriage and joins us in wishing you a very happy married life. How about a picture of your sweet little "better half."?
>
> Sincerely,
> Mr. & Mrs. John Ross & family

I have two pictures from their wedding (fig. 1). One is black and white and the other is in color, although with color photography barely existing at this point, it is likely that their picture was tinted color rather than color photography. Ben wore a dark suit with a white shirt; later I found that this is considered a "Brethren suit" because it is very simple and very conservative. His hair was parted on the far left and he had a boutonniere of a carnation. His face was happy and friendly; he appeared confident and kind. Miriam wore a loose-fitting dress with long sleeves and a very modest V neckline trimmed with a bit of white lace. The bodice was "blousy," for lack of a better explanation, with wide pleats that trimmed to her natural waist. The skirt fell loosely from there. She had a large corsage pinned to her front. Miriam's face was also happy and friendly, but she also looks very shy and a bit nervous. Miriam wore a traditional head covering over her pinned-up hair with the strings hanging untied down her front. This covering was a white, semitranslucent bonnet that covered her head from just in front of the crown down to her neck. Conservative Christian women in many different denominations, including Brethren and Mennonite, wore these head coverings or prayer coverings as part of the traditional garment. Today the practice continues in Old Order Brethren and Old Order Mennonite denominations as well as the Amish.

They were both very, very young.

Ben and Miriam built a small home on his father's property, fairly close to Benjamin Sr. and Lulu's house. I am told that on the morning after their wedding

FIGURE 1. Ben and Miriam on their wedding day, April 5, 1942. The photo of Ben and Miriam standing was color tinted with a yellow background and Miriam wore a robin's-egg blue dress.

and first night as husband and wife, Lulu awakened them by banging on the bedroom window and yelling, "Benjamin! Why aren't you up yet?!" Benjamin Sr. loaned them part of the money to build the house, so not only did they live cheek by jowl, but they were beholden to Ben's parents financially. This created a fair amount of discomfort, particularly for Miriam, in the early months of their marriage.

Then in September, only a few months after being married, Ben received his draft card.

CHAPTER 3

Conscription, Nonresistance,
and Civilian Public Service

The camp which we are privileged to enjoy was one of our Greatest Blessings. I would rather be with you at home, but I'd also rather be here than in another kind of camp preparing to Kill fellow man instead of helping him. what this whole world needs is more fear of God in their hearts.

BEN, NOVEMBER 25, 1942

IN ORDER TO CONTEXTUALIZE BEN AND MIRIAM'S SMALL-H HISTORY, AND to craft a fully woven family history narrative, I did extensive archival digging and secondary source reading. This chapter develops the historical context that Ben and Miriam found themselves a part of as conscientious objectors (COs). Drawing information from large-H histories enables a richer and more nuanced understanding of the choices that Ben and Miriam made; it contextualizes their individual story in the larger social history. Conversely, including and interspersing details of Ben and Miriam's lives as I recount the larger historical details enables us to visualize what it was actually like for two people caught in difficult circumstances amid a world at war.

Ben received his military conscription in the summer of 1942 in accordance with the earlier Selective Service Act of 1917 and the Burke-Wadsworth Selective Training and Service Act of 1940. Saved within the archive is his Notice of Classification, a postcard that has faded to a dark orange (fig. 2). It is dated September 9, 1942, and stamped with the approval of the Local Board No. 2 Elkhart County Court House in Goshen, Indiana. This postcard is D.S.S. Form 57, which Selective Service issued to each man at the time he registered with his local board. Unofficially known as "draft cards," these small literacy artifacts contained the fate of every man over the age of eighteen and changed an entire generation.

Here is when the small-h history of their relationship, letters, love, and lives during World War II really began.

Included on this card is the class that indicated how the man would serve his country. The majority of men's cards indicated a classification of 1-A: "Available; fit for general military service." But Ben's card, by a vote of three to zero by the local board, classified his status as 4-E, indicating that he was deferred from military service. Classification category 4 indicated that he was "deferred specifically by law or because unfit for military service." The E in his classification

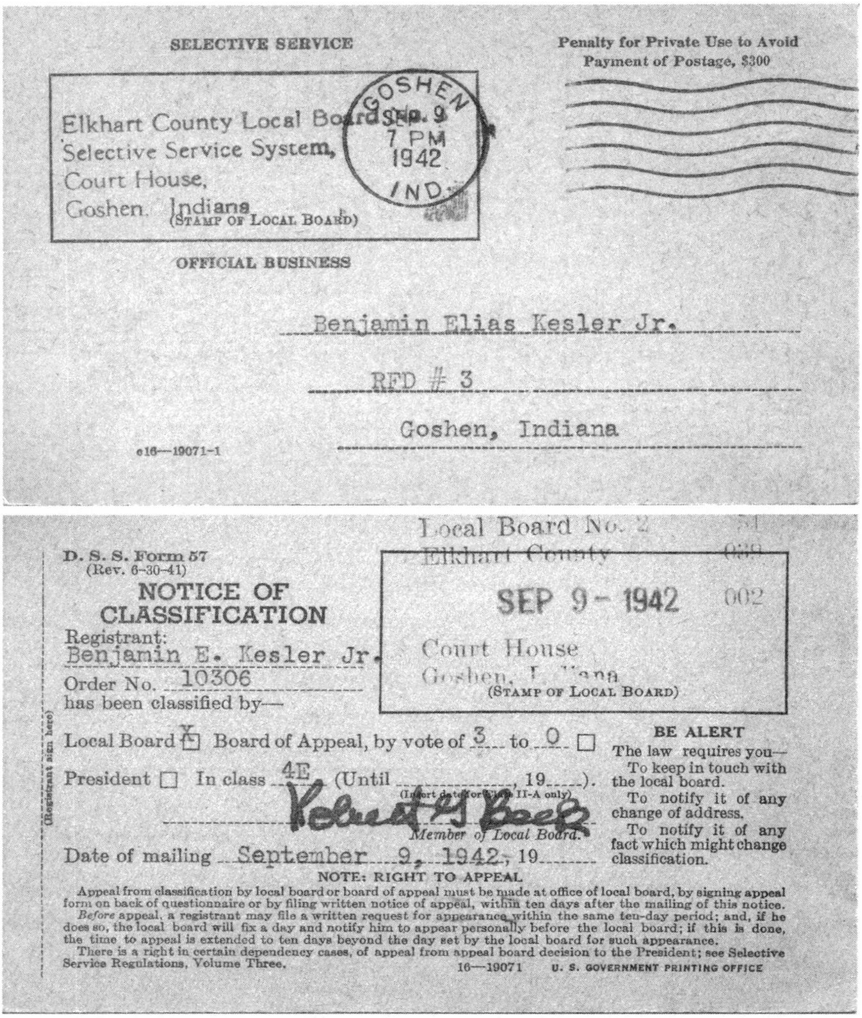
SELECTIVE SERVICE

Penalty for Private Use to Avoid Payment of Postage, $300

Elkhart County Local Board
Selective Service System,
Court House,
Goshen. Indiana
(STAMP OF LOCAL BOARD)

GOSHEN SEP 9 7 PM 1942 IND.

OFFICIAL BUSINESS

Benjamin Elias Kesler Jr.
RFD # 3
Goshen, Indiana

e16—19071-1

D. S. S. Form 57
(Rev. 6-30-41)

NOTICE OF CLASSIFICATION

Registrant: Benjamin E. Kesler Jr.
Order No. 10306
has been classified by—

Local Board No. 2
Elkhart County
SEP 9 - 1942
Court House
Goshen, Indiana
(STAMP OF LOCAL BOARD)

Local Board [X] Board of Appeal, by vote of 3 to 0 [ ]
President [ ] In class 4E (Until ...., 19....).
(Insert date for Class II-A only)

Member of Local Board.

Date of mailing September 9, 1942, 19........

(Registrant sign here)

BE ALERT
The law requires you—
To keep in touch with the local board.
To notify it of any change of address.
To notify it of any fact which might change classification.

NOTE: RIGHT TO APPEAL

Appeal from classification by local board or board of appeal must be made at office of local board, by signing appeal form on back of questionnaire or by filing written notice of appeal, within ten days after the mailing of this notice.
Before appeal, a registrant may file a written request for appearance within the same ten-day period; and, if he does so, the local board will fix a day and notify him to appear personally before the local board; if this is done, the time to appeal is extended to ten days beyond the day set by the local board for such appearance.
There is a right in certain dependency cases, of appeal from appeal board decision to the President; see Selective Service Regulations, Volume Three.

16—19071 U. S. GOVERNMENT PRINTING OFFICE

FIGURE 2. Ben's draft card shows his classification as 4E, a conscientious objector, as determined by the local draft board.

indicated he was a "conscientious objector available only for civilian work of national importance."[1]

Men received their draft card and simply followed the directive. They had been taught to act in obedience to the government and in keeping with their duty to country. You could say, then, that heritage literacy played a large role in the reaction to draft cards: "Heritage literacy is an explanation of how people transfer literacy knowledge from generation to generation and how certain practices, tools, and concepts are adapted, adopted, or alienated from use, depending on the contexts. It is lifelong, cross-generational learning and meaning making; it is developmental and recursive; and like all literacies, it builds over time. . . . [It] describes how literacies and technology uses are accumulated across generations through a decision-making process."[2] Their draft cards, as literacy artifacts, reflect their choices to adopt the practices of previous generations. The draft card said go, so they went. The same could be said of Ben's reaction to his draft card. His heritage literacy practices put duty and obedience to God, the Bible, and specific biblical scripture above duty and obedience to one's country. So, because of his faith, as a member of the Dunkard Brethren Church and because of his adherence to nonresistance, Ben chose to declare himself a CO of World War II. He and twelve thousand other men chose to follow a faith tradition that had renounced any form of military participation for hundreds of years.

Some might call his choice a noble one, since he felt he must answer to God first and could not kill another person, even for something as important as the fight of WWII. Some might (and did) call him a coward for not performing his military duty as an American, but whatever others thought, Ben stood firm in his convictions. In contrast to the 373,000 men investigated for evading the draft, Ben did not try to hide or actively protest; instead, he took his place as a citizen and served his country, albeit in an alternative way.

The classification for COs was a significant and hard-won concession to the historic peace churches. Within the Selective Service Act of 1917, Congress included an exemption from battle for individuals who were members of long-established and well-recognized peace churches. These historic peace churches included the Mennonites, Brethren, and the Society of Friends (Quakers). However, the exemption Congress included was not well-defined: "No person so exempted shall be exempted from service in any capacity that the President shall declare to be noncombatant."[3] The noncombatant classification during World War I had included service in the medical, quartermaster, and engineering corps—three areas that while not in direct conflict are still closely connected to combat. Many COs in WWI refused to cooperate and were automatically convicted in court-martial. Others filed claims for noncombatant service but were found medically unfit for service. Many eventually abandoned their CO status, leaving only about four thousand COs on record. About a third of those four thousand COs eventually entered military noncombatant service, and eventually, in 1918, "because of a labor shortage, the government offered the remaining conscientious objectors an alternative for service unrelated to the military—furloughs to perform farm labor or to work on Quaker war relief programs in France. The government offered no guarantee of pay, but conscientious objectors finally got the chance to engage in civil occupations and pursuits—albeit still under supervision of the armed forces."[4]

When compared to the 170,000 recorded draft evaders and almost 3 million men inducted into the armed forces during WWI, it is clear that COs who stuck with their convictions made up a very small minority. Of those who were convicted, most were jailed. "Not until 1933 did the government grant the last of the court-martialed objectors a full and free pardon. Some conscientious objectors hardly had time to catch a breath of fresh air before the winds of war began to blow again."[5]

Between the wars, the peace churches banded together to form a joint committee of the historic peace churches. This committee, later formalized into the National Service Board for Religious Objectors (NSBRO), agreed to promote a plan that would provide COs with furloughs from the military for alternative service beyond military influence or control, spiritual care for the men in these camps, and financial support for the dependents of the COs.[6] In February 1937, President Roosevelt agreed to meet with committee members. They presented a plan for COs to serve under civilian direction that the peace churches themselves managed. They would perform overseas relief aid for sufferers and refugees, rebuild war-torn areas, and help to resettle refugees.

Instead of accepting this proposed plan of the historic peace churches, the draft legislation introduced into Congress, the Burke-Wadsworth Bill, made no mention or concession to COs and instead proposed only noncombatant service within the military. This bill reverted to the troublesome treatment of COs during WWI and created the first peacetime conscription in US history.[7] And yet, "contrary to recent myths, although many volunteered or accepted conscription as their duty, the draft was not universally popular; American men did not enthusiastically embrace conscription. . . . But even those who did not serve in the military overwhelmingly supported the war effort, taking the good-paying jobs in the industrial machine that tooled up to produce armaments and supplies for the Allied forces and buying war bonds."[8] By contrast, COs both objected to conscription to war and refused the well-paying jobs that supported the war effort.

Representatives of the Joint Committee of the Historic Peace Churches presented a letter to President Roosevelt in which "they expressed their concern at the trend of events and their hope that for sure some adequate provision would be made for conscience. They proposed a scheme of alternative civilian service and complete exemption for absolutists."*[9] Finally, concessions to the peace churches were made and the Burke-Wadsworth Selective Training and Service Act of 1940 was finalized. In this finalized version, the peace churches did not receive everything they asked for. Just as the government made concessions for COs to have alternatives to military service, the churches made concessions to the government. It was, as Sibley and Jacob call it, "an experiment in tolerance."[10] The law

* "Absolutists" were those objectors who objected to conscription entirely. They believed that the government should not be able to compel its people to serve or to go to war. They were requesting to be entirely exempted from conscription or service.

"contained no provision for absolutists, [but] it did offer religious conscientious objectors alternative service outside the military in 'work of national importance under civilian direction.' The law also presented a broader definition for objection—one based upon religious training and belief—which opened the door to those who did not belong to the historic peace churches. A third unique offering allowed the draftee to file an appeal in the event the local Selective Service board refused him conscientious objector status. And finally, a provision removed the control of alternative work from the Armed Forces and gave it to civilians."[11]

There were costs, both literal and figurative, to these provisions for COs. The most significant was that "Congress made no appropriation for compensation to conscientious objectors."[12] In fact, Sibley and Jacob write that for the duration of the US involvement in the war effort, a period of six years, COs worked between forty and ninety-six hours a week without receiving any pay from "the government which conscripted them, the institution or agency which benefited from their service, or the religious organizations which sponsored or administrated their work."[13] Instead, COs relied heavily upon themselves and their families to support their time in service. Further, COs had no life or health insurance; should they be injured or die while in Civilian Public Service (CPS), their families received nothing. Perhaps most egregious, no funds were made available to support the wives, children, or aging parents of COs. Matthews notes that if the men were paid at all they "received two dollars and fifty cents a month for their services. Politicians rationalize that the virtual work-without-pay balanced the sacrifice of the men in uniform. General Hershey was convinced that if CPS men were paid, 'it would destroy the best public relations.'"[14]

So in 1942 when Ben was before *his* local Selective Service board, declaring himself a CO was not done lightly. By making the choice to join CPS, Ben and Miriam faced many of the same trials as any other draftee going to war; like any soldier and his wife, they faced years of separation and an unknown future, they faced physical and mental harm (many COs died in service, though they did not participate in the military), and they faced the same fears of instability, loss, and harm. By declaring CO status, they also faced public ridicule and censure. And they faced financial ruin as a result of their choice.

The most benevolent of historians call CPS "a deliberate experiment to discover how far a nation dedicated to democracy would tolerate freedom of conscience under the stress of bitter ideological and military conflict."[15] At the time, however, many citizens and many of those who made up local Select Service draft boards were not nearly as benevolent toward COs. Draft board members would pepper COs with questions meant to trip up their perceived faulty logic (at best) or cowardice (at worst). Matthews gives some examples: "'Would you just stand there and let a Nazi rape and kill your mother or sister?' was a typical question skeptics asked to corner a CPSer into taking a hypocritical stance. Many citizens believe that conscientious objectors had no logical argument to back their views. Intolerant Americans verbally insulted and sometimes physically attacked the conscientious objectors, who often heard the epithets 'yellow belly,' 'slacker,' and 'coward' shouted behind their backs and sometimes to their faces. They were frequently spit on or had to dodge stones thrown by teenagers or older irascible patriots."[16]

Some might wonder what possible reasoning these individuals could have that would prompt them to take such a drastic step to stand still against the rushing current of the war effort that consumed the nation and the world. In a biweekly newsletter printed at the Sideline Hill CPS Camp where Ben first served, one author wrote, "Now more than ever before, each one of us should take inventory of ourselves to see what we can do to improve conditions in the world. While the war is going on and many people are on the battle field taking life, we, as Christians should be working for peace, trying to save life instead of destroying it. In order to do this, both now and after the war we must prepare for what may come after this great conflict is over. We must prepare ourselves to overcome the great forces of evil that are at work."[17]

As I note in the introduction, the Brethren Church, similar to the Mennonite Church at that time, had a doctrine against war and the use of force called *nonresistance*, a term based upon the fifth chapter of Matthew in the Bible. Matthew 5:38–39 reads, "You have heard that it was said, 'Eye for eye, and tooth for tooth.' But I tell you, do not resist an evil person. If anyone slaps you on the right cheek, turn to them the other cheek also."[18] Sibley and Jacob have an excellent explanation of Mennonite nonresistance that captures the essence of what Ben and Miriam also believed:

> Nonresistance, Mennonites were careful to point out, had nothing to do with the "nonviolent resistance" so often associated with modern pacifism; there was no affinity between nonresistance and the techniques used by Gandhi's movement in India. . . . "Nonresistance" meant the refusal to use force or pressure of any kind in human relations. . . . If the non-resistor found he could not consciously do what the state commanded him to do, he would simply refuse and take the consequences, without any attempt to use concerted action in opposition. Nonresistance ruled out both strikes and lockouts in labor disputes; indeed since pressures of various kinds seemed inevitable in industrial society, it virtually required agrarian communities and modes of life for its full observance. Repudiation of war was thus only one facet of Mennonite social doctrine, for conscientious objection itself was but one expression of a way of life which, consistently and rigorously applied, clashed with almost every point with modern industrialism and with the state that was so largely associated with industrialism. . . . The primary objection of most Mennonites was to war, not to conscription.[19]

Ben and Miriam, then, were a part of what Matthews calls a "rich tradition of nonviolence that had its roots in early Christian belief. The followers of these churches took the Gospels of the New Testament literally, believing that the words of Jesus superseded the sometimes-violent accounts set forth in the Old Testament. In explaining their stance of nonresistance, they quoted passages from the Bible, such as Luke 6:27–36, a passage in which Jesus admonishes his followers: "Love your enemies, do good to those who hate you, bless those who curse you, pray for those who mistreat you. If someone slaps you on one cheek, turn to them the other also. If someone takes your coat, do not withhold your shirt from them. Give to everyone who asks you, and if anyone takes what belongs to you, do not demand it back. Do to others as you would have them do to you."[20]

Eisan, a historian of the Brethren Church, notes that the church's history and commitment to nonresistance dates back to 1708. He writes that the Brethren Church "can be conceived as involving the following principles: 1. War, and its allied activities, are out of harmony with the teachings of Jesus. 2. The Christian faith calls for constructive service to all mankind. 3. In cases of hardship, assistance should be rendered one to another. 4. The threat of suffering and oppression should not deter the doing of what is right. 5. Loyalty and service are the due of the government, but should its demands run counter to the will of God, they cannot be met. 6. The overruling of conscience is wrong."[21] Thus, "at a time when all the world seemed engaged in a work of destruction they sought to render a positive service of peace."[22] And yet, nonresistance should not be confused with passivism because passivism actually takes an active stance; it "pushes back" against war. Instead, nonresistance is likened to letting the river of the war simply wash over. It is a rock in that river that is unmoving and unwavering, but it does not stand in the way of the river.

In thinking through Ben and Miriam's choice to become COs, I find myself reflecting on what I call "the glorification of war" as part of large-H histories. When only large-scale, impactful events like war are celebrated, the small histories of men and women like Ben and Miriam are lost. In American culture, we seem to be enamored with war, with displays of military might, with winning. We erect monuments and we memorialize battles, those who fought, those who died, and those who won. We have holidays to remember and honor veterans, (yet, we treat them like baggage when it comes to benefits, rehabilitation, health, and continued emotional and mental support after the war has been waged). Large-H histories are never lost as they are resplendent with documentation of the war experience.

Jesus said, "Blessed are the peacemakers, for they shall be called sons of God."[23] What exactly is a peacemaker? On the one hand, a peacemaker, a maker of peace, implies someone who actively pushes toward peace, establishing peace by any means necessary. I will make you mind. You will be peaceful *or else.* Such a perception of peacemaker might even fit the pacifist model of commitment to peace and opposition to war. Such pacifism includes peaceful versions of the same actions as more aggressive activists take. Martin Luther King Jr. is one well-known Christian pacifist who both abhorred all forms of violence and also actively resisted segregation and racism.

On the other hand, a peacemaker, a maker of peace, might be considered a practitioner of peace, an artisan or craftsman of peace. A peacemaker embodies peace such that peace is not something they *do* but instead is something they *are*. This is how I understand nonresistance, and this is the basis for understanding the convictions of men and women like Ben and Miriam. Such conviction meant that in WWI, before CPS was an option, drafted COs were usually jailed. For those who ended up in the military in spite of their efforts, they refused to pick up guns, sometimes literally sat on their hands, and calmly accepted the consequences of nonresistance. This conviction continued even in the midst of a war that was called the "Good Fight" and a moral fight against tyranny. Was returned violence justified to stop such tyranny? Nonresistant citizens like Ben and Miriam would say no; violence is never justified. So, they sought other ways to obey the draft that compelled them to serve.

CHAPTER 4

Leaving and Nesting

T HEIR TIME APART BEGAN ON NOVEMBER 5, 1942, WITH A SQUEAK AND hollow "thunk" of a car door closing, gravel crunching under tires, and the fading of an engine. Both wrote later that they were proud of how they survived this event with stoicism, a stiff upper lip and so on.

> I was ^so proud of you this afternoon. You looked so nice and took your going away so bravely. You were swell darling. [Miriam]

> I made up my mind that I was going to take things on the chin and do the best I could under the circumstances. And when I faced the realities as they really were it wasn't half as hard as I tho't it was going to be. [Ben]

Ben's leaving lacked the fanfare of a soldier going off to war. There were no cheers, no waving flags, no pomp, or any of the other commotion a bus or train of soldiers leaving might have. His leaving was quiet, subdued, and sad. There were other differences in the leaving from what I surmise a soldier leaving might entail. Ben was leaving for an indeterminate amount of time, true. But he was not going to war; he was not facing his own death, necessarily; and most importantly to their way of life, he was not facing the horror of causing the death of another.

This chapter concerns itself with the processes that Ben and Miriam experienced of leaving, separating elements of their lives, and establishing their new realities. They, who had so recently married and "become one," now had to figure out how to live a life physically apart from one another. Their letters, as conduit and platform, enabled them to make sense of this new landscape. Ben's life was a strange new world, and it changed in the most obvious ways as he physically left his home and the familiar. His life became one filled with strangers (at least at first). He was surrounded by men whose faith practices differed somewhat from his own; he did work for which he was not previously trained (menial though it was); and he lived a newly regimented life with a strict structure that exceeded the work routine of his former days. Miriam's life at home changed but in less obvious ways. Hers was a strangely altered old world, familiar yet foreign, exhausting and scary. She did not continue to live her previous life and simply subtract her husband from the equation. Instead she moved, worked as a hired girl for various families, and, in spite of the pressures she faced from her in-laws, sold her home, and took control of her and Ben's financial future.

Their early letters represent a type of epistolary "nesting" in which they extensively, exhaustively described their new lives to one another. "Here is where I am now, what it looks like, what I will do, what I will eat. Here is how we will convey our love over the miles." They clucked and shuffled and rearranged their feathers, so to speak. I think this helped them make sense of their individual experiences and their mutual heartache. They further began to establish how they would make decisions, some of them significant, without the other present. "Here are the choices I am making; I hope they are OK because you are not here to discuss it."

In this way, we can clearly see both the platform and the conduit as they constructed one and opened the other. Their detailed descriptions of their physical environment, their nesting, laid a foundation for the platform, and it was clear that this was a new aspect of their letter writing and relationship. They described their physical surroundings—Ben's bunkhouse or Miriam's kitchen—in order to create a pattern, a representation of their material spaces portrayed in immaterial words. The conduit was something already established both in earlier letters between them and in their relationship since being married. There is no obvious start to the conduit, at least not in the same way we can see the platform being built. Instead, the outpouring of love began as it would continue. At first, they did not sound so desperate, so despondent, as they did later on. Their separation was new and unfamiliar at this point, so their expressions of love were simply a continuation of how they expressed themselves when in person. As the weeks passed by, their writing took on a different tone, as if the conduit opened more fully as the only means by which they could share their love.

In her opening letters, as part of her conduit of expressed love, Miriam praised Ben for what I call "standard masculine practice." As the opening quotes of the chapter indicate, Ben left bravely without crying or making a fuss. I know in future correspondence he defied this brave masculine norm, at least to her on paper, by admitting to crying into his pillow and being depressed and lonely. But in leaving, particularly in front of their families and perhaps members of the church, he subscribed to what was expected, perhaps because they were not alone and perhaps because leaving was made all the harder by making that fuss. Montgomerie notes that "1940s masculinity was not always hard-edged and rooted in a separate male culture."[1] Through letters, men expressed a "heartfelt desire to stay connected to home" and showed that they "value[d] domesticity and family connections."[2] Ben clearly displayed the desire to remain connected, and the letters were the primary way of doing so.

Prior to his leaving on November 5, 1942, the couple made plans to close down their home and property in order to sell it. They made plans for Miriam to return to living with her parents and to procure work. They made plans for seventeen-year-old Miriam to take on the entirety of their financial future, since Ben would not have access to their accounts. And they gathered the supplies required for Ben's service at Camp #20 at Sideling Hill, Pennsylvania. In Keim's illustrated history of CPS, *The CPS Story*, he includes a list of what campers were instructed to bring to camp:

What to Bring to Camp
From Instructions Sent to Each Camper

1. Not more than one suit of clothes suitable for Sunday wear.
2. Not more than one camp suit; these clothes suitable for wearing evenings and Saturdays.
3. Overcoat.
4. Raincoat.
5. Work Clothes:
    a. Three pairs of good quality blue denim trousers.
    b. Three good quality work shirts.
    c. Three good quality blue denim jackets.
    d. Light sweater or similar windbreaker garment to wear under jacket when necessary.
    e. Two pairs of gloves.
    f. Two good pairs of work shoes.
    g. One pair of overshoes (arctics).
    h. One warm cap.
    i. Six pairs of work socks.
6. Three shirts for good wear.
7. One pair of good business shoes.
8. Several pairs of Sunday socks.
9. Underwear:
    a. Two pairs medium weight long underwear with long sleeves and legs.
    b. Lighter underwear if desired for camp purposes.
10. Two pairs of pajamas.
11. Linens:
    a. Three bed sheets good quality; at least 63 by 99 inches when finished.
    b. Two pillow cases, same quality material.
    c. Three hand towels.
    d. Two bath towels.
    e. Two wash cloths.

12. Personal items—supplies may later be replenished in camp.
    a. Shaving supplies.
    b. Dental supplies.
    c. Toilet supplies.
    d. Shoe polish supplies.
    e. Stationery and stamps.
    f. Literature supplies—notebook, devotional literature, Bible, etc.
    g. Musical instrument if desired.
    h. Hand mirror.
    i. Mending kit, needles, thread, pins, buttons, etc.
    j. Other personal items, that you consider indispensable.

Do not bring a whole wardrobe, that is too many supplies. They will be a burden to you in camp. This clothing NEED NOT BE NEW but can be supplied from your present wardrobe; the above list is to guide you as to quantity and quality.[3]

So they packed him up, buying a few items to supplement his existing wardrobe and making or purchasing the bedding and linens. Miriam packed his trunk for him, and throughout his letters, Ben wrote of things he discovered that she had tucked inside just for fun: a small photograph of her as a child, a few silver dollars, and a potato.

They also made plans for how Miriam would support herself while Ben was gone. Without any sort of income, Miriam would have no way to pay the home loan and other bills. As newlyweds without much savings, planning was key to keeping Miriam from being destitute. They decided to sell their home on his parents' property. Benjamin Sr. and Lulu felt strongly that they should try to rent the home so that it would still be there when Ben returned from service. Ben and Miriam opted against this for two reasons. First, they had no way of knowing how long Ben would be gone, and Miriam did not need the financial millstone of the mortgage around her neck. Would they be able to rent it for enough money and with enough regularity to cover it? Second, I suspect that after living next door to his parents for a few months, Miriam and Ben had had enough of their meddling.

Ben's first item of correspondence was a postcard that he sent as he traveled between Indiana and Pennsylvania. The card's written message was simple.

Hello Honey—
    Everything is O.K. thus far. Just had Breakfast here in Pittsburg. Our Bus leaves in about 15 minutes we had supper at Fort Wayne at aprox. 6:00—the time now is 8:00. Heaps of <u>LOVE</u>
               Your Hubby

FIGURE 3. Ben's first postcard to Miriam after departing for CPS work, postmarked Pittsburgh, 10 a.m., November 6, 1942.

The postmark says Pittsburg, Pennsylvania, November 6, 1942 (fig. 3). Ben had only been gone a few hours at this point, it seems maybe overnight, since he just had breakfast but talked about last evening in Fort Wayne, Indiana. Logically a postcard was unnecessary for any practical purpose this early in his trip, but this began their daily correspondence of the next five months. Furthermore, in this postcard we can see what will become a key aspect of their conduit and platform: descriptions of food and eating.

What is most interesting about this card, beyond it being the start of their extensive correspondence, is that it makes visible the contradiction that they must live out over the course of the war. The card is a picture of the Pennsylvania Turnpike that he likely picked up at a road stop. The message was quick and loving as this conscientious objector (CO) ventured toward alternative work of national importance. Yet, it is ironic that next to the postmark there is another stamp saying in large letters: "BUY DEFENSE SAVINGS BONDS AND STAMPS." Even the simple act of sending a quick note was overlaid with the cultural imperative of supporting the war effort.

Miriam's sense of leaving began the moment Ben's car drove away:

Nov. 5, 1942
Hi! Honey!

Well I wonder if this will find you located in your new life. I haven't just too much to write to you as it has only been 5½ hrs. since we parted. But after you left we made the payment at Montgomery Wards and then went "home" to pack some things. I took down pictures & put things away. Dad packed the fruit & vegetables, jelly & quince honey that was in the cellar away. Gran washed dishes & mother & I were busy at other things. . . . We brought your instruments, the plants, fish, silverware and dirty doilies & scarfs. . . .

We are going to finish with the things over at our house tomorrow and I don't know what I'll do with the house yet. We'll hope & pray that what ever is done will be God's will. We have to trust him now more than we ever did before and believe that everything will be for the good of everyone concerned. Honey please pray for me that I may do the right thing.

I'll send the payment to Hostetler tomorrow so that will be out of the way for this month.

Miriam's entire family engaged in moving her out of her and Ben's house into her old room at the farm. We can see here that already she was working through how to manage their finances and future. In this first letter we also see her trying to face the reality of their situation and the emotional work ahead:

I miss you so much it don't seem right that we aren't together where we can love one another. Charles is very light-hearted but the rest of us are far from it. . . .

Everything is so different here from our home. I can't say I'm not glad I could come but I wish that it was different. Just you & I.

I am so glad for the few minutes we had alone to-day although they were so very few. It was so hard to go home without you. Well I mustn't talk like this or I'll give you the "blues."

I was ^so proud of you this afternoon. You looked so nice and took your going away so bravely. You were swell darling. And I caught the kiss you threw me & have tucked it away with every thing else that you have given me to cherish. . . .

I don't know what to do with such long evenings. But I reckon you're the same way. So we'll just have to do things for one another even tho we are several miles apart. I'll write again to-morrow night & tell you how we got along. So don't worry honey as everything will be OK I'm sure. and you'll come home before long. Every day makes one less you know.

In the week after Ben left for camp, Miriam's letters describe how she and her family worked together to close up the home in Goshen and move her back to her parents' home in Shipshewana, Indiana.

Nov. 6, 1942
Dearest Darling:

Well how is my youngun' by this time? It's only Friday evening but I spose it'll be Monday by the time you get this small book. What time do you get your mail? Ours comes at ten so you'll know how anxious I get about that time.

Well honey, I suppose you're wondering how the moving progressed. Well if I can collect my thoughts enough; I'll tell you how every thing was. In the first place the weather was splendid for which we were very thankful and dad got a small truck from Mr. Curtiss for which we were glad as it was bigger than the trailer. . . . Of course we had a truck full to bring home. There was the davenport & chair, rocking chair end table & that little table that was under your picture in the living room, your saw (electric one) and a box full of tools, a big pasteboard box full of empty cans, all the small rugs and I don't know if that's all or not. Mother had to come home in time to get the children at school so I came home in the truck. Boy was that some ride, we didn't drive more than 30 and the thing made so much noise we could hardly hear ourselves think.

In addition to describing the process of moving back to her parents' farm, Miriam described the financial situation they found themselves in. Miriam began to assert herself as an independent person and representative of her and Ben's new little family, and she took important matters into her own hands, much to the dismay of Ben's parents.

I went to Roy Rensberger this P.M. but he wasn't in. So will have to see him tomorrow as we have to go back in the morning & finish up a few odds and ends. Dad will putty the window & fix the roof & we'll get the mail box & I'll mop the kitchen & take down the curtains upstairs. . . .

Still I won't have to worry about that until we rent or sell it will we. I spose you'll wonder why I decided to turn everything over to a real estate agent. I didn't intend to until it was forced to that by the neighbors actions. I didn't want renters in our house like has been & still is in there's. Your mother has told me what to do with everything all day until I am most nearly crazy. So if I say anything that you don't quite know what I mean please overlook it tonight honey. as I am so tired & wore out I hardly know what I'm saying or doing. She told me last that I should take curtain rods & blinds.

Well you know why we decided to leave the curtain rods and it is customary to <u>always</u> leave behind the blinds. She said I should leave the key there so they could show people around. Well . . . Rensberger can sell it. I'd be more than glad to pay the commission to have him fix all the legal papers so I wouldn't have to worry about them.

Benjamin Sr. and Lulu were set against the young couple selling, and they had definite ideas of how the young couple ought to be doing just about everything. Lulu was not shy about telling Miriam what to do, to the point that Miriam felt "most nearly crazy." Lulu told Miriam to take the curtains, and Miriam noted that it is customary to leave those for the new owners. Lulu wanted to keep a key to the home so they could handle the showing of the home, but Miriam was not about to allow that. Further, Benjamin Sr. and Lulu wanted Ben and Miriam to rent the home, with the expectation that they would live there again once Ben completed his time in service. Instead, Miriam decided to hire a realtor to show the home and to sell it so they could bank the money. Miriam's assertion here at the beginning of Ben's service set the stage for a number of misunderstandings over the course of the next few years.

Along with Miriam asserting herself about the house itself, she began to manage their finances.

I have found there were a few things we over looked so I must definitely get a job at once or I won't be able to meet them all. Well . . . Honey what do you spose I better do. I know the folks think I'll help them here for awhile & I just simple can't as far as financial matters are concerned because if the house isn't rented or sold there won't be any money to make the payment. Don't you think I had better go on the way we planned?

You'll have time now to think a little more about it so what do you think we ought to do. Rent or Sell?

She was assertive about what she must do, but she was also uncertain and anxious as well. While she had a lot of spunk and independence, she swung from being firm with Lulu, and confident in front of her own parents, to writing, "Honey what do you 'spose I better do," and asking Ben to guide her choices.

Miriam also shifted from confident to impossibly sad and worried as she expressed her love for Ben and lamented their new, hopefully very temporary, life:

> Well honey I must quite rambling on and say good. night as it is nearly eleven and I'll have to get up <u>early</u> in the morning. I glad that you can't see how the house looks now. It doesn't seem like our home anymore it's so bare. But we still have our furniture to make any house a home when you come home to me Darlin'. And until you can come I hope that God will watch over you & keep you safe for me. We know that what ever is done in the future will be his will. Honey I've missed you so. It's seems like years since I seen you & in reality its only a little more than one day but that makes it one day less until the time when you'll come home to me. I wish you could put your arms around me & tell me you love me and that everything will be all right. It don't seem right that two people who love one another as much as we do should have to part.
>
> My heart aches and I'm lonesome and I want you. But I mustn't feel like that I must feel that what you are doing is for the Heavenly father who loves & cares for us and keeps us safe for one another. So darling we must have more faith & trust Him more to do everything that is his will.
>
> Well honey I must close as you know & I'll be waiting for your letters darling to help me be brave & to reassure me of your love although I do know how much you love me. and my love for you is even greater than I had realized before. It's growing more & more So I must close and you'll find enclosed every bit of my love & if you were here I could show you how much there is.
>
> Good night Honey!
>
> <u>All</u> of my love <u>Your</u> "Mimmie"

This fluctuating back and forth from confidence and, perhaps, false bravado and a feeling of utter helplessness continued. The next day, on November 7, 1942, she wrote, "I feel so small and helpless. Please pray for me often that I might do the right thing in everything. There isn't an hour that goes by that I don't ask God to watch over you & keep you safe that you can come back to me." Miriam's confidence teeter-tottered from resilient, firm, and full of sass, to worry, anxiety, and powerlessness. She clearly was sorting through their lives, their things, their finances, and her own emotions to find stability and equilibrium.

Ben's first letters contained a great number of descriptors of his new surroundings. First, he explained the details about his trip. He had certainly traveled before (remember the early letters before they were married that he wrote while traveling with his family), but being on a bus headed toward a new, regimented life was clearly something different. Ben described the bus trip itself:

> Sideling Hill Camp.
> C.P.S. Camp #20
> Wells Tannery, Pa.
> Well Darling:
>
> Here we are about 500 miles away from home and I'm wishing I could be right back where we started from, but since it is not within our power to change things we must be brave and make the most ^of everything.
>
> Ill give you a detailed account of our trip starting when we said Goodbye ^or (so-long) you understand Honey I know.
>
> I made up my mind that I was going to take things on the chin and do the best I could under the circumstances. And when I faced the realities as they really were it wasn't half as hard as I tho't it was going to be. . . .
>
> We had supper in Fort Wayne and were alowed 75¢ worth of eats nearly all of us filled our quota, I did—ha—we were in Fort Wayne about an hour. . . . I had sirloin stake with salad and french fried potatoes a cup of coffee and a piece of mince pie and Buttered Toast.
>
> We left Fort Wayne about 7:00 and rode all night to Pittsburg. But I'll tell you about that ride I got on the bus carrying my Guitar and there was a bunch of young people in the back of the bus who wanted me to play. So I let them beg awhile (you know me) then I played a few songs. And Theron Christophel and I sang. (by the way—I sat with Theron that night). We sang and played "You are my Sunshine", "Wabash Cannon ball" and some of those we played "The Great Speckled bird" and "farther along." I suppose we played a dozen pieces or more then we settled down to sleep. . . . I slept about 3 hours.
>
> Well we finally got to Pittsburg and had Breakfast. We were allowed 75¢ for Breakfast and I used 65¢ of mine (There were no refunds) I had ham and ^two eggs—buttered toast, glass of milk, wheat krumbles, and a glass of orange juice. everything was all good. . . .
>
> The crowd on the bus today was much different than the one last night we stopped at Midway (that is half way between Pittsburg and Harrisburg.) for about 30 minutes that was only 20 miles from Sideling Hill Camp. And there is a Tunnell called Sideling Hill Tunnel.

The letter, from the very beginning of their time apart, included descriptions of food and eating; Ben and Miriam both relied on food to help build their platform. It was a comfortable and comforting topic. Then after his account of their two-day bus ride with few stops, Ben described his arrival at the camp itself. Just as his leaving had been inauspicious so was his arrival to camp.

> It was raining when we got our baggage off the bus. We just put it along the roadside and went across to a small house ~~and~~ to ~~called~~ called the camp. . . . And there was no one there but the camp was only about 200 yards. So they walked over and come back in a pickup truck. The driver took a Picture of all seven of us boys beside our baggage with my cammera I hope it is good but it was pretty dark.
>
> At camp we were assigned our beds. The beds are arranged two together and the fellow next to me is named Orie Miller I don't just know where he comes from, but he has been here 9 months. First tho we ate dinner, we got in camp about 1:15 oclock. we got straightened out and I unpacked my stuff. Boy oh Boy! Honey, you sure never left out a thing. But you should have kept that two dollars which I found in my trunk. I took a shower and cleaned up, then the bunch of us went exploring around the place there is a recreation room with three ping pong tables a piano and organ. A work shop with power saw and jointer that is all the power tools except an emery wheel. . . .
>
> We had our supper and right after, ~~we~~ we had to take a shot for Typhoid Fever. There is to be another next Fri. then the next, (3 altogether). I needed some blankets and was given two I have three army blankets beside the sheets. I am right across the aisle from the stove. The water is really good and scenery is pretty.
>
> Three fellows were playing while ago one had a Guitar, Fiddle, and the other had a mouth organ. I played a couple songs for them on the fiddle and ~~th~~ told them I had a banjo. they wanted me to get it. So if you could find out if it could be sent by parcell post, (There is no railroad at all near here.) and tell me then if I want it I can get it.

Ben found comfort in music on his trip to Pennsylvania. I think the familiar feeling of an instrument and his fondness for entertaining others helped him both pass the time and feel more settled. Ben finished this first letter with the first instance of conduit. It was an outpouring of emotions as he worked through the newness of his environment and his loneliness for Miriam.

> Well Honey! That brings us down to the present. And if you can't under-stand some of the things I wrote you'll just have to ask me about it and if I think of something else I'll tell you. You must tell me <u>sweetheart</u> how everything is at home and who the house is rented to or sold to. I know you'll do what is best. If things go hard and you're undecided what to do, ask our God about it because we have the same one. . . .

Darling, Things have been happening so fast and everything is so different, that I haven't had time to be very lonely. But Sweetheart I miss you more than I can even tell you.

Honey, try to be brave and courageous and trust in me and we'll get along O.K. I know you'll take care of things the very best. It's now 8:10 P.M. so I'll close. A chorus sings at 8:30 and I want to hear it and I can tell you all about it.

So goodbye now sweetheart. Oh! How I love you. Darling think how much you love me and you'll know how I LOVE YOU.

I'll close now and write soon again.

Your Darling Loving "Hubby"

Ben Kesler Jr.

Write Honey

Bye Bye

Xoxoxox
I LOVE YOU [in a heart with arrow]

The next letter from Ben described both the emotional work he did and the physical changes he underwent to fit into his new life. The letter, again, was filled with descriptions of his new environment.

C.P.S. Camp. #20
Sideling Hill Camp
Wells Tannery, Pa.
Sat. Nov. 7, 1942
Sweetheart:

I'll try to write again, But I feel pretty bad. That Typhoid shot that I told you about last nite, is and has sure been taking effect. I ache all over, especially my right arm, and my head has ached all day. (unusual for me). I will have my two other shots in my left arm if they will let me. All three shots are for Typhoid. . . .

It took me about 10 or 15 minutes to go to sleep. I have both the pictures you put in my trunk on a shelf at the foot of the my bed My head is next to the aisle and Orie my partner has his head at the other end. That is selective service rules that two cots side by side should have the head facing opposite directions. The closet we have is toward the foot of the bed. The shelf where the picture is fastened on it. When I lay down, I can just lay and look at your picture and our picture and somehow it doesn't seem quite so far away as it really is, that we are separated.

Two bells ring for bed time a warning at 10:00 and last bell at 10:10 P.M.

There are two bells for breakfast of course one to get up, we get up at 6:00 A.M. then first breakfast bell is at 6:15 then last bell is 6:20. So we have

20 to dress and wash up before breakfast. This morn. I didn't hear the first bell and I had only 5 minutes to get to breakfast so I didn't have time to wash. My arm hurt so I didn't feel like hurrying. This morn. I cleaned up the office, swept and scrubbed the floors and washed one window took me about 3 hours and 15 minutes then the rest of today was off. Played my Guitar a little before dinner and subscribed for the "Turnpike Echo" That is the name of a little paper they publish. it cost 50¢ per year and comes out every two weeks. I read my copy since dinner and am mailing it home to you. and you can keep them for me, (I mean <u>us</u>). HA HA.

Maybe you'd like to know what we eat. I know you would. for dinner yesterday we had fried beef tounge, tomatoes and bread together, cookies (chocolate) and Gravy, lettuce and potatoes and bread & water oh yes <u>peaches</u>. <u>We all ate our fill.</u> for supper we had Liver, Gravey and potatoes ^green beans and ice cream ^and pretzels. for Breakfast we had cornbread and Gravey made from the grease from the fried tongue I suppose because it had tounge in it. Coffee bread and pears and oat meal. for Dinner we had bread, vegetable soup with lots of little pieces of beef in it, rice with raisins in, applesauce, celery and potatoes Well! so much for that. . . .

Oh yes! There are two Bells for Dinner, I forgot to tell you the warning Bell ^5 till 12:00 and then last bell at 12:00 The supper Bells are 15 minutes apart 15 after 5:00 and last at 5:30. This afternoon I lay down a little while then played checkers with Melvin and Theron They Beat me about as much as I beat them.

Ben's description of camp life does not sound all that terrible or scary, a stark contrast to men going to war and facing camps filled with the smell of death and the sound of guns. The reality is that the camp at Sideling Hill was pleasant by comparison, but that did not make the emotional work any less challenging for Ben. It did mean that a sense of unreality settled on Ben those first days:

<u>Honey</u> I just can't seem to realize that I'm way out here and you're oh! so many miles away. Sometimes it seems a long way away Then ~~other seems~~ other times it seems like you're just as tho you were home with your folks and I was in Goshen. But we're a long ways apart.

<u>Darling</u> I love you so much and think so much of you but I'm trying not to get blue. I had to cry a little last night as I lay looking at us together in the picture, and then knew that we couldn't be together like that for a long time. But Sweetheart I'm hoping and praying for the time to come when we can be in each others arms and tell our love to each other.

There quite a few married fellows here, some of them haven't been married as long as we are.

Well sweet,—I'll try to close now and save a little to write tomorrow. I've written about all up to now only I'd like it if you would make me a nice size laundry bag—not to big but, oh well—you know how to make them <u>ha ha</u>, here I am trying to tell you how to sew.

Bye Bye now Darling
God Bless you and may he
Keep us safe for each other
is what I pray.
Sweetheart I love you

Your Darling one and only
Ben Kesler Jr.

<u>I Love you truly</u>

Ben's letters were filled with newness. Everything at the camp was different and noteworthy, so his letters were lengthy at first. The letter on November 9 continued the same trend of explaining the environment of camp in great detail and also began the discussions of their financial future.

Sideling Hill Camp
Wells, Tannery
Pa.—Mon. eve.
Nov. 9 '42
Darling:

I finally got your letter. Two come today our mail comes about 1:00 P.M. to the office and then it is delivered to the dorms. about 4:00 P.M. so I just got them read before supper I read the second one twice but I'll bet you that won't be the last time. But I haven't had time ~~for~~ to read yet 'cause its not quite 6:00 and supper is at 5:30.

Darling your letters were the sweetest and I know you meant everything as for our Love, honey. I'd like to share it with you as much as you would but since we can't sweetheart we can tell each other as best we can in our letters and make that as interesting as possible.

After what will become a typical start to his letter, Ben promptly shifted into financial matters, but since their separation was so new, even within the paragraph about finances, he slipped back into sending her his love through the conduit over the miles.

As for the house, I don't believe I would take less than $3000 for it, and if you can sell it for that Sweetheart, let it go, we can build another, "We did it once, and we can do it again", you know, and Darling when I get the chance there's nothing in this whole wide world I wouldn't do for you. You're really such a pal and I'm sorry I had to leave such a large responsibility, not that I don't think you're capable, 'cause I know you'll do what's best and what's right as best you know and I'd rather have you than anyone else in charge of me (OUR) business, Oh! Darling I love you so much I wish I could fly to your arms and relieve your mind of all its worries. And just live in your love. And try to comfort your troubled heart.

After this brief comment upon their financial situation back home, Ben dove into descriptions of the new camp life. The newness of his life seemed exciting to talk about at this point, whereas later his letters describing camp life were pretty boring because it was the same thing day after day.

Well Honey, today went pretty good—I didn't do anything all day break-fast this morn. Then got my laundry ready. Dorm 1 and 2 has their wash on Monday—Dorm 3 on Tues. Dorm 4 on Wed. and Dorm 5 on Thurs. (There are five Dormitories) I got my 1 sheet and underwear back this aft. but socks and shirts don't come till tomorrow. By the way I don't have any tags for my blue sox that Grany gave me. . . . Please send me some tags and I can mark them. . . .

Well on with the happening of the day. After getting laundry ready went to the recreation room and played Ping Pong. They have three tables. There is also a shuffle board and we played on that. It's really fun. We didn't get a call yet to be examined and no call to work, seems like I'm wasting my time when I could be loving you if you were only near. Had dinner and then went back and played a while. There is a player piano in one little room at the end of the recreation room and we started to play it but found out it wind the roll backup so I tore it apart and fixed it, Don't know how long it will work. . . .

I haven't weighed yet, but I don't think I've gained anything yet, although the meals are very good. I only had 4½ cake of sausage for supper beside (catsup) on all of it (the catsup tasted a lot like that you made) it is sure good. We also had cabbage, scalloped potatoes lettuce and pears which were cooked in brown sugar syrup with raisins it was all so good.

Honey it's only 6:30 but I don't know anything else to write, except to tell you and reassure you that I love you love you love you and am living only in hopes for I know someday God will let us be together and then Honey we'll make up for all the sweet times we're losing. Oh! Sweetheart pray for me, to help keep me courageous and to help keep me going on. . . .

Well Honey I'll say So-Long for tonight it's already black dark outside.

Bye Bye Honey and Goodnight

I DO LOVE YOU

Your "hubby"
Ben

A couple of things are worth noting in this letter. First, Ben had absolute confidence that Miriam, who was only seventeen years old, was more than capable of handling their finances, the sale of their home, and the host of responsibilities that came with that. Throughout his letters he sometimes offered advice, then promptly returned to the phrase "do as you think best." It is as if he wanted to perform his duties as the man of the family by directing the finances, then he remembered he could not do any of it from across the country. So, he reverted to supporting her. It is an odd mix of assertion and passivity that I think annoyed Miriam at times.

Second, in this letter it is apparent that there is a systematic delineation of the daily lives of campers. One of the oddities of an already out-of-the-ordinary situation like Civilian Public Service (CPS) is the fact that it had two very different, sometimes conflicting, objectives. The camp was part governmental camp and part church camp, part forced labor camp part kum ba ya. On the one hand, like military camps throughout the world, the men were told when to sleep, when to wake, when to eat, when to work, and when to go to the bathroom. Their beds had to be made with military precision each day or they would earn an infraction. If they were late to work, they would earn an infraction and penalty. If they refused to work or left camp without permission, they were marked as AWOL and faced jail time. Camp life was filled with peeling potatoes, scrubbing the latrine, waxing floors, and shoveling snow. It was, ultimately, strictly structured, boring, and mundane.

On the other hand, camp life included plentiful food, church services, prayer meetings, Bible studies, choir practice, hymn sings, guest lecturers from churches throughout the Midwest, ping pong matches, ice skating, and even the occasional bowl of ice cream. There were the church services on Sunday morning, Sunday night, and Wednesday night. Monday night was prayer meeting; Tuesday night was choir practice. Then there were guest sermons or lectures by ministers from neighboring churches, Mennonite church leaders, and occasionally CPS officials. There were courses offered for personal growth or enrichment by lecturers on topics such as first aid, typing, nature study, photography, physiology, and anatomy. Men in the Sideling Hill Camp were generally like-minded in their worldview, so fighting and resentments were minimal.* The comradery of the men was founded in their Christian beliefs and in the shared circumstances. It was, ultimately, a peaceful, if boring and mundane, place.

And like camps throughout the world, there were significant amounts of down time with simply nothing to fill it. Ben filled such times, each day, with writing letters to his Mimmie. Some days he added in writing letters to his parents

* Reports from other camps throughout the United States were not so pleasant as Sideling Hill, and infighting, frustrations, and conflict were not uncommon. Mennonite-run camps seemed to have been the most harmonious, and both the Sideling Hill camp and later the camp at the State Mental Hospital in Rhode Island did not have significant, reported issues with conflict.

or her parents. But mostly, he wrote to Miriam, thought of Miriam, prayed for Miriam. What was she doing today? Was she working too hard? Did she miss him as much as he missed her?

Through letter writing, Ben and Miriam settled into their new lives. Their letters, even at the start of their time apart, demonstrate the commitment they had to one another, to God, and to their nonresistant way of life. Their earliest letters set the stage for the months of separation that were to come, and the nesting they did through those letters demonstrate conduit and platform.

CHAPTER 5

Ben's Work and Camp Life at Sideling Hill

*I have been here only a short time, but already I have become aware of the fact
that life at Camp is much better than were my expectations. I had an idea that
the camp here, being in the mountains, would be isolated from all contacts with
normal life, and would be such a lonely place that time would seem long and go
slowly. True enough it seems much longer since I left home and loved ones than it
really is, but to me the time passes very rapidly.*

BEN KESLER, ESSAY EXCERPT IN *TURNPIKE ECHO*,
VOL. I, 20 (DECEMBER 8, 1942)

T HIS CHAPTER MORE FULLY EXPLORES BEN'S FIRST CIVILIAN PUBLIC SER-
vice (CPS) assignment in camp #20 at Sideling Hill, Pennsylvania, by framing
the contents of Ben's letters with more official, archival data. When employing
family history writing (FHW) methodology, large-H historical data bolster and
contextualize personal information like the letters. The quote from the camps
newsletter above is both part of Ben's small-h history and part of the larger narrative of CPS. Additionally, as part of the FHW methodology, this chapter includes
some detail about my research process in procuring archival data; unlike more
traditional qualitative research, the researcher is an engaged and visible participant
at times. In this chapter specifically, I want the reader to visualize the camp and
its surroundings to be fully invested in Ben's experience, so including my own
experiences of seeing and walking among the remains of the camp enables such
visualization.

I traveled to Fulton County, Pennsylvania, where the camp was located, in
the summer of 2016. As often happens when doing research using FHW methodology, there is a sort of serendipity to the information one finds. Okawa notes
the value of "disappointment, success, spontaneity, and serendipity in research
and the importance of being open to any encounter."[1] One piece of information
leads to someone who knows someone who has another piece of the puzzle. It is
like a snowball sample with much less systematic deliberateness. You meet people
in elevators, at coffee shops, and even in line at the grocery who know something
worth adding to your collection.

The main CPS website civilianpublicservice.org contains basic information
about each of the 218 CPS camps, data about each man enrolled in CPS, and
some relevant images. When first researching CPS Camp #20, the name of a

Pennsylvania Department of Conservation and Natural Resources ranger Shawn Lynn was listed as being willing to provide tours of the camp. I contacted Shawn via email and arranged a visit and tour for my husband (my much-appreciated research assistant) and me. Shawn met Dave and me at the ranger station, drove us the twenty or so miles into the hills, and walked us through the remains of the camp. What remains of the camp are the stone foundations of the barracks, the chimney of the rec hall, enough remnants to indicate an area was once the latrine, most of the officer's log cabin, and elements of the buildings where the work equipment was stored. In pictures from the 1940s there were trees that were barely waist high; now they are more than one hundred feet tall. The Sideling Hill Tunnel and that stretch of the turnpike is no longer in use and is heavily graffitied. We walked and Shawn talked; his knowledge of the area and history was substantial and revealing. He offered to lend us his own private collection of the *Turnpike Echo*, the newsletter put out by the CPS camp on a biweekly basis.

The next day our visit took us to the McConnellsburg library, home of the Fulton County Historical Society, where Dave scanned the *Turnpike Echo* collection, and I dug through their limited information on the camp. I purchased copies of the Fulton County Historical Society's two-part publication on the camp. Dave made still more copies. We talked to the research librarian but learned nothing that Shawn had not already told us. We then returned Shawn's collection, drove forty minutes through winding roads to a local brewery in a neighboring town, ate entirely too much pizza, and came in last place at trivia night in spite of our two PhDs.

I provide these details from our research trip in part because they are amusing and interesting and in part because they reveal some important aspects of the FHW methodology. Archival research is not linear. Transcribing interviews and doing statistical analyses of quantitative data often has a set pattern for how research is done and ought to be done. In contrast, family history research follows a meandering path, takes turns and switchbacks, and often ends up in a vastly different place from where you expect it should. It is both solitary and collaborative, requiring others to provide information but requiring solitude to make sense of that information. It is both past and present with historical details, the letters themselves, and the images taken of the camp juxtaposed with our present-day read of those elements and the crafting of a document about those elements. It is questioning "how can we be accountable for someone else's story, especially when that someone cannot tell the story on her own."[2] What follows, then, is a brief history of the camp, as best as can be put together from the different threads found in Fulton County, in Mennonite Central Committee (MCC) Archives, in other published materials, and in Ben's letters.

CPS Camp #20 at Sideling Hill, Pennsylvania, was located two miles away from Wells Tannery, Pennsylvania, in Fulton County. The camp opened originally as a Civilian Conservation Corps (CCC) camp in the summer of 1933. As part of President Roosevelt's New Deal, unemployed and unmarried men lived on rural lands owned by federal, state, and local governments to perform unskilled manual labor jobs related to soil conservation and natural resources. The original campers cleared the land and constructed the campgrounds. When the six-month enlistment in the CCC program proved successful, the government decided to winterize the camp for year-round use.[3] The October 26, 1933, *Fulton Democrat* gives these details:

> Preparations for the winter are in progress at the camp. . . . Six wooden Barracks are being constructed. Five of the buildings will be used as quarters for the men and the sixth building is being built for headquarters, dispensary, infirmary, and supply room. . . . Over 123,000 B.M. feet of lumber and 21,000 pounds of other materials are being used in the construction of the new buildings.
>
> The mess hall . . . will be made over for winter use. In all buildings, including the mess hall, there will be double flooring, wall lining, and roofing felt on the outside.
>
> The shower and bath room, made originally of frame work, has already been made over. The pump house will be reconstructed for winter. A log cabin is being built in the "Vermont" style for the officers.
>
> The heating for the barracks will be furnished by stoves. It is planned to have the buildings at the camp lighted with electricity. The men will be issued warm clothing and everything possible will be done to make them comfortable in their winter quarters.[4]

The camp buildings were constructed in a layout similar to military camps. As in military camps, at Sideling Hill, a road or path separated men's barracks, the mess hall, and the recreation building from the officers' housing. The buildings were set in tidy rows, and the latrine was located some distance from the other buildings.

The CCC camp was decommissioned in 1937. It was then used for another New Deal purpose of housing Works Progress Administration (WPA) workers and engineers whose main task from 1938 until 1940 was to convert the nearby abandoned railway to a limited access highway that would stretch from Harrisburg to Pittsburgh. The Sideling Hill Tunnel is located about one-half of a mile from the campgrounds and was the longest tunnel of the turnpike at that time at 6,782 feet. On October 3, 1940, the highway opened to the public at 12:01 a.m., and thousands of cars quickly clogged it. While "the paving of the turnpike was completed and it was open to traffic, . . . much additional work remained to be done."[5] This additional work was to be completed by CPS men such as my grandfather.

Also, in early October 1940, Gen. Lewis B. Hershey became the deputy director of the Selective Service System. Based on the revised Burke-Wadsworth Bill, CPS camps were born throughout the United States. Hershey liked camps such as the Sideling Hill CCC camp because they were in out-of-the-way locations where CPS men could be housed for "work of national importance" but be out of the eye of the public. He wanted to be sure that CPS men were in no way honored, commended, or even noticed for their convictions and stance against the war effort. Keim notes that the general felt that putting conscientious objectors (COs) into the military would be a disaster. It was better to put them in camps such as Sideling Hill, away from populated areas. "'The CO, by my theory, is best handled if no one hears of him.'"[6] Keim writes that Hershey also said, "'And CO's are working for the national welfare at almost no cost to the American taxpayer.'"[7]

Under the direction of the government, and funded by churches and individuals, the camp was finally designated as CPS Camp #20 at Sideling Hill (fig. 4). Records exist showing the official commissioning of the camp. The camp location was considered ideal for a CPS camp because of its remote proximity to larger populations ("the nearest town is Wells Tannery, a very small hamlet"), its proximity to the recently opened turnpike, and the existence of barracks for the men and cabins for the leadership, and because the plumbing and fixtures were 75 percent present and other repairs were fixable with fairly minimal costs.[8]

In a memo, the CCC headquarters sent a detailed list to the commanding general of the district. The list included the supplies that the camp still had, for example, "(1) Four (4) barracks, 20' x 110', capacity 37 men each, based on 60 sq. ft. of floor space per man. Total capacity—148 men. (2) One (1) Mess Hall, 20' x 120', with kitchen. . . . (4) One (1) Officers' Quarters, 19' x 39', with two (2) wings 10' x 10', including living room, 3 bedrooms, kitchen and bath (log cabin)."[9] In total there were twenty-seven buildings.

They also included in the report the cost estimates for rehabilitating the camp. The sewage and waste disposal system needed $258 in repairs. A pump house needed to be constructed, with costs estimated at $286. Roofs needed replacing,

FIGURE 4. A view of CPS Camp #20, Wells Tannery, Pennsylvania, taken in 1942. Courtesy of Mennonite Church Archives, Bethel College, North Newton, Kansas.

estimated at $760. And so it went for six pages of descriptions with estimated costs associated with each element. The total estimated cost was $9,025.99.[10]

General Hershey approved the camp in an August 22, 1941, order. The order stated the "Sideling Hill Camp project to be work of national importance. Said camp . . . will be the base of operations for soil conservation work in the State of Pennsylvania, and registrants under the Selective Service Training and Service Act, who have been classified by their local boards as conscientious objectors to both combatant and noncombatant military service and have been placed in Class IV-E, may be assigned to said camp in lieu of their induction for military service."[11] These orders lasted the duration of the war, in spite of the original expectations of those conscripted. "When the CPS program began, CPS men expected to serve one year and then be released from service. However, after Pearl Harbor on December 7, 1941, a complete readjustment took place and the time element was removed. Men in CPS would stay in service for the 'duration' of the war."[12]

The camp was sponsored and managed by the Mennonites. Copies of the *Turnpike Echo*, which Camp #20 published every two weeks, still exist in the Mennonite Central Committee Archives. Just after Ben arrived at camp, in the November 12, 1942, issue, the following notice appeared in the *Turnpike Echo*:

> Food, as well as all other expenses (technical excepted), is paid for by the Mennonite Central Committee which acts as the agent for the Mennonite Church in the administration of C.P.S. Camp # 20. The MCC receives its support from the Church as a whole. The Assignee pays for his own clothes and medical attention and other incidentals. In case the assignee is not able to do so, the MCC furnishes the essentials. Assignees not affiliated with MCC affiliated churches pay their own way or if not able to do so are taken care of by the MCC or other service groups. All work done—a minimum of 8½ hours a day, six days a week—is designated by the Government of the United States of America as Work of National Importance. The Assignee gives his time and work without financial compensation in the hope that it will be a benefit as well as being a constructive force in alleviating the conditions brought about by various destructive forces which are at work in our country today.[13]

This paragraph sums up the realities of Ben's situation quite well. Note that it differentiated between those who affiliated with the Mennonite Church and those who did not. Ben, being Dunkard Brethren, was to "pay [his] own way." All campers were to work eight and a half hours a day, six days a week, with no financial compensation, no medical care, and no life insurance. Yet, the paragraph ends with a nod to just why these men were doing this work: "In the hope that it will be a benefit as well as being a constructive force in alleviating the conditions brought about by various destructive forces which are at work in our country today." Even in a formal declaration of the purposes and composition of camp life, conscientious objectors stood firm in their convictions.

The next issue of the *Turnpike Echo* gave a directory of the newly assigned campers. Ben's name is listed along with twenty-four other men who arrived between October 27 and November 17. The last column on the list indicates church denomination. Every other camper was a member of a Mennonite-affiliated church: OOAM (Old Order Amish Mennonite), OO Amish, OO Mennonite, and Mennonite are the terms listed. Ben's designation as "Dunkard Breth" stands out as different from the others.[14]

Because Ben was a member of the Dunkard Brethren Church, the MCC did not cover his expenses. It is unclear exactly who paid his way. My guess is that his home church, over which his father was the minister and the patriarch of the larger denomination, covered his costs. Later, when Ben was in Camp #85 in Rhode Island, he petitioned the larger Brethren in Christ denomination for a stipend to help cover expenses for his dependents. So both the smaller Dunkard Brethren Church and the larger Brethren in Christ Church contributed to Ben's time in CPS. I discuss those financial issues in more detail in chapter 13.

Ben's letters reveal that life in CPS camp was ordered and disciplined much like life in the military. According to Selective Service mandates, the layout of men's barracks was to be arranged like military barracks. Beds were arranged two together, head to foot, with the idea that it would keep certain illnesses from spreading. Each camper was assigned his bed/bunk and had a trunk or closet, a shelf, and little else to call his own (fig. 5).

The organization of the CPS camp mirrored the life of a military camp in terms of how time was regimented as well. "With the Army as a model, Selective Service comprehensively ringed the daily life of the CO's with its regulations."[15] The campers rose at a specified time, ate at specified times, and slept at specified times. In Ben's letter from November 7 (discussed in the previous chapter in more detail), he noted that there were bells to signify each time of the day.

> Two bells ring for bed time a warning at 10:00 and last bell at 10:10 P.M.
>
> There are two bells for breakfast of course one to get up, we get up at 6:00 A.M. then first breakfast bell is at 6:15 then last bell is 6:20. So we have 20 to dress and wash up before breakfast. This morn. I didn't hear the first bell and I had only 5 minutes to get to breakfast.

The reality of CPS camps and the lives of the campers is perhaps best understood by the following excerpt:

> From the time an assignee reports to camp until he is finally released he is under the control of the Director of Selective Service. He ceases to be a free agent and is

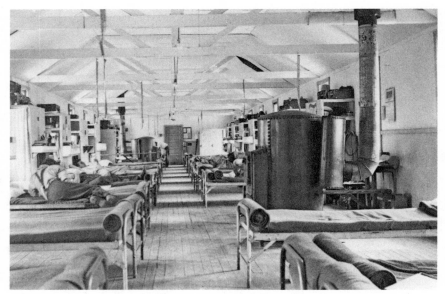

FIGURE 5. A look inside a residential cabin at CPS Camp #20, equipped with bunks, stoves, flypaper strips, and not much else. Courtesy of Mennonite Central Committee Collection, Mennonite Church USA Archives, Akron, Pennsylvania.

accountable for all of his time, in camp and out, 24 hours a day. His movements, actions and conduct are subject to control and regulation. He ceases to have certain rights and is granted privileges instead. These privileges can be restricted or withdrawn without his consent as punishment, during emergency or as a matter of policy. He may be told when and how to work, what to wear and where to sleep. He can be required to submit to medical examinations and treatment, and to practice rules of health and sanitation. He may be moved from place to place and from job to job, even to foreign countries, for the convenience of the government regardless of his personal feelings or desires.[16]

Also, as in the military, Ben was given a physical and a series of immunizations, including a series of three for typhoid. Ben's first shot was administered on November 7, just after arriving. The next was a week later. "I'm sure sore This eve. we all had our second Typhoid shot This afternoon at 1:15 and it sure has taken effect. It took action before the first one did so I hope it won't last as long." His final shot was administered on November 25, and the following day he wrote, "This letter finds me feeling pretty Punk. I Just had a tooth Pulled yesterday and last night I got my last shot for Typhoid. So consequently I am staying in from work." Camp work records indicate Ben was "SQ" on this day, which signifies "sick in quarters."[17]

Fellow campers noted this absence, and some good-natured teasing followed. The *Turnpike Echo* from November 28 included a section of funny comments about various camp members. One stated, "Ben Kesler seems to be having trouble with his arm even though all his fellow men are asleep." This section also included a large blank space with text in the very center that said: "This space is reserved for what John Brenneman has to say on any subject." Seems Mr. Brenneman was a pretty quiet guy.[18]

The National Service Board for Religious Objectors (NSBRO) served as an intermediary between the peace churches and Selective Service; as such, camps reported on the work done each month to NSBRO, which then formulated larger reports to send to Selective Service. The reports from Camp #20 at Sideling Hill are available in the MCC Archives and Records Department. These records indicate that in November 1942, a total of 2,199 man-days were worked. "Man-days" refers to the number of campers who worked a full day totaled over the course of the entire month. The records also indicate that weather prohibited work for 65 total man-days. In the Sideling Hill Camp, men did not work on the Sabbath and generally only worked a half day on Saturdays. From December until March, however, men worked whatever days the weather allowed except Sundays.[19]

In November, Ben's individual record indicates that he spent four days "conditioning," which meant he arrived at camp, was given various instructions on how camp worked and the work he would be doing, received a physical examination, and was generally acclimated to camp life. He then worked thirteen and a half days, had four days off for the Sabbaths, missed one day for weather, and missed one day sick in his bunk. Ben's foray into "work of national importance" was no more glamorous than any other COs. His first day on the job, he wrote, "This morn. I cleaned up the office, swept and scrubbed the floors and washed one window took me about 3 hours and 15 minutes then the rest of today was off." Because he had not yet been assigned a team, he was given tasks at the camp itself to start with, along with other "conditioning" activities.

As General Hershey's letter commissioning the camp indicated, Sideling Hill was the base camp for "soil conservation work in the state of Pennsylvania." Soil conservation was a mainstay of the various CPS camps throughout the country (fig. 6). Ben's letters state that the main task put to campers was to plant trees and bushes on the steep inclines of the newly opened turnpike in order to prevent erosion. The campers planted rose bushes, bittersweet, honeysuckle, locus trees, and barberry (fig. 7). The work was indeed boring.

[November 12, 1942]
This Morn. we went to work about 25 miles up the Turnpike east of Camp, no west, cause it's toward the Direction from which we come when we first got here. We Planted Bittersweet, Honey Suckle, Roses, & Locus trees on a steep

FIGURE 6. Laborers at CPS Camp #20, perhaps returning from soil conservation work near the new Pennsylvania Turnpike, ca. 1941–44. Courtesy of Mennonite Central Committee Collection, Mennonite Church USA Archives, Akron, Pennsylvania.

bank we didn't have to use ropes tho. in The forenoon I dug holes for the Plants (about Three feet apart) and in afternoon I Planted them.

[November 16, 1942]
My work isn't hard Darling not half as hard for me as yours is for you. We worked almost 50 miles from camp today and will again Tomorrow. We Planted Roses, and Bittersweet today. Tomorrow we will Plant Barberry. I haven't seen any of it yet. This winter The boys say we will cut wood and clean up the woods, I think That will be better.

One of the more unique aspects of the work the men at Sideling Hill Camp did was due to the steep incline of the Allegheny Mountains that framed the

Figure 7. Laborers at CPS Camp #20 planting trees, ca. 1941–44. Courtesy of Mennonite Central Committee Collection, Mennonite Church USA Archives, Akron, Pennsylvania.

turnpike. Men would work in teams of two: one sat in a harness, or what they called a "saddle," down the side of the hill to do the actual planting, and the other was responsible for holding the rope at the top. The top man's purpose was not necessarily to bear the entire weight of his partner. Rather he guided it and provided stability for the times when the saddled man would lose footing. When first confronted with this configuration, Ben wrote:

> [November 11, 1942]
> My Job was holding a rope from the top of the bank which was fastened to one of the boys who were planting. The banks are almost straight up in some places and the boys have to be held up. There are saddles in which they sit which fasten around their waist and under each leg. They said they were pretty comfortable but they cut in a little. It's pretty dangerous and it's quite a feeling to have a man's life in your hands. One of the new fellows holding a rope let go and the boy on the other end fell about six feet before he caught the rope again. That's pretty bad. But don't worry I'm heavy and probably won't be put in one of the saddles.

Ben was not, in fact, heavy enough to keep him from the saddle. On November 21 he wrote, "Yesterday I worked in the saddle Its fun I think I had Warren Meyers holding my rope."

Because the work sites were as many as sixty miles from camp, work teams often returned only just before dinner. This meant that the work of maintaining the camp was neglected. So, the camp director, Sanford Shetler, sometimes had teams stay "in" for a workday to work around the camp.

> [November 14, 1942]
> This morn. some of us had to stay in camp and work. Some of the Boys (mostly new fellows) had to Peel Potatoes and wipe Dishes. I had to help clean out the Bathhouse and sweep and Dust the Latrine (Toilet) There are 16 holes in our toilet Pretty big isn't it? Sometimes it's Pretty Crowded too. After that we moved the water Barrells in the buildings They are in case of fire. ∧There was 14 of them It was about 20 above and we had to dip part of the water out of the Barrells so we could carry them in, and the water froze on the outside of the Buckets. We got thru about 10:15 quite a bit earlier than the rest.

The only other work that Ben did in his first month of "work of national importance," aside from planting on the turnpike and working in camp, was to cut down brush. On November 28, 1942, Ben wrote, "This Morn. it was too cold to Plant trees so we cut Brush along the Power line that follows the turnpike. The first time we've worked at anything else except tree planting."

All the work was menial, tedious, and boring, and life in camp maintained a regimented schedule in order to satisfy the government and in order to keep men focused and purposeful. So along with the regimented daily life of campers came consequences when a camper failed to follow the rules. There were daily inspections of dormitories and bunks, of latrines and the kitchen. There were also penalties for tardiness. Ben wrote on November 22, "I was late so I had to wash all the dishes as a Penalty. I Kept five fellows busy wiping so I got along O.K." He further explains the inspection process in a later letter.

> [November 25, 1942]
> Maybe I'd better explain that inspection business. every morn. about 9:00 the nurse goes thru all the Dorms and looks the beds and closets over and if everything isn't ne[a]t she gives you a ticket and then the [penalty] is sweeping the Dorm next morn. If your Pillow is Just a least Bit wrinkled or if your sheet is wrinkled and shows thru the Blanket she gives you a ticket or if your curtains to your closet are not Pulled or if your shelves are dusty you get a ticket. I have not had a ticket yet. I try to Keep everything neat as possible.

For the most part, Ben was a tidy and careful camper. But on New Year's Day 1943, he received his first ticket for failing to have his space as tidy as prescribed. After ending the workday a bit early because of weather, Ben wrote, "When I got in I found a ticket Pinned on my closet. It was because my Pillow was a little Dirty so I'll have to sweep two times now. This week end I have to help in the kitchen we start at 5:00 tomorrow eve and all thru Sun. so I'll be busy."

December's NSBRO work report totals were similar to November, though Ben was there the entire month. It is at this point that weather became a more critical aspect of daily life and work in camp. The total number of man-days worked dropped to 2,139 as there was a loss of 790 man-days because of weather. Ben only worked 17 days of the month, missed 9 because of weather, and 4 days for the Sabbaths. Ben's letters mention the weather more often as winter settled in.

[December 2, 1942]

Dear Miriam:

How are you tonight Honey? It's pretty cold here. it was 10° above 0° about 20 min. ago and is getting colder. I think I'll be glad I moved down by the stove. It was snowing and blowing, so we didn't go to work this morn. Kenneth Blosser and Warren Meyers wanted to go to McConnellsburg to get Gas tickets but couldn't go unless there were enough fellows who had business to make a load. So Louis Delegrange, Sanford Yoder, Allen Landis and Myself went along I didn't have much business but I went anyway. we left about 8:00 and got back about 11:00 or a little after. IT was 16 miles to town. Kenneth Blosser got enough Gas tickets from Goshen to get back to Camp. He lives near Goshen. I wish I could come along but I don't have enough furlough days yet.

[December 3, 1942]

Hi Mimmie;

Its Just me knocking, may I come in? I won't stay very long, for There isn't much news. We didn't work again today. It was a little warmer this morn. than last night, but was still cold. And snowing a little. There isn't much snow on the Ground it was mostly blowing around. I was down in the shop most of the day Playing around. Didn't get much accomplished but wasted some time. About noon it cleared off and was pretty nice. I guess Probably when we will work in the Morn.

[December 5, 1942]

We only worked about 2 days this week. Pretty good I'll bet you didn't get by that easy.

In addition to writing letters to Miriam and various family members, Ben spent his days off writing for a larger audience.

[December 1, 1942]

This afternoon when I got in from work, I finished that essay I was working on, then after supper I moved. I moved all of my stuff from one end of the Dorm, where I was, the place where you have the picture of, to the other end. It is a single bed all to itself so I like it better. I have a closet all to my self and I can fix it anyway I want it. I had to build my self a shelf and change all my clothes from one place to this one so I've been busy this eve. again.

Ben wrote for the *Turnpike Echo* a few times while he was at camp. His father wrote a great deal for the Brethren's *Messenger*, so it seems understandable that Ben also would feel comfortable writing for a broader audience. Ben was outgoing and personable. Though he was not Mennonite like most of the other men in the Mennonite-run camp, he became the director of Sunday School, led prayer, and even spoke on occasion. His essay ran in the December 8 edition of the *Turnpike Echo*. The epigraph to this chapter is from the first paragraph:

What I Expect from C.P.S.

I have been here only a short time, but already I have become aware of the fact that life at Camp is much better than were my expectations. I had an idea that the camp here, being in the mountains, would be isolated from all contacts with normal life, and would be such a lonely place that time would seem long and go slowly. True enough it seems much longer since I left home and loved ones that it really is, but to me the time passes very rapidly. When a week has passed by, it is hard to realize where the time has gone.

The influence of the camp is also something which should not be overlooked. We have our regular church services where we can all take part and bring Praise and Thanksgiving to a God who has so mercifully provided a way of escape for His children here in the world who are striving to do His will. It should be the aim and desire of every one of us to cooperate to the fullest extent of our ability, and to make our camp a shining example to the world, that it may see the Christ life reflected in us, as Christian followers of our Lord and Savior, Jesus Christ.

How will this camp help us? This question may be answered by every individual. As has often been stated, "A person can get no more out of a thing, than what is put into it." This statement is very true as applied in our cases here. Some effort is required on our part if we are to receive any benefit from our experience.

I expect through my experience to come in closer contact with God, to attain greater heights in Godliness, to be more resigned to His will, and ready to do His bidding. It is my desire that I may truly say with Paul, "I press toward the mark for the prize of the High calling of God in Christ Jesus." Phil. 3:14.

—BEN KESLER[20]

Ben sent a copy of this article to Miriam a few days after it was printed. He continued to write of his workdays (or sometimes his lack-of-workdays) for the duration of his time at the Sideling Hill Camp. In general, his work rotated between planting, digging, brush burning, and maintaining the camp. Because he wrote daily, his letters seem almost repetitive. On January 22, 1943, he wrote, "Same old thing burning brush out by Fort Littleton Interchange That's perhaps 15 miles from camp." In fact, the work became so monotonous that Ben wrote in that same letter, "I'm sorry my letters of late have been short. But there Just isn't hardly anything going on unusual or worth mentioning." Similarly, on January 25, 1943, he wrote, "Sweet it sure doesn't take much space to tell the happenings in one day here. It's the same thing over and over."

In late January, the monotony was broken with work on the turnpike itself. On January 30, 1943, Ben wrote of work they did in a tunnel on the turnpike about thirty miles from camp. It offers a glimpse of what Sideling Hill Tunnel and others like it would have been like at that time.

> We worked today in spite of snow. It snowed Pretty lively all day but we kept right on Picking ice and shoveling snow. we worked out at Twin Tunnels today about 30 or 35 miles from camp, at noon The Tunnel Guards let us eat our dinner inside the office at the entrance. after we were thru eating he took us all and showed us the whole interior of the office. at each end of the ~~tunnll~~^tunnel there are large fans which Pull the fumes out of the Tunnel he showed us those and quite a few other little things. The Motors that Pull the fans are 50 horse power and They turn 18 revolutions per second so that is Pretty fast.

> [March 16, 1943]
> We worked at a new Project today. It was a nice spring day so we worked on some grades along the turnpike. Grades [were] made when hills were cut down where the turnpike passed thru, They froze and as they thawed caved down and rain washed them so we were grading them and smoothing them up. It is tiresome, monotonus, work. That is what we'll be doing for a while till April then tree Planting season will start.

The work Ben performed while at the Sideling Hill Camp could be summed up as "uneventful." Similar to the boredom and tedium of military life and other large-H historical accounts, CPS had times of vigorous effort and long spans of playing a waiting game.[21] Added to the monotony of his work was the reality that supposedly they were doing "work of national importance." Ben's letters rarely spoke negatively about his experiences, but occasionally he would include a sarcastic note about his feelings toward work that seemed so futile, for example in a letter from March 8, 1943: "Today we were busy with our work of National Importance. 'Burning Brush' It seems like a waste of time fooling around like all that. But It's orders."

One might wonder why Ben continued to write daily to Miriam if his work was so wretchedly boring. His days were monotonous, and he could only rephrase a description of planting greenery or digging holes so many times. But write daily he did for two reasons. First, Ben mentioned more than once in the letters that he did not need to keep a diary or journal because he wrote down every detail in the letters. He sought to capture the monotony as an important detail, a memory worth keeping, whether described in a diary, a journal, or in letters home. Second, he wanted to maintain the conduit and platform with his sweet wife at home. The conduit flow of love and connection and the stability of their platform depended upon consistency and effort. Investing the time in telling of his days, over and over again, demonstrated a commitment to their marriage and to maintaining closeness with Miriam. In this case, the content of the letters did not matter so much as the effort behind writing them and the tactile sense of them. Miriam did not care that she read yet another description of hole digging. She was just excited to see another letter from her Ben in the mailbox.

In all, Ben's time doing work of national importance at Sideling Hill was spent doing soil conservation. Sibley and Jacob note, "One out of every six man-days worked by CPS was devoted to the battle against soil erosion, and the record of accomplishment was substantial[:] . . . 1,455,000 yd. of bank sloped; . . . 1,070,000 trees planted or moved. . . . Much of this work was hard, menial, and tedious."[22] CPS did not consider men's skills and aptitudes. Instead, the men were uniformly assigned work throughout the country to keep them busy and keep them out of the public's eye, which frustrated many CPSers because, while they were not being asked to kill another human, they were not serving mankind in ways that they would like. The government turned down all suggestions for relief work in war-torn France or Belgium because all transportation overseas was dedicated to military efforts. While at camps, some men did find other ways to help the neighboring farms and churches. As his letters indicate, Ben was in a men's chorus that traveled to various churches (fig. 8).

One of the few alternative options given to those in Sideling Hill was to join a camp dedicated to hospital work, either in regular hospitals or in mental hospitals. Since medical professionals were desperately needed on the war fronts, the staffing in hospitals and mental institutions became quite desperate, and the government agreed to alleviate the staffing needs with CPS men. In February and March of his time in CPS at Sideling Hill, Ben heard of this option and was intrigued. More intriguing was that women workers were as desperately needed (if not more so) in hospital and mental institution work. If he chose to change camps, there was a possibility that Miriam could join him and work alongside him. Thus, chapter 9 details the decision-making process Ben and Miriam went through in determining whether to work in a mental hospital. However, before

FIGURE 8. The chorus of CPS Camp #20. Ben is in the back row, second from the left. Courtesy of Mennonite Central Committee Collection, Mennonite Church USA Archives, Akron, Pennsylvania.

they were to go to Rhode Island and work together at a mental hospital, Miriam worked at home to try and support them both. Her story fills an important gap in the history of CPS because little is known of CO wives' lives back home, and it is detailed in the following chapter.

CHAPTER 6

Miriam's Story—the First Six Months

OFTEN THE LARGE-H HISTORIES OF WARS ARE ALSO THE HISTORIES OF white men. The term history itself is "his story." So in respecting and sharing small histories we find the stories of women, minorities, and people of color. Those with racial and gender power determine what gets valued in archives. Jennifer Sinor writes that "we value the new, the aesthetic, the whole, the extraordinary, the masculine, the Anglo, and the fast—not because our dumpsters are filled with these but rather because our textbooks are."[1] Even within small histories, there are still issues of power, gender, and race. While the histories of Civilian Public Service (CPS) are small-h histories compared to the larger war narratives, the focus in them is still exclusively on men, their experiences, and their perspectives. The experiences of women and minorities have been neglected in CPS histories. This chapter helps fill that gap with one small history of one CPS woman's experience during the war.

Women conscientious objectors' (COs) experiences during the war differed greatly from most American women's stories. Women were not conscripted into service, but the entire nation was mobilized for war with a focus on industrialization and militarization. "Propaganda campaigns made wartime jobs and services appear fashionable and glamorous while also emphasizing that women would earn more money supporting the war effort than in other professions. . . . Due in part to the success of these efforts, 6 million women joined the workforce and another 350,000 joined military services between 1941 and 1945."[2]

Whether they worked to fill in labor shortages or not, women were still "required to maintain order and stable conditions"[3] at home in part because men were "more often told that they were fighting for 'apple pie, mom, and the girl next door' than for political independence, freedom from political tyranny, or their country as a political community."[4] Women were now the heads of their households and were expected to be frugal and conservative. This meant that women "reinvented the way that they fed, clothed, and cared for their families."[5] Domestic work carried with it the social and cultural expectation of supporting the war through victory gardens, victory mail, war bonds, and rationing. "Preventing waste, avoiding black markets, producing food, and abiding by food rationing, however trivial they may have seemed, allowed Americans to contribute to, and feel a part of, the war effort in daily physical and communally oriented ways."[6]

While millions of American women on the home front filled in factory, clerical, medical, governmental, legal, and journalism positions, Miriam and other COs had to find work elsewhere because their consciences would not permit them to work in any position connected to the military or that supported the war. While millions of women volunteered at their local chapter of the United Services Organization (USO), wrote letters to soldiers for victory, and bought war bonds for victory, women like Miriam did not. And while most Americans found themselves stretched and uncomfortable with rationing, Miriam and other women of the Plain Anabaptist Christian tradition took it in stride as they continued to garden, preserve, and maintain their already-frugal and simple lifestyle.

That frugal and simple lifestyle was stretched to the point of desperation for most CO wives and dependents. Whereas COs were conscripted into service just as most of the men in the country were, they were not paid as other conscripted men were. COs chose not to dodge the draft; most were patriots and were willing to serve their country. Since they could not take human life or take part in the military, they were left with limited options. They could be jailed or they could choose to serve in an alternative manner. Whatever their decision (to work in CPS or to be jailed), COs faced years without a source of income. Unfortunately, their dependents were in the same financial situation regardless of what avenue they chose. Hence, "in practice, men had to pay for their conscience by the impoverishment not only of themselves but of their families. More than any other factor, depriving COs of reasonable financial compensation impaired their service and violated the just observance of civil liberty."[7]

Crespi did an extensive study to understand public opinion of COs during the war years. He notes that the attitudes of the general public were not as bad as one might think: "Four-fifths of the general public accepted the principle of alternative service for C.O.'s and three-fourths believed that C.O.'s should receive wages and dependency allowances."[8] Recall that General Hershey selected CPS camp locations based on their distance from populated areas in order to minimize the spread of their point of view and the social impact they might have. Similarly, the government wanted to be silent about the financial conditions under which CO dependents lived, but many COs and dependents were vocal about the situation, writing letters to newspapers, state representatives, and even to the First Lady.

Eleanor Roosevelt, lauded humanitarian, condemned COs and spoke harshly about their dependents during the early years of the war. In one of her "If You Ask Me" columns in 1944 in *Ladies Home Journal*, Mrs. Roosevelt answered the question "Why don't the innocent dependents of a conscientious objector who has been called up by his draft board receive an allotment?" She responded,

> I am afraid the conscientious objector can make no allotments to his family because he does not become part of the Army. The allotment to families comes

from the Army and is the direct result of the service of the man for his country. The conscientious objector is not preforming any service for the country and therefore is not entitled to any pay. If he goes to a civilian camp, they agree to pay him a small sum of money for work in that camp, but that is work which he chooses to do and is not work which the Government is asking him to do as a citizen. He is not forced to do any work because the Government considers he has a right to his own convictions, but neither can he expect that he will be paid for something which he is not doing. It is hard for the innocent dependents who must suffer, but that is part of the burden which a conscientious objector assumes when he lives up to his beliefs.[9]

Note here that she was asked "why don't the innocent dependents . . . receive an allotment," but her response avoids the question. Instead of saying "innocent dependents do not receive an allotment because they do not deserve it," she responded only to criticize CO men. Though she does acknowledge that dependents were "innocent" and set apart from the decision to declare CO status, they also carried no independent value as citizens of the United States. It is as if women, children, and elderly parents were worthy of note and worthy of the financial support of their government only because of their relationship to a man. Though it is false logic, she was convinced that dependents' suffering was justified because COs made a choice she disagreed with. It is indicative of the era and of Western culture's fixation on men that Mrs. Roosevelt's responses are entirely focused on the male experience of war.

Stunned by her callous perspective, particularly toward innocent dependents of COs, Paul Comly French, executive secretary for the National Service Board for Religious Objection, wrote to Mrs. Roosevelt to protest. He noted that the "Selective Service Act provided that CO's perform 'work of national importance' and they had provided the country with many invaluable services. The C.P.S. assignee had no free choice about his work, and if he chose not to perform it, could spend up to five years in prison. . . . Mr. French questioned whether it was fair to 'extend a man's punishment to his wife and children.'"[10]

In a letter on June 14, 1944, Mrs. Roosevelt continued her fixation on the male experiences of war and responded that "when a country is at war and drafts its men, it drafts them for the one service which it needs—and that is men to fight. When a man's religious beliefs make it impossible for him to render the service which his country expects of him in time of war, he is naturally considered a *less useful citizen* than those who respond to the country's call in time of crisis" (emphasis added). She finished the scathing letter with: "One feels very sorry for the conscientious objectors who are obliged to live up to their religious convictions because one knows how they must dislike letting other men die so that they may be free to exercise these religious beliefs."[11]

Later that month, on June 21, Mrs. Roosevelt published similar sentiments in her "My Day" papers. She wrote,

> It is true that conscientious objectors have earned and saved much money for the government. It is true that they have made the lives of patients in state hospitals more bearable than they have ever been before. It is true that those who are willing to work in factories or military medical establishments, and some of them actually in danger zones or in the field of battle, have done heroic deeds and are fine people. But they are doing what they want to do. *They are not the same kind of citizens as are the men in the armed services.* For this reason, Congress has not appropriated money to pay them or to help their dependents on the same basis as the men drafted into the armed services. . . . It is hard on the families, but that is the price of doing what one believes in.[12]

In 1944, Mrs. Roosevelt considered COs to be second-class citizens. Because she regarded them as second-class citizens, she initially remained unfeeling and harsh toward the needs of the women, children, and elderly parents left behind. It was only once the atom bomb became a reality that the First Lady changed her perspective. Just over a year after her "My Day" publication above, she wrote on September 5, 1945:

> I found it very hard during the war to have much patience with the young men who were conscientious objectors. I knew that in those cases where they belonged to religions which did not permit them to take part in war, it often required more courage on their part to live up to their convictions than it would have taken to go into the services and serve with the majority of their friends. In spite of that, it was hard to keep down the feeling that they were exercising this freedom to live up to their religious beliefs at the expense of some other boy's sacrifice.
>
> Now we face the fact that scientists have made it possible for us to do such a successful job of exterminating other human beings that, unless we stop doing it in the mass way we call war, the human race will commit suicide. I hope we are going to have the courage to give up war and find ways of living peacefully together. It is not going to be easy, and the amount of self-discipline it is going to require is quite appalling. It is also going to require more thinking on our part and some real convictions—two things that most of us don't find easy.[13]

And after the war, when Mrs. Roosevelt had become a strong voice against nuclear warfare, she wrote,

> It is quite evident that, in the case of true conscientious objectors, we have no right to interfere with their conscience. But they will suffer, of course, because

until the whole world comes to feel that war is really mass murder, the great majority of men are going to feel that they have an obligation to defend their country in time of war.

The problem may become obsolete if modern weapons prove, once and for all, that any war in the future will mean destruction of the whole race, and if we therefore use our intelligence to prevent this final destruction. *Nevertheless, as long as the conscientious objector exists in relation to a majority opinion, he illustrates the point that we must preserve the right of individuals to be different. And we must very carefully guard against legal processes under which human beings can be punished for holding different ideas from the majority of their fellows.*[14]

Being able to look back at history and see how Eleanor Roosevelt's perspective on COs changed over the years does not change the fact that during the war, the dependents of CPS men were in a very precarious financial and emotional situation without hope of financial assistance from the government that had conscripted their husbands, fathers, and brothers.

Miriam's story, and the stories of those like her, present a gap in the research surrounding CPS. Historical accounts and government records of the CPS system agree that there were approximately twelve thousand men who served in camps across the United States during World War II. These same accounts sometimes also note that the "refusal of Congress to make any provisions for assistance to dependents of drafted CO's exposed the wives, children, and aged parents of men in CPS to extreme hardship and insecurity."[15] In 1978, Frazer and O'Sullivan wrote that "twelve thousand men participated in the program, and although a good deal has been written about them, there has been no systematic analysis of the impact of their decision on their wives and families."[16]

Twenty years later, in 1997, Rachel Goossen published her important study, *Women against the Good War*, which notes that a rich historiography has been compiled of women workers on the home front during World War II. But she also notes that this rich

historiography of American women and World War II thins considerably when one adds the dimensions of pacifism. Women who took part in Civilian Public Service were not drafted and therefore received little official or public notice. In subsequent years, few of them published memoirs or spoke publicly about their wartime experiences. Accordingly, scholars of the peace movement and of the American home front have excluded their experiences from historical accounts. Peace scholarship has focused instead on prominent antimilitarists who took a radical stance against the war [such as Dorothy Day, Jane Addams, Jeannette Rankin, Mildred Scott Olmsted, and Dorothy Detzer].[17]

She also points out that while "most chroniclers have assumed that Civilian Public Service was exclusively a man's world[,] [t]o the contrary, approximately two thousand women, and perhaps half as many children, lived in and near Civilian Public Service Camps."[18] Goossen's *Women against the Good War* stands alone as a text focused exclusively on the lives of women working in and around CPS camps.

I found Goossen's text invaluable; however, it is important to note that her text concerns itself primarily with the approximately two thousand women who *worked in and near CPS camps*. Miriam herself fit into that number later when she and Ben moved to Rhode Island to work in the State Hospital for Mental Diseases. But what of Miriam's first six months? What of the stories of "wives, children, and aged parents of men in CPS [left] to extreme hardship and insecurity"?[19] Just how many dependents were there? I have been unable to find any record of even a broad estimate of the total. For example, Gingerich's 1949, 508-page volume *Service for Peace* mentions women only seven times according to the index, and while it offers numerical estimates for where men were from, how much education they had, their prior occupations, and a host of other details,[20] nowhere does it offer information about the families left at home. The publication called *The Conscientious Objector* was in print during the war years. It notes that "over one-third of all men in C.P.S. were responsible for dependents."[21] So, there were a minimum of four thousand dependents left behind in sometimes very precarious situations, but it is far more likely that that number was double, triple, or quadruple. Census records indicate that the average household population in 1940 was 3.67 people. If it were true that only one-third of CO men were responsible for dependents, those 4,000 men had 14,680 dependents. It is clear, no matter the exact numbers, that the number of dependents far surpassed the total number of CO men in service.[22]

The reality was that twelve thousand CO men were conscripted and then worked more than eight million days without pay, without health insurance, and without workman's compensation when even German POWs were receiving eighty cents a day for their labor.[23] Further, "if the United States Government had paid for this work at the same rate as for its Army, it would have spent over $18,000,000."[24] Those unpaid work hours meant the men had no money to send home to support their dependents, and even if there was time at the end of a workday, they were not usually allowed to work for pay outside their CPS duties. Even more egregious, the COs' dependents were denied the financial allotment given to all other conscripted men's families, leaving many almost destitute. In spite of numerous attempts by the peace churches and individual COs to rectify this, funds were never made available to the families. What Miriam's letters from November 5, 1942, to March 17, 1943, represent is a written record, a perspective of one of those dependents, of how the lack of financial support impacted her and her family, what she felt about being left behind, and the realities of her daily life.

I struggled with how to represent Miriam's story. Her letters were generally longer than Ben's and bounce from topic to topic. Her life continued on in their community as well, rather than at a remote camp. She had much to report about the goings-on from home, from church, from their friends and acquaintances and of what she did each day. Ben's letters, in comparison were systematic and easily explained chronologically. Chronology would be somewhat confusing for Miriam's story. The themes I see over the five months include the hard work she did to earn a living, particularly the experiences working for the Holderman family as a hired girl, descriptions of food, her worrying and efforts to stay positive, her managing their finances and the selling of their home, the death of her grandfather, her loss of weight and possible loss of a pregnancy, and the fact that many of her letters included shorter letters from members of her family. Thus, I have organized Miriam's story by theme and not necessarily by chronology.

Another challenge I found with Miriam's letters is that Miriam only labeled her letters with the day of the week. For example, she would write "Wed. evening." Often she would write in the morning and evening on the same day, then not at all the following day—due to when she had time to write and how tired she was at the end of a given day—so trying to organize her writing chronologically was difficult. The sheer volume of correspondence from Miriam, and the lack of definitive dates, forced me to create my own calendars of the months during 1942 and 1943. Because there are no dates on the letters themselves, I initially organized according to the postmark date. Then, I shifted the days of the week in order along with the postmarks. For the most part this worked well enough to figure out her chronology, but occasionally, there was a letter that just did not make sense in either the postmark or the day of the week. In these instances, I adjusted the chronology as best I could according to the content and context described in the letters.

Miriam was just seventeen years old during their first year of marriage. She had left high school early, much to the dismay of her teachers, to marry Ben before he was conscripted. From what my father tells me, she was on track to be the valedictorian had she finished. Without a high school diploma, she would not have qualified for office work, and because of her own religious convictions, she would have been unwilling to work in any defense industry job. Both of these factors limited Miriam's options for employment. She had been raised, however, on a farm by people accustomed to hard manual labor. (If there is one thing Keslers know how to do, it is *work*.) So working as a "hired girl" in someone's home was the logical choice.

Miriam's first venture into the work world occurred while she lived at home with her parents and siblings. She worked for a neighboring farmwife. On November 9, 1942, she wrote: "To-morrow morning I'm going down to Dawson's to work. She wants me Tues. & Wed and either Fri. or Sat. I'll be making 20¢ an hour. (Some Pay ha!) or $8.00 a week. She says when ever I want an afternoon off I can just go or if I don't feel like working just not work." I suspected, based on her joking comment, that the pay was pretty low for the amount of work she was to do. This suspicion led to some digging to find out comparative data.

The US Department of Labor Wage and Hour Division website notes that in 1939 the minimum hourly rate of pay was $0.30. In a 1940 study of female domestic workers in Washington, DC, the "weekly schedule for full-time workers ranged from 42 to 105 hours. The median daily schedule for full-time white workers was 12 hours and 50 minutes; for Negro workers 11 hours and 33 minutes. The weekly cash wage for full-time resident employees ranged from $3.50 to $18.75. The median weekly wage for 564 women [both day workers and residential] was $8.10."[25] Miriam's pay for this first position was at that median. The *Occupational Outlook Handbook* from 1949, put out by the US Department of Labor, does not have descriptions of the position, outlook for a career, or average earnings for a domestic laborer. The closest I could find was a description of the job of hotel housekeeper. "Earnings of housekeepers, according to limited data for a few large cities, were about $150 to $350 a month in large hotels and $75 to $100 in small hotels in early 1946."[26] Clearly, there was a range in pay for the job of housekeeper.

Later on, when working as a live-in housekeeper for the Holdermans, Miriam's pay rate does not match the 1940 study, given that she probably worked sixteen hours a day, six days a week. Fox notes that "wages showed no consistent relation to hours of work. Women holding full-time jobs demanding over 80 hours per week were represented in every stage of the wage scale, receiving $3.50 to $18.75."[27] Even though "resident employees were in general the better-paid white women who were given comfortable living quarters and some provision for social life"[28] and even though the more schooling a woman had the higher her wages, the Holdermans paid Miriam a flat amount and sometimes even less than the amount agreed upon when they hired her.

Ben made a very good friend, Lewis, while at camp. Miriam and Lewis's wife, Amanda, corresponded a bit. In a letter on January 18, 1943, Amanda wrote, "A week after Lou left the people I worked for before we were married ask me to work for them, so I've been here for eleven weeks now. They give me $18.00 a week I'm their maid. All I do is dusting and cleaning and wash dishes at night." Amanda was located in northern Indiana as well, though in a more populated area. The difference in their pay for similar domestic labor was significant.

Miriam worked very, very hard at the jobs she took on. She likely worked to avoid thinking or feeling the pain of missing Ben. As was her custom (and one that I apparently inherited, according to my husband), Miriam regularly worked to the point of exhaustion. Whereas Ben had to find things to occupy his downtime to stave off boredom, and he lamented that there often was too much downtime, Miriam had no such difficulty. Boredom was not possible when she worked twelve to sixteen hours a day. On Friday evening, November 13, Miriam wrote,

> I was down to Dawsons to-day to do what I thought was their Saturday's cleaning. I got there and to-day I cleaned three rooms. "Nice" wasn't it. I'll try to tell you about what the size of them is. The front room is about 11 by 15 and the next one is about 15 by 14 and a bedroom about 12 by 12. I washed wood work around 12 window casings and 1 door besides the mop board around the rooms. swept down all the ceilings and walls. They are fiber board (brown) like the folks put on in the kitchen and little pieces of "stuff" kept coming down all over me & everything else Then I swept (with a broom) a 9 x 12 ^living room rug. & then I rolled it up and ^swept & mopped that room & that other big one and had to move the piano to sweep behind it and change the davenport & overstuffed chair from one room to another and changed a desk ^& bookcase from one side of the room to the other and pa turned the rug around from what it was & laid it back in place. and mopped the biggest room. Then swept the bedroom down (wall & ceiling) then I took off the inner spring mattress and washed the springs there we 99 coils. I know! and then the mattress had to be put back on & I helped get supper and then washed the dishes & wiped them. It was seven o'clock by that time and I had gone to work at 8:20 this morning. Then she said she would give me $2.00 for the work and I worked 11½ hrs. at 20¢ an hr would be $2.30. But she takes off the time when I'm eating. I'm rather fed up with everything.

A repeating theme of Miriam's work efforts is to be overworked and underpaid for her time. After working for the Dawsons for only about two weeks, Miriam found a position that was for a longer period of time. The Holderman family, who resided in Goshen, Indiana, was in need of a woman to clean, cook, and take care of their young daughter for a few months. Mrs. Holderman was to have an operation, so part of Miriam's time there would be spent running the household and watching the child on her own. As much as Miriam thought she had finally found a position that would not be as difficult, she was to be sorely disappointed. The treatment by the Holdermans was considerably worse, though it started well enough.*

[November 17, 1942]
This morning Mrs. Holderman of Goshen called. Mother answered & she wondered if . . . mother had a daughter who wanted to do house work. Mother said

---

* Everett Holderman was the owner of Everett's Grocery Store, where my father worked for twenty-eight years, starting at age fifteen. Several of his brothers also did. I myself worked in the store from the age of thirteen until I was seventeen or eighteen.

Yes Mrs. Ben Kesler. She said, "Ben Kesler's wife why I know him." and then I talked to her & I understood her to say she was Everett Holderman's wife and he's the man who runs the Royal Blue store. You know—the fellow you talked to about the job she wants some one for 2 months. She is going to have an operation and I would be there to run every thing alone for 2 weeks or until she came home from the hospital. I don't know what to do about anything. I'm so "befuddled," I hardly know where I'm at. So I'm going to pray some more about everything and I'm sure God will show me the right way.

[November 18, 1942]
I wrote a letter to Mrs. Holderman and told her that I would come & work for her if ~~m~~ she would give me 12$\underline{00}$ a week Imagine me making that much money in one week. Some "punkins." I don't know what she'll say but I think she'll give me that much because she can't find a girl and she has to have an operation so there isn't much choice. She'll call me up before Sat. evening & tell me what she has decided.

[November 19, 1942]
I will get $12.$\underline{00}$ the two weeks that she is in the hospital and $10.$\underline{00}$ the rest of the time. With Saturdays & Sundays off. And I think evenings when ever I wish. But I won't want any off because there isn't any place I'd want to be without you along so I'm waiting for you to come home & my evenings will be spend writing to you & sewing until then. They are both very nice people and have a little girl who is three. She's cute. Has black curly hair and black eyes and is tall & slender for no older than she is.

At the beginning, Miriam was promised twelve dollars for the weeks Mrs. Holderman was in the hospital, ten dollars on the weeks she was home, and Saturdays and Sundays off. Based on her letters, I do not believe she ever got twelve dollars, and she never got Saturdays off. She worked well into the evening most days of the week, caring for the child, and she even worked Sunday afternoons on occasion, all for the same pay.

At first her time with the Holdermans was very good. She cleaned and cooked and was given afternoons off. She also thought that Mrs. Holderman and she would be the "best of friends." Monday, November 23, 1942, she wrote,

Well here I am my first day's work completed. (I think). This forenoon I did the washing with Francis' (Mrs. Holderman) help and I have so many things to remember that I hardly know where anything is. Today we had chicken, gravy potatoes & tomatoes. Then I got supper and we had creamed chicken on toast; cabbage (fixed the way you like it with cream) and jello with ^mixed fruit in it & whipped cream on top.

This afternoon from about 2:30 until 4:30 I had off to do as I pleased. I felt about half condemned to not be doing something but it just wasn't there to be done. So I put my hair up again and swept the side walk (By the way it has rained (rather misted) all day so it wasn't just too pleasant outside. I think that Francis and I will be the best of friends I am so glad because I like to have friends. She seems more like a sister than my mistress. And they are Christians for which I am so thankful. Rhonda their little girl is sweet and very brilliant for no older than she is. Everett & Francis have lots of fun just like we did (& will). They like to tease one another it brings back to me all the swell times we've had together darling but I put that out of my mind & dream of the ones that will come in the future.

And on Tuesday she wrote,

This is a nice place to work. The work isn't hard just ordinary housework but it isn't "home" to me. I have everything anyone could nearly wish for to make the work easier. Washing machine Laundry room, drying room, electric iron toaster, waffle iron, electric mix master, electric (mangol) ironer, sweeper, furniture sweeper, electric stove, rifrigerator, a swell piano, a radio in the kitchen & a combination radio & recorder in the living room, a new sewing machine & a modern room for my self. So I should be happy but I'm not. I rather envy Francis & Everett. They call each other honey! just like we did & every time they say it, it just sends an ache right through me.

But by Friday, November 27, the amount of work she was asked to do increased. She wrote,

I am dreadfully tired & about half sick to-night.
To-day I did the Saturdays cleaning and I mean cleaning too. She is very particular. and there are three big bedroom upstairs & the long hall & the bathroom. And downstairs there is Rhonda's play room (They have their desk in it too.) And a living room that is about 16 x 30 and dining room & big kitchen & breakfast nook & the bathroom downstairs & another hall and of course the venetian blinds to clean every place. Then after dinner she went up town & I did dishes and then . . . I had to put Rhonda to bed and read her some stories and Then I washed her pajamas that she had wet in last night and straightened up some things and took time out to read the four letters I got from you & the card from mother. And then I woke Rhonda & dressed her and I thought it was pretty cool in the house for her so I went down & put some coal in the furnace & it got a head start for me & got too hot & I was just scared stiff and then it puffed out & I got soot all over me & then they came home & there was smoke & fumes all over & it was so hot & everything I am most nearly

a nervous wreck. & then I got supper & he made all sorts of remarks about the hamburgers & then her brother came just as we were ready to sit down to supper & we didn't have anything but tapioca cream & hamburgers (with all the trimmings) fixed and so finally they go started & I finished my dishes & at last—here I am. Whew!

Mrs. Holderman was to have a hysterectomy, based upon Miriam's descriptions of the operation. Mrs. Holderman had a cold the first two weeks so the doctor would not operate for fear of pneumonia. Because of this, Miriam's time there was extended as well. Sometime the following week (though this was a letter with a mystery date and possibly incorrect day of the week so I cannot be sure, but it is possibly around December 1, 1942), she wrote,

Thursday Evening
9:40
My dearest Hubby:
    I'll tell you to begin with that I'm pretty blue so you'll know what to expect altho I'll try to cheer up for your sake. Darling I miss you more than tongue 'can tell. And it just makes my heart ache to have to be away from you my dearest— oh I just can't find words to explain But then you know how tis. Cause your my better "half" and so you feel the same way. I was terribly blue & lonesome after the mail man came & didn't bring me any letters and today I ironed a good share of the day so I had plenty of time to think about us. Francis was sick and most of the things I did didn't seem to please her very well and then Rhonda was naughty & in to everything & I don't think her mother likes it very well if I correct her or make her behave. Her daddy isn't like that. I wish I had complete charge of the house as it is I have to do what she says the way she wants it done & if I don't do it ^quite that way then that's something else. In way I hope she doesn't need me very much longer I'd rather work in a store. Then you get to meet more people & you don't just have one or two bossin' & the only ones you're around all the time. . . .
    I keep losing weight ^except but ^around my waist the size is increasing I don't get it. I was just thinking to night when Everett had Ronda. How sweet you would look holding & talking to our little son or daughter. I just closed my eyes & lived in sweet dreams for a little bit. Darling our children will have a daddy to be proud of.
    Honey you have no idea how very, very, Very, much I love you. . . .
    So nite now and I'll be with again fore very long. Although it's on paper that's better than not at all. So cheer up—as the robin says (and me too) and remember my "love" is all "yours" and always will be. Your loving, adoring wife; Mrs. Kesler (ahem! surprise ending ha!)

In this letter we can see the emotional upheaval Miriam was in, a forecast of how difficult the work at Holdermans was about to become, and that she might be pregnant. Note that Miriam was losing weight "except . . . around my waist the size is increasing I don't get it." She spent a moment daydreaming about having a baby. A few days later, on December 4, she wrote,

> Quite a little mother I am getting to be. . . . But then I'd better be getting in practice you know cause I may need the experience. Oops! Who knows? I'm sure I don't. I have been having some mighty peculiar feeling in my tummy lately that have been given me some-thing to think about. If I still proceed to get bigger this month then I shall go to the doctor and find out whether there is or isn't something the matter. . . . Darling if we are going to have one (maybe two ha!) would you mind just too much to postpone your furlough until that time so you could be with me then. Cause then I would need & want you more than any other time & you know they say you never begin showing until the fourth or fifth months so maybe it will be in the spring. "ok mimmie cut it out or you'll really convince him there is going to be one & you don't even know yet your-self."

But on December 8, only a few days after that, Miriam wrote,

> Tues. Eve.
> Hi Honey!
> Here I be! Your Mimmie has been feeling pretty punk all day. She has had her usual monthly occurrence. Yes you guessed it! I'm in the red. (as you used to say). I had cramps so bad that I was nearly tied up in a knot. I would have liked to crawled in bed & stayed there but I can't do such things now. Instead I ironed all forenoon, then got dinner and wash^ed dishes and then washed 30 windows that were about ~~seves~~ 7 by 15 (on both sides) . . . and then I ironed some more and then I put clothes away I made 3 trips up stairs and had all I could carry each time. And then I called Roy Rensberger and then I mended some things and finally got supper and washed the dishes . . . and sewed a little bit and her I am. Whew! I'm all out of breath.

Miriam noted the next day that her period was unusually heavy. "I don't quite understand it," she wrote on December 9. Based on her explanation of how she had felt in the preceding weeks, how heavy her period was, and the sheer exhaustion from overwork she experienced, there is a possibility that she was pregnant and miscarried. The following day she wrote,

> This week I have worked the hardest I have since I came and of all "weeks" I should have taken this one "easy." I don't hardly see how I could be ^an expectant

mother. I rather imagine I would have lost it before now if I had been. This forenoon I cleaned up stairs. They have hardwood floors all over the joint (I mean house) and so there is nothing but scatter rugs up stairs. Guess how many. Wrong! <u>20</u>. don't hardly seem like enough does it. My back began to ache before I had all of them shook. and of course all the window sills had to be cleaned. The floor dusted; the waste paper basket emptied and the furniture dusted and then in the bathroom all the chrome fixtures have to be polished and I have to put "drain-o" in the tub and lavatory drains & Plumite in the stool and wash of the window sills and clean the bathtub, lavatory, & the stool (on the outside) and then clean the floor in the shower & the bathroom linoleum with a damp cloth and so on. . . . Any way I got done before dinner and so after dinner Francis went up to the store to help and so here I was again. And then this afternoon I washed more wood work. six doors and the stairway and of course the mop board all the way around and numerous ^other little things to small to mention.

A week passed by and Miriam was still not being treated well, working too much, and feeling very unhappy. On December 16, she wrote,

Isn't it terrible to be in a place where no one cares about your feelings or whether you are happy or not. They never show any more appreciation than if I were an old broom stick. I'm here to work not to have a personality of my own. You wondered last week why I didn't let the scrubbing on the wood work go until an other day. Well I had to do it. She knew how I was feeling & she had felt the same way the week before but she crawled in bed & stayed there. But me well that's different! She doesn't care about that where I'm concerned. If I hadn't promised I'd stay I wouldn't cause it's not all it was "cracked up" to be. She had said she didn't care if the house work didn't get done as long as I took good care of Rhonda while she was gone. That was the first time she talked to me. Now it's a different story. I'm supposed to take the best care of their darling cherub. and—do the washing, ironing, thorough cleaning on Thursday & Friday, Give Rhonda a bath every other day. el defrost the refrigerator clean out closets, wash wood work and all the hundreds of little things that a person does mechanically that are connected with a days work.

And on December 17, in addition to the "usual" household chores, caring for Rhonda, cooking, and cleaning, Miriam found that the Holdermans expected her to do other work.

To-day I was all set to clean the upstairs as usual and a fellow came & began brushing snow off of the windows outside and in a little bit he came to the door & sto said he had come to put on the storm windows. And they weren't washed!

So—you can imagine how they looked. They had putty and paint & just plain dirt on them. I got thirteen washed on both sides. They would average about 27 by 54. Some bigger and some smaller. My back aches from washing so much & there are still about 8 to wash (I think!) Besides doing that I gave Rhonda a bath this morning and of course got her breakfast and then after dinner at 2:00 I put her to bed and washed some more windows and I had to get dinner of course & wash dishes and then this afternoon I made a cherry pie and baked two crusts too.

Finally, Mrs. Holderman was approved for her surgery. Then Miriam found herself tasked with not only taking care of the house and the child but also being a "special nurse" in the hospital for Mrs. Holderman.

[December 18, 1942]
You'd be surprised to see what your wife has been doing this afternoon. I have been the special nurse for Ms. Holderman at the hospital. They couldn't find a special nurse so it happened to fall to my lot to be just that.

And I had to hear all about the operation and the whys & what-for's of this & that & the other thing and I had to tell her ^all about the things here at home. The dear lady would have had a backset if I'd told all that's happened. She thinks her darling daughter is so sweet etc. I wish she could have seen the way she acted this af evening. Positively horrid! I put up with it as long as I could and I tried to make excuses for her behavior but when she kept right on bawling & hallowering and wouldn't eat her supper. Well—that was just a little too much. I gave her a good old fashioned spanking! And then she wouldn't stop crying & was holding her breathe & being stubborn so—I just took her in the bathroom and dashed cold water in her face. Ah but she was naughty. Finally I got her to bed & came down stairs to do breakfast, dinner & supper dishes. more fun! I finished those at nine o'clock & then in about 15 min. Everett came home & wanted to know what time I put Rhonda to bed and I told him & then he went to bed. He said he was going to get up at 3:30 in the morning. There is so much work to be done at the store. I haven't gotten any of the cleaning done this week and I'll only have tomorrow forenoon to get any done. Cause in the afternoon I'll have to go to the hospital and stay until (I imagine) about midnight. Then come home (here; rather) and get up in the morning & get Rhonda ready for church & give her a bath & take one myself and goodness knows what else. Oh well such is life.

The good that came out of the experience working in the hospital was that Miriam was much more confident about the possibility of working in a hospital with Ben in CPS service. After going home for Christmas, Miriam came back to work to find that nothing had changed, except that things were possibly worse than before.

[December 27, 1942]
My "gorsh" I came back about four-thirty and I have worked until about seven. And on Sunday Eve. yet in the bargain. The "Boss" came back last evening from the hospital. And now the <u>fun</u> has really began. Did I say "fun"??? Well when she says "Frog" every one jumps or else! And goodness knows she's off to a flying start. I dread the weeks to come. I have been up and down ^the stairs about a dozen times since I came ~~up stairs~~ and I had to prepare a "special" supper for her and get Rhonda's and then I washed the dishes and wiped them and got oodles of things for Francis and boy was the house ever in a mess when I got here. It doesn't look like the same place now. Quite a transformation .

[December 28, 1942]
    Well I'm so tired that I honestly haven't enough ambition to hardly even sit up. It's 8:45 and I have just finished my work. And I have been nearly running every [minute] since 6:30 this morning. And when I say running I mean running. Honestly I don't think I have ever hurried so much (all in one day) in all my life as I did to-day. I might try to tell you what all I did but it would take pages so I won't even begin. Except a few things. I got the washing done and part of the ironing and did some cleaning and washed oodles of dishes and cleaned out the refrigerator, fixed special things for Francis and Rhonda to eat. Took their meals to them in bed and of course got an altogether different meal for Everett and I.
    I had to take Francis the bed pan when ever she wanted it (and then empty it too) Boy that is one <u>nice</u> mess! I'm telling you! Then one time this afternoon she missed the pan and I had to change the bed (sheets, pillow cases and her nightgown). She can hardly move yet at all by her self. So I had to do the moving.
    And this afternoon the nurse came and gave her an anemia and a bath and changed her bed. I had to get things for her and then I had to fix some binders for Francis' abdomen and I had to look for the material and make them and of course I had to put away ^all the things the nurse had used and put away the clothes I had ironed.

After the new year, Miriam began to look forward to leaving the position. In addition to the extra work, Miriam received less than the money agreed upon.

To-day was New Year's Day and I "shore" started it out right. Up to my neck in work. And to-night Everett gave me my pay for this week. It was <u>ten</u> dollars. And after all I have done this week and beside that I have to stay to-morrow.

(Saturday) and work and I wont even have time to go up town. Cause I have to stay right here. . . . My (I mean "our") mother called just as we finished looking at the pictures. She is all worried about me working so hard. She said I should tell them I wanted fifteen dollars or else I'll quit. But boy I can't get up enough nerve. I did tell them though that I would only work three more weeks. Francis seems to think I should work for her just as long as she wants me to. But she's got another thing a coming.

Miriam's mother, Maureen, wrote to Ben the same sentiment she gave to Miriam,

[January 3, 1943]
I'll be so so glad when she is thro there at Holderman's I won't know what to do. It makes me just plain M.A.D. they impose on her good nature the way they do. I'm afraid she wont spunk up & tell them she cant stay for the same wages as when she was helping with work before going to the hospital. . . . I sure hope your Mimmie gets some good breaks pretty soon or her lonliness & work I fear will break her. Don't tell her I said so tho. I have been watching pretty close & it worries me. Let's hope & Pray that her luck changes very soon & that the sun will soon shine thro. I don't know what she would do if it wasn't for your letters & your faith in her.

Finally, on January 13, Miriam wrote,

This is my last week here. Yippee! So be absolutely sure you don't forget and send some of my mail here, cause then I might not get it. . . . I am going up to the folks and recuperate for a week or two so maybe I'll weight 200 when I come out to see you. I'll have to gain 73 lbs though if I do. Well night now honey and I'll be back with you again to-morrow evening and in the meantime my precious darling: take care of yourself for me and soon I'll come to you and we'll just love & love & love, I bet-cha! I am getting ^oh so anxious.
                    Your lonesome little pal; "Mimmie"
                    Here's a great Big squeeze and a Kiss
                    my arms → (you)X.

Though Miriam knew it was her last week of work, her time at the Holdermans' ended rather abruptly. I believe she stayed the duration she promised to, given the way things were there after Mrs. Holderman's surgery, but I think they wanted her to stay longer. However, Miriam was more than ready to be done with the demands of that household. And her own family was soon to need her to help as her Grandpa Carpenter's health rapidly declined.

Friday Eve 9:30
[January 15, 1943]
Hi Honey!

Guess where I am? Up at the folks. Mother called up about 1:30 and asked me if I could be ready by 5:00. So I told her I could. And I sure did hurry. I practically have "run" since yesterday morning. I am not going back to the Holdermans again. Hurray! Am I ever glad it's over with. . . .

I don't know whether I can get rest or not. Cause everyone up here is at a pretty high tension too. Mom got me some vitamins tablets. So I'm going to get real strong right away quick ^(I bet-cha).

In the days after Miriam came home from her time at the Holdermans' house, Grandpa Carpenter's illness got worse and worse. Even though Mother and Dad (the folks) thought Miriam would be home to help them with the house and the butcher shop, Miriam found herself taking on the tasks of keeping her grandparents' home together as her grandfather approached death.

[January 17, 1943]
I told grandma that I would be glad to come & help out if they need me. so She wants <u>me</u> to take charge when grandpa dies. See that the house is in order and tell the neighbor women & friends etc. what to do and then straighten up. I am glad that she <u>wants</u> me too. But that's a pretty big undertaking for even an experienced person. But if it is God's will that I should help out that way. I will do my best with "His" help. If I can have the courage & strength to keep on. I am going down with mother to morrow night when she goes after dad and if they need me then I will stay. Some one has to be with him all the time (nights & day).

In a letter, Mother (Miriam's mother, Maureen) shared more information about the state of Grandpa and the living conditions within the grandparents' household.

[January 20, 1943]
We are <u>so</u> glad to have our dear girl home again. What a worry gone since we know she doesn't have to be imposed upon and treated as tho she was an ignorant slave. We hope she soon feels real good. She says she eats more since she got home. Right now she is down to Grandpa's as I suppose you will know before my letter reaches you. I hope her stay there wont make her feel any worse physically. I know there is bound to be some mental torture. Perhaps she has written you how Grandma is acting. Surely she is letting the devil rule in thots and

actions. She has hurt several of the children so bad by her ugly talk and actions and poor grandpa in his dying condition hears almost all that is said and done. He is just as rational as can be. Our hearts ache. . . . He is anxious to die, we wonder why God spares him to suffer so & have to endure all the plans for death & burial etc. If you have a card or greeting you mite send him one. He realizes all and mite cheer him a little if it would get here before he's gone.

Miriam stayed at her grandparents' household to help, but she commented regularly that there was not much to be done. She noted that she did not see a reason to be there, but she was wanted, so she did her duty. She continued to create a sense of place and space by commenting on the materiality of her letter, specifically that her pen had had some issues. The letter was smudged and blotted with ink, a departure from her usual tidiness.

> Thurs. Eve.
> [January 21, 1943]
> Hi Honey!
> Here's your "little wifey." It's time for our evening chat. I hope you'll be able to read this. I went & "screwed" the cap on my fountain pen & it's on so good that I can't get it off.
> Don't be surprised if there is soot all over this paper cause just before supper I lit the lamp in the dinning and when we were eating supper Elsie said she thought she smelled smoke and so we looked—and there the lamp was smoking and blazing clear to the ceiling and there is soot all over the dinning room & kitchen. So—tomorrow I'll have a "JOB" I bet-cha! I never did like to clean up such messes. But then I guess I shouldn't complain. Although after all I'm not compeled to stay here. I am my own boss now. ^Nobody Except you can be my boss. Want the job?

Grandpa Carpenter passed on January 26, ending Miriam's time caring for the household. Then, all of February and into March, Miriam was back in her parents' home. Her letters were considerably shorter, since there was not much to tell Ben about. Because by this time the house had sold (see chapter 7), her financial burden had lightened considerably, and she was able to stay home and help around the house. She painted ceilings, cleaned, made clothing, helped at the butcher shop, and did a host of other "normal" activities on the farm. The letters during February and into March were also filled with a sense of expectancy and perhaps unease because Ben was considering transferring into hospital work so that Miriam could join him. Miriam did not take another job for fear that she would finally get word that she was to move to wherever Ben was stationed (see chapter 9).

While Miriam's experiences from November 1942 to March 1943 were mostly mundane housework, through her letters we are given a glimpse inside one CPS woman's story when left at home. The letters serve us now, decades later, as a material reminder of an ordinary life lived during extraordinary times. They enable us to immerse ourselves in the experiences of one woman, the heavy work, the exhaustion, and the worry and anxiety. It is easy to get lost in Miriam's story, in the day-to-day grind. But her story is more than interesting. Stories like hers have been experienced over and over and over again by women throughout history. Indeed, even those Rosie the Riveter women working in the military industrial complex during the war worked harder and longer and were paid less than their male coworkers. And so, while Miriam's story fills a gap in the historical data about CPS, it also allows us to understand some of the experiences of women in America at that time. It is a small-h historical account that adds texture, nuance, and context to the larger historical narrative.

CHAPTER 7

Finances and Interpersonal Conflicts

A T THE SAME TIME MIRIAM FACED THE CHALLENGES OF BEING A "HIRED girl" and earning enough money to support herself and Ben, she also faced the daunting task of selling their home in order to release them from that financial burden. As I note in chapter 6, Miriam simply could not afford to keep the house, given the low-paying work that was available to her as a conscientious objector. What were the challenges of selling a home in 1942? The US home front was immersed in supporting the war effort, impacting finances, housing, and employment and initiating the rationing of gas, food, and clothing. Because women and minorities filled labor shortages, people moved and needed new housing options throughout the country, but it is unclear how the market was in Goshen, Indiana, at that time. We can know certain aspects of the housing market overall. First, the median home value in Indiana in 1940 was $2,406, according to US Census Bureau records for Housing Values, putting in perspective the $3,500 asking price Ben and Miriam originally put on their home.[1] Second, rationing of metals and other materials limited building new homes and halted the recreational vehicle factories across Elkhart County. These pieces of large-H historical data, available in public and governmental records, impacted the housing market. Based on Ben and Miriam's correspondence, I suspect that the housing market was not good for sellers in Goshen, given that they had to reduce the price of their home and it took more than eight weeks to sell.

Letter writing as a main form of communication proved to be especially challenging when it came to dealing with Ben and Miriam's financial situation. The financial and business content of Miriam's letters are another way of understanding her small history and how conduit and platform function. The conduit, that outpouring of love and devotion I describe in chapter 1, never stopped between them, but a large part of their relationship at that time concerned their financial future—a very unromantic aspect of marriage. This helps us understand that conduit functions as more than just shared love between two people; yet, the financial content of these letters was also more than a formulaic business transaction as in ars dictaminis. The letters were not just "love letters" and neither were they just "business letters"; they were both. Here the business of living intersected with love and devotion, making visible what Bazerman aptly calls "an open-ended transactional space." We often hear the word *transaction* in business and financial matters. The transactional space Bazerman describes is a two-way conduit flow of information that "can be specified, defined, and regularized in many different ways. . . . Moreover, letters can and often do explicitly describe and comment on the relationship between the parties and the nature of the current transaction."[2] The combination of romantic love and discussions of finances demonstrate how in such a transactional space "the genre itself expands and specializes, so that distinctive kinds of letters become recognizable and treated differently."[3]

This transactional space is also one in which we can see an intersection of the conduit flow of information and the materiality of platform. The platform functions to make physical the intangible or abstract. When discussing business dealings like the selling of their home, Miriam and Ben used the conduit transactional space to decide things that had very real, very physical ramifications. Because the letters merged the two different types of letter writing, the path Ben and Miriam took to financial stability was not as clear-cut as it might have been with formal business writing. There were emotions involved in the decisions, so the conduit flows got "crossed" more than once over the months it took to sell their physical home.

Recall that the home was located on the same property as Ben's parents' home. Benjamin Sr. and Lulu did not want the young couple to sell the house, believing that it could simply be rented while Ben was in service, and then the couple could live there once again. A major issue of selling the house, then, was a three-way conversation via letters that had delays between writing and reading and that did not always arrive when expected. Additionally, Miriam's grandmother got involved because she had some business experience, and the realtor, Roy Rensberger, was caught in the mix as well. There is a great deal of angst, frustration, and exasperation evident in letters from and to each member of the conversation.

From what I have pieced together, Benjamin Sr. and Lulu fronted some of the money and land for the home. Miriam and Ben sought to sell the house in order to pay back his parents and the bank what they still owed then pocket the rest to help support them for the remainder of the war. I think that because Benjamin Sr. and Lulu were the financial lenders, they felt like they owned the home and should have a say in how and when it was sold. Additionally, I think that Lulu was having an extremely difficult time "losing" her only child to a spirited young woman like Miriam. Her letters have a sense of "hand wringing" concern for her "baby boy." At this point in time, Benjamin Sr. was eighty years old, a father thirteen times over, a grandfather many times over, the originator of an entire church denomination, the head of various church organizations, and a teacher. He was very, very used to being in charge, to offering "wisdom" and sage advice. He addressed Ben in his typed letters as he would any of his parishioners it seems. I know he had a sense of humor, but it does not come across in his letters. Clearly, he did not appreciate a seventeen-year-old young woman telling him no or making decisions without him.

Ben and Miriam referred to Benjamin Sr. and Lulu as "Pop" and "Mom" in their letters to distinguish which set of parents they are referring to. Miriam's parents, Kenneth and Maureen, are "Dad" and "Mother." Ben often referred to Miriam's parents as "our folks" because they seemed to support the couple more. There are many indications in the letters that Ben and his own parents had a strained relationship. On the one hand, Benjamin Sr. and Lulu managed to raise a confident, kind, and hard-working son with a tremendous sense of humor. On the other hand, they fussed and meddled and frequently said and did things that hurt Miriam, complicated the young couple's financial affairs, and showed mistrust of the fact that Ben and Miriam were independent, married adults. At one point, Miriam even heard Lulu say to someone at church she wished Ben had married someone else. Added to these tensions was the fear and strain over the ongoing war and the fact that Ben was 1,500 miles away, and they all loved and missed him. Emotions were high, and letter writing fanned the flames of miscommunication rather than aiding in coming to a peaceful agreement between all parties.

Knowing that at seventeen she simply did not have the knowledge to handle a house sale on her own, Miriam hired real estate agent Roy Rensberger to handle the showing and sale. The first time she met with him, her mother went along, and Miriam spoke highly of his knowledge and demeanor in several letters. Roy seemed entirely competent at his job, but he ran into obstacles at every turn from the meddling and sometimes controlling Benjamin Sr. and Lulu. Miriam reported an issue with Mom and Pop on November 26.

> Your father called up Mr. Rensberger and asked him what we asked for the property. He told him $3500^{00} and pop says, "Well it's only worth $3000.^{00}" So you can see what a mess things are in because Mr. Rensberger doesn't know what to do. I told him he shouldn't pay any attention to what they say just go ahead & do like I said. But if he sends someone out to look at the house (& you know how your folks are) and they tell who ever comes that it's only worth $3000^{00} How on earth are we going to get $3250 or $3500 for it. I haven't wanted to say anything but if things keep getting worse I guess I'll have to. I'll try to reason with them but if they won't reason I'll just have to tell them what's what. I don't want to because I know they won't take it from me like they would from you.
>
> Your mother is calling every day so toward evening I'm going over to the house and then on to their house and see them for a little bit. So after I come back I'll tell you what all was said.

But Ben already had heard of this same problem in an earlier letter from Miriam's Granny, so letters with similar information are beginning to cross in the mail. Ben wrote on November 24,

In the letter from your Grany today, she said "Pop" had been talking to Roy Rensberger and told him "That the house should be sold for $3000 instead of $3500." I think he's butting in where he's not wanted and I am going to tell him so as soon as I finish this letter. I'll try not to say it so he'll get offended too much but if he does get offended, he'll Just have to go ahead. I've got to think about my family not theirs, and our future is at stake. And Darling I want to make it the very best I can for The Most lovely, Darling, sweetest, angel I know and you are mine Darling. If we can sell our house for more it's absolutely none of his business. He'll get his money as soon as I can get it for him and I'll Pray the Father above that I won't have to depend on him anymore to help me. I appreciate all he has done

But I think he has overstepped his bounds. Please tell Roy Rensberger not to Pay any attention and Don't let the folks have the Key. If you did someone might come to look at the house and They would say Discouraging things instead of encouraging ones. I wish They would cooperate like your (our) folks do They're sure a swell family.

The next day he followed up with a copy of the letter that he sent to his father. "I wrote that letter to Pop and I am sending you and exact copy of it so you can see whether or not I said the wrong thing. I hope it will not cause too much offence." In the letter to his father, Ben attempted to bring up the issue almost casually with "Say Pop, I hear . . ." but then Ben was pretty direct about the issue:

Say Pop I hear that you are not cooperating like you should. Ray Rensberger says he can sell the house for $3500, and you go to work and tell him he should sell it for $3000. I wish you would let Miriam tend to our business affairs. I know you intend to be helpful But something like that is not. She has Placed the house in Rensbergers hands and if she needs any help from you, she'll ask you. I want to sell the house and if you ^"or Mom" try to stop it, you are not doing me a favor. I think you should ask me what to do about my business instead of going ahead and then I find it out thru some other source. I appreciate what you have done for me. And know I can depend on you if the situation calls for it. But Miriam feels bad that she cannot be free to do what she wants to without someone finding fault or trying to oppose what she is doing.

Please do not get offended at this ~~but~~ for I don't want any more hard feelings what ever. And I do want to hear from you.

Love—your Son

Ben

So, only one day after Miriam sent her letter explaining the problem, Benjamin Sr. received the letter from Ben asking him to butt out of their affairs.

Benjamin Sr. reacted fairly strongly and visited Miriam at the Holdermans. She was clearly upset and hurt by the whole affair.

[November 27, 1942]

Now I'll tell you what pop had to say. He was very angry. Oh he talked nice enough only he said everything sneeringly & insulting. Honey, please for my sake don't say any more to them about anything. I have been hurt so many times that I'm getting used to it and it only makes them hate me more cause they blame me for every thing you say to them about anything. He thinks I told you what he said to Roy R. about the house. I told him I hadn't said any thing until yesterday (& you know I just sent that this morning & you couldn't have gotten an answer back to me yet.) But I know he didn't believe me & didn't know granny wrote to you. I wasn't even going to tell you I thought it would just be another thing for me to worry about. Will you please tell them that I didn't tell you about it so they stop blaming me, but honey please don't say anything more about it. Will you? for my sake darling. I ask God to help to not say anything unkind or rude or I don't think I could have talked with him at all. I don't know if they realize it or not but they are killing all the love & respect I ever had for them. But that doesn't change my love for you one bit. It is just as great, no greater, than it ever was & honey I don't blame you for writting cause I know just how you felt. You thought they were hurting me & you don't want anyone to do that. No, I won't let them have the key as I want it. Pop went right up to Rensberger as soon as he left here & was going to talk to him. He said he didn't say it wasn't worth more than $3000.⁰⁰ and went on talking just like he did that time after he said what he did about the Pleasant Ridge church out at West Fulton. You know he said he hasn't said a thing about the Pleasant Ridge church & we both heard him say it.

After Ben received Miriam's November 26 letter that told him the same story that Granny had told him, Ben started to doubt himself and his letter to his father. It is pretty clear he second-guessed himself. Additionally, he wanted the matter to be resolved soon. On November 28, Ben wrote,

Darling, How is Roy Rensberger coming with the house? If he doesn't do something soon, Try again to rent it. If he can not sell for $3,250 then sell for $3000 if you think best, if not do as you think will be profitable. You are there honey, so do what you want to I know you'll use wise Judgement. Probably better that if I was there. "You're the Boss you know" ^HA HA remember how we used to tease didn't we get along swell Darling? I'd give everything I have in the world if I could Have you with me all the time in a cozy little Home all our own. Sweetheart That is my Ideal and my only hope for our Future Together.

Ben frequently said to Miriam "do as you think best." He often offered ideas of how to handle a particular situation but just as frequently backed away from the advice and said she should do what she thought would be the right thing. It is an interesting dynamic.

Miriam first thought she had a buyer for their house in early December.

[December 3, 1942]
I am so excited I can hardly write. Guess what? Darling I've done it. The house is sold! Have you got your breathe yet? Boy am I tickled. Soon I'll be able to forget about the things that have been puzzlin me.

    I am a little disappointed as ~~I am~~ ^we are only getting $3000.00 for it. But I have been thinking even at that we'll come out ahead in the end although I don't think we'll clear much more than $1200. But that's better than nothing. And after all until the house would be completed it would take about $200 now and I have been afraid that the pipes would freeze and then think how much it would take to fix them. So I guess all & all it is a good bargin. . . . My head is practically swimming it had been trying to absorb so much about deeds, mortgages, abstracts, etc. The technical points you know. And I want to do it right so you'll be proud of me. and so the people won't have any fault to find or be able to make any trouble later on. God has answered another one of our prayers.

Miriam handled the details of this first potential sale with a lot of care. She figured out how to mail him papers to sign and have notarized by "express" so that they could get the ball rolling with the sale. Even though she handled all the details at home, his name counted as more important in the transaction. On December 5, she wrote: "This paper ^(the deed) should not be written on at all until you have it before the notary. Then you only write where the X is. And sign your name—B. E. Kesler Jr. I thought I would tell you so you would know what to do. I'm not supposed to sign it until after you have."

Then the couple had the issue of what to do with the money after the house sold. In the age of internet banking it is hard to think about a time when money was only available at one physical location. If Ben needed cash, he had to ask Miriam in a letter. The letter would arrive to her approximately three to five days later. She would have to go to the bank, and then the return letter would add another three to five days. So, if he had an immediate need, there was a minimum of a week that he had to wait. And while they both wanted to save as much of the profits from the sale of the house as possible, Miriam had to budget for buying her own things.

[December 8, 1942]
Honey don't worry about the money [from the house]. I'll put it in the bank in

one of those deposit boxes like we planned and don't hesitate to tell me if you
need any thing. I love to get things for you and now since I don't have to pinch
every penny, I'm going to get some things for my self to. I'm ashamed to have
Francis see any of my under clothes they're so ragged. My good Sunday pants
have the crouch nearly all worn out of them and my slip is getting to be pretty
well plastered with patches. And my good socks have sewed up runners in them.
So I'll get rid of a few dollars.

The weight of making most of the major decisions took its toll on Miriam. In
any given letter she shifted from confident and decisive to uncertain and anxious
that she had done something wrong. This emotional tug of war was not helped
by the fact that Benjamin Sr. and Lulu continued to try and meddle in the sale
of the house. It seems that Lulu especially was still trying to find a renter for the
home, though Ben and Miriam had a pending sale already. On December 10,
Miriam wrote,

I was glad for your letter to-day. I have been so anxious to know what you
thought about the selling of the house. You wondered if I was getting cash for
it. Yes! I have been wondering since if I should have agreed so hastily to taking
$3000. or if I should have insisted on more than that. Some times I think every
thing is wrong & that I can't do any thing right. But I thought that would be a
way to end all of our financially worries and my mind was ^is so jumbled up that
I hardly know what I'm doing.

But I think that is the best thing any way. This way if any thing should
happen to Pop (or us) he'll have this money and there won't be any trouble
about it. . . .

I understand Mr. Rensberger to say that these people (Pletchers) who are
buying it live in Middlebury but your mom declares up and down that they live
in Millersburg so—as far as I'm concerned I don't care where they live as long as
they live up to there end of the bargain. I was under the impression that they intended to live there themselves but your mother says they have asked "them" to
rent the house for them. She seems just to gloat over the idea that these strangers
are letting them do that and we didn't. She certainly doesn't act now as though
she ever had cared whether we lived there or not. But since you aren't here to
be bossed around I come next in order & she proceeds to tell me what to do.

She called up twice this afternoon & tried to get me to let her have my
key to show these prospective renters the house. Well I'll be dog-goned if I'll
let her or any body else have my key. Mr. Pletcher has one of his own and if he
wants to rent the house OK but he can use his own key and any way they have
absolutely no right even to consider renting the house yet. Because it is still ours
as long I don't sign my name to the deed. And for that matter I don't have to

if I don't want to. Goodness knows that if the house was situated in any other place than it is; I wouldn't even consider selling it. But I know we could never really be happy and enjoy one another the way we should (and will) so close to your folks. Cause they complained & talk and goodness knows what all until I was nearly crazy last summer. I know I wasn't the good wife I should have been but I'll make up for it one of these times when I get half a chance. When I know my every move isn't being watched & judged by someone then I can just be "me" and I know we'll be happy. darling. We'll be just the pair of sweethearts we always were; only more so. And we have; in the short time we were married; learned to know one another better so that we can enjoy just being to-gether. You'll never know every thing that your folks have said to me. I haven't wanted to be bitter toward them and I know you thought I was unfair but you had their side of the story.

Unfortunately, the sale fell through just a few days later.

[December 14, 1942]

Your Mimmie can hardly write to night. She is just sick all over in side. I have had some dreadful news for you. But I know you can take it; so here it is. Mr. Pletcher went back on the bargin and isn't buying the house. So we're right back where <u>we</u> started from. And right now I can't seem to think anything right or try to plan what I'll do now or nothing. My brain is all jumbled up and I want you-you-you. So I'll have to make this payment and the one to Montgomery Wards and so I'll have to borrow money again. I don't like to. I already owe dad $17.00 & Granny $5.00 and then last night I borrowed $1.00 from her cause I knew until I paid the bus fare home I wouldn't have much more than enough for stamps left this week. I'm sorry I won't have more ^money cause I wanted to get some more thing for you But I guess I can't do it now and then too all my plans about coming to see you will just have to dry up and blow away cause it'll take all I make to be able to make the payment. Oh what is there to look forward to. All I can see is a blank wall. Everything just goes round & round and I want you to reassure me and love me. Oh why is every thing in such a mess.

I've been trying to think that God has some plan in mind. But right now I don't see how this can all be for the best.

But after all we still have each other and where there's life there's hope so we shouldn't be too discouraged; cause we'll get along some how. And as long as we both have enough money for postage & stationary we can be comparatively happy and we'll both pray that whatever happens will be pleasing in God's sight and for the best.

Mr. Pletcher ^had given Roy R. $50.00 to reserve the right to the house & Roy said this afternoon he was going to keep it. So we'll still be $50.00 to the

good. I don't know if Roy will keep it for his ex-penses or not. I'm going to try
& not worry to much about it one way or the other. He sure felt terrible about.
When you come home I want you to meet him. I'm sure you will like him. I
think he is a very nice gentleman. I should imagine he was about 50 or maybe a
little older and he has a funny little grin and a twinkle in his eye & I know that
he has been doing his best to take care of our houses. He said, "I hate like the
dickens to have to tell you!" and I know that he tried to get Mr. Pletcher to re-
consider. He said I should try and not worry and then he would do things as tho
he were my father. I certainly appreciated having someone who cared whether
or not <u>our</u> business transactions went OK. or not and I feel sure that he is our
friend and not just a real estate man who is only interested in a commission.
    Well that's enough of business.

The loss of the sale shook Miriam enough that she started to consider renting
the house instead, which would have kept them encumbered with the financial
situation with his parents and encumbered with the house payment if no one
rented.

[December 16, 1942]
I told Mr. Rensberger that if he couldn't sell the house in a week (or two) that we
would rent it for the time being. There was a fellow to see him; about renting it;
the other day. He offered him $30.⁰⁰ So if we could do that we could get along
(& I could come out too!) Especially if I didn't have such a great financial burden.
Other wise it would take all ^(nearly) I make a month to make the payments. But
I'm not going to worry about that yet for a while. Anyway not until we see what
progress Roy R. makes about selling the house.

Ben and Miriam worked through the disappointment in their letters. There were
a lot of reassurances written back and forth that no, Ben was not upset at Miriam
and that no, Miriam did not blame Ben. In the midst of negotiating the emotions, as ever, Benjamin Sr. and Lulu continued to meddle. On December 17,
Miriam wrote,

You wondered to-day (in the letter I got) if you should say anything to your
mother or not! Well honey if you don't mind I'd a little rather you wouldn't
cause she never can see where she has done anything wrong & thinks I am altogether mistaken. Please don't say any thing to her. And I'll tell you something
else. Of course I don't have any actual proof but I have a sneaking suspicion that
the reason Pletchers backed out of their part of the bargain was on account of
her. Cause she was making such a fuss over them & took it in her hands to rent
it for them.

Miriam's suspicions seem to be well-founded, based on what Lulu wrote to Ben a few days later:

[December 22, 1942]

I was so suppised that Mr. Pletcher went back on the deal he came here and wanted us to rent it for him, had me put an add in the paper and I had several good chances to rent it for him but I did not want to rent it for sure till I seen him. as he told me to hold them off a few days as they might take a notion to come here themselves. I had a real good chance to rent it $30.00 a month and I tried to call him at home and he had gone to Goshen the folks said. so I thought maby they was coming in to fix it all up, so I called Roy Rensburger and ask him if he might see him as I had a good renter in view he told me he had been to the office and he was not in, but left word that he would be back. he said I think he is going to go back on the deal, I was so suppised as he had told me to rent it. now dont you think I had any thing to do with his going back on it, for I did not. I just made the explanation how it was so you can know I had nothing to do with it. Mr. Rensburger told me it was his wife that caused it to fall through—he ^Mr. Pletcher said he wanted us to rent it as we would want to know what kind of neighbors we would want to live by. Mr. Rensburger said also he had another man in view. to buy it. so I never heard any more about it.

The fact is that it was not Lulu's house to rent. It does not seem reasonable that the potential buyer would consult with Lulu; nor does it seem reasonable that the buyer would want to rent the home to someone else. The entire explanation from Lulu sounds like a fabrication, and I can only imagine the stress, frustration, and anger that this caused Ben and Miriam. Benjamin Sr. backed up Lulu's claim in his accompanying letter by saying, "Wife tells me the property deal fell through. I do not know why. . . . Your mama tells me they had the papers all fixed up and the man went back on the deal. They think his wife was the cause of the miscarriage of the deal. Your mama says she could have rented it to two different parties for $30. Bur she thinks Mr. R. is trying to sell it to some one else."

Benjamin Sr. and Lulu both responded to Ben's letter requesting that they stop meddling. Both parents defended themselves and declared their innocence. Benjamin Sr. insisted that he and Lulu were innocent of any meddling but then proceeded to explain just exactly how they meddled:

[December 27, 1942]

Now Benjamin I am sorry you think I have interferred in your business. You know I told you I did not think you could sell for $35000. only two parties have been here to see us about it. I told the man it was in the hands of Roy Rensberger, that he had advertised it for $[3,500], and he went toward town Don't know if he saw Mr. Rensberger or not. Mrs Holderman who lives just east of us came to see me about it. I told her Mr. R. had it in hand and he had it advertised for $[3,500], but Miriam reserved the right to sell it, and if she would see her perhaps she would make her a reduction as she could save the commission. Your Mama did not talk to those parties nor any one else about the matter. So she has not hindered the sale either.

I took your letter and showed it to Miriam yesterday, and she said we had not interferred [in] the matter. She said "Mom" did not want you to sell it, which is true as you know. Of course I would rather you would keep it but I have not stood in the way of its sale, and will not.

I talked with Mr. R. and he told me I had not stood in his way or hindered him in any way. But he told me a party came to him and he told him the price was $3,500. the man told him you had offered it to him for $[3,000], but he meant to hold it at $3,200 until Miriam gave him different instructions. Then after I had talked with him over the phone I took up the paper and saw he had it advertised for $[3,200].

Now I hope you will not think we are standing in the way or doing anything to hinder the sale.

In the same envelop, Lulu wrote her own defense:

Dear Benjamin—I have had nothing to do about the business. or price—some have asked me what you are going to do with your house I said you were going to sell or rent. Sister Cara Rensburger asked me and I told her you were talking of selling and she said I would not sell it and Effie and Paul were up for the meeting and they ask me and I told them you was talking of selling it they both said they would not sell it. other wise I have had nothing to say about the business. I don't want you or Miriam to think hard of us for we have not—I think I am right in my view for you to keep it and let the rent pay out all it can for you know how hard you worked for what you have in it. but I have prayed over it and if it is the Lords will to sell it I say His will be done.

Essentially, the more Benjamin Sr. and Lulu said they had nothing to do with the conflict, the more apparent it was that they did just that.

Finally, in early January, the house had a buyer. This time the buyer stuck. Miriam wrote with excitement and joy:

[January 4, 1943]
Hi Me Dearling!

I have some swell news to tell you. Hang on to your hat! Well here goes. We have sold the house again. I was both surprised and pleased and tickled tea-kettle pink. I had just rather taken it for granted that we had a "white elephant" on our hand. In other words we had the house and probably would forever & always. The fellow that is buying it I̶ is reselling it right away to some fella. (on the contract.) H̶e̶^We are only getting $2900.⁰⁰ for it. But I thought that would be better than nothing and then too we have Pletcher's $50.⁰⁰ too, So realy it will only be $50.⁰⁰ less. (Than the $3000). And what pleases me so much is that I will have all this business finished up before I come to see you. So I shouldn't have a w̶o̶r̶r̶y̶^care in the world. And I can devote all my thoughts on you. I have just figured up how much our debts amount to. We owe $734. to "pop" and $800 to the church; $87 to Roy for his commission; $6 to Granny, $17.⁰⁰ to Dad and $26.⁰⁰ to Montgomery Wards. which makes a total of a debt of 1̶6̶.̶7̶ $1670. Will say $1680. which would leave a balance of o̶v̶e̶r̶ $1280.⁰⁰ But I have the money saved to pay Montgomery Wards off. So we clear over $1300. Not bad I'd say! I'm getting to be quite a mathematician or business woman or something. As soon as I get up town I'm going in to Bert Kings and cancel our insurance and then I'll get a refund. Well good-for me. I mean "us"! . . . I wish I were coming to you this week but even if I could, there are countless things to be done first. I have to sort a lot of things and get some clothes fixed up for my self. I think perhaps I will get a dress or two and I just simply must get some new under clothes. The whole seat of my pants is just one big hole; it's about a foot long. Sounds bad. I wasn't eating beans either. I bet-cha! Ha! . . .

Roy R. said I should tell you that you should take the deed to a notary this time. Because Mr. Shetler did not fill out the other [deed] at all satisfactorily. and anyway if a notary does it the people won't have any cause to question the legality of it. I hope you get this letter before you sign the deed. . . . Oh honey my heart just seems to be bubbling over with love for you and I'm going to give you a loving you soon won't forget when I get the chance. So be-ware. You can't say I didn't warn you! ha! Nite now honey.

Over the next week, Miriam wrote of the business of selling the house: how Mr. Rensberger was a great help, how she settled various debts, and of their final financial picture.

[January 11, 1943]
And while I was getting supper Mr. Rensberger came (and I got the deed to-day) so I went and got it and signed it. And he is going to finish up everything tomorrow. He is going to pay off the mortgage and what we owe "pop." And he took care of all the other numerous little things and the taxes. I am so grateful for everything he is doing. I think that all in all he deserves the money which he will get for his commission. I have got to figuring some more and I don't believe we will clear so very much more than $1200 since some other thing have loomed up

that I had forgotten about. After the expenses are all paid the rest of the money will be put in a bank check made out to you and I. And I won't be able to use any of that money until after you have signed it and me to. So I will try and get along with ^the money that I make. Cause I think now that I can get along on that.

[January 12, 1943]
I came down and had just started to iron~~ed~~ the dampened clothes when the phone rang and it was Roy R. He wanted me to come up to his office right away and get the papers & "money."

So I ask Francis if I could go if I would iron to night to make up for the time I lost this afternoon. She said I could so I went right away. I was going to take the bus but it was so cold I didn't want to stand still to wait for it. I saved 7¢ anyway. Well good for me. I walked up and back. It isn't just so very <u>warm</u> out doors. And I didn't have any gloves either and the hole in the back of my boots made them air-conditioned. I bet-cha!

Well any how here is our expenses and the balance. I am sure they made a mistake about the church mortgage. So I ^have just finished writting another letter to Webb H. to find out if his figure & mine checked.

If I am right. We'll be $50.<u>00</u> richer. So let's be hoping I am. Well here is a list of the expenditures ~~and~~ etc.

Sale of the house $2950.<u>00</u>

Abstract	$6.00
2 Deeds (1.50 apiece)	3.00
Taxes	11.50
Commission	88.50
Revenue Stamp	<u>3.30</u>
	112.30
Mortgage	$825.00
Int.	<u>28.40</u>
Total	$853.40
	112.30
	853.40
Note—$734.<u>00</u>	<u>734.00</u>
	$1699.70
	$2950.00
	<u>1699.70</u>
	Bal. $1250.30

The balance was made out in a bank check to both of us. And it can't be ~~checked~~^cashed until both of us have our signatures on it. So we won't be able to cash it until you come home. So I won't be running off to Florida or some place with all our money. ha! I wouldn't any how. You know—.

I went up to see Burt King and I got a check for $20.33 from him So altogether I have $1280.72 in my pocketbook. I'll bet that's the most money I'll ever have in it or ~~any~~^otherwise. I bet-cha.

But that nest egg in her pocketbook was almost immediately reduced when a pump at the house froze and she had to pay to get it fixed before the new owners could move in. Further, part of dealing with the finances for the family included taking the responsibility for purchasing things and deciding when to spend money and when to wait. Miriam, perhaps, waited too long to get herself new clothing. She had commented early on in November that her underclothes needed replacement, but she did not actually do so until mid-January. And she seemed to feel some measure of guilt at the purchases, needed though they were.

[January 17]
Here it is 11:10 and I'm not to bed. Isn't that terrible? I fixed Charles a pig trough & some things and then I proceeded to make out an order. One to Sears & one to Montgomery Wards. Altogether it all came to over $16.$\underline{^{00}}$ Isn't that a <u>nice</u> way for me to spend all our hard earned money. I'm not using any more than I have to. Cause I'm going to have to earn some more now before I'll have enough to come out there. I didn't realize that nearly <u>all</u> of my clothes were worn out until I began to figure up what all I needed. I sent for material to make myself a new dress and a skirt and two blouses 2 slips, two pairs of bloomers, 2 brassiers (I wonder what for? ahem!) three pair of stockings, a big box of Kotex (52 pads) (don't hardly seem like enough, does it?) a pair of gloves.

I'm not going to tell you what the dress & skirt and blouses will look like. I'm going to let you <u>see</u> if you like them on me.

In all, the sale of the house took almost two months, which does not seem that long. But in light of the fact that they had little money saved and the fact that Miriam worked for such low wages, those two months probably felt like a lifetime. If the home had been rented, the rate per month would have been about thirty dollars, so it is likely that the mortgage on the home was a similar amount. Miriam made only forty dollars a month working for the Holdermans, and there were other bills to cover should the home not be rented out. Though Benjamin Sr. and Lulu desperately wanted them to keep and rent the home, if they had done so, Miriam would have barely stayed afloat financially, leaving little she could send to Ben at camp and little she could use to buy necessary items for herself.

Letter writing proved to be a complicated, frustrating way to conduct business and to maintain relationships with family members during a conflict. The conduit and platform continued to function between Ben and Miriam. Between Benjamin Sr. and Lulu and the young couple, however, the conduit admitted angst and hurt feelings through the letters. The family's larger relationship was shaken when Benjamin Sr. or Lulu personally confronted Miriam, then again in letters between the parties. It is unclear whether fences were entirely mended after the sale of the home, though they all continued to write to one another through the duration of Ben and Miriam's time in Civilian Public Service.

CHAPTER 8

The Holidays

H OLIDAYS DURING THE WAR YEARS WERE, OF COURSE, DIFFERENT FROM
what American families were used to. Rationing meant that traditional holiday foods were sometimes altered, limited, or missing altogether from celebratory
feasts. The rationing of gas meant fewer could afford to travel "over the river
and through the woods to grandmother's house," and the majority of tables set
in celebration on the home front were missing one or more place settings. For
Ben and Miriam and other COs, Thanksgiving focused on the Lord's provision
of alternative CPS service, food, faith, and family. For the majority of the nation immersed in the war effort, in addition to being thankful for food, faith,
and family, Thanksgiving celebrations focused on supporting the war effort, the
soldiers overseas, and the American way of life. Soldiers were told they were
fighting to preserve this way of life. Norman Rockwell's iconic image *Freedom
from Want*, which he painted in 1942, best illustrates the odd juxtaposition of
thankfulness and war.[1] The image appeared in the March 6, 1943, issue of the
Saturday Evening Post. The painting is also known as *The Thanksgiving Picture*
because it has become an iconic representation of the holiday meal in the United
States. It depicts a group of smiling people, presumably family and friends, gathered around a holiday table that has been set with what I call "Grandma's fancy
dishes." Plump and smiling grandparents stand at the head of the table, and the
aproned grandmother holds a platter with a holiday turkey. Below the image is
the inscription "Freedom from Want." The painting was a marked contrast to
meals in war-torn Europe.

It is not surprising that holidays that first year were challenging for Ben and
Miriam, but by examining the ways that they negotiated being apart in their
letters, we get a more complete picture of who they were individually and as a
couple. These were Ben and Miriam's first holidays as a married couple, and of
course, they were emotional. The conduit and platform of their letters proved to
be a poor substitute for being together, more so on Thanksgiving and Christmas
than other ordinary days, so here we see the limit of what letter writing could do
for them.

By Thanksgiving Ben was fully integrated into camp life and Miriam was
fully immersed in working for the Holdermans. The day before Thanksgiving
Day, Ben wrote

[November 25, 1942]

we had our Thanksgiving meal tonight. our prayer meeting is to be a Thanks-giving service it is Just about time for the Bell to ring for it. It is to begin at 8:30 and my watch says that now but it is 2 minutes fast. Well I'll tell you what we had for supper then after Prayer meeting I'll tell you what happened. We had the tables pushed together. each one sets 8 but ~~we~~ they were put two together and seated 17. the Dining Hall was decorated with Pine branches and oak leaves. There Prayer meeting Bell so I'll be back in a few minutes

I mean when it is over bye for now.

Just got back it's 9:25, lasted nearly an hour. back now to the menu each table had two Platters with a roast chicken on. (Clarence Hooley carved ours). Then Mashed Potatoes, Gravy, celery, pickles, corn, cranberries, mince pie, cake, cupcakes, apples and oranges, candy, peaches, and in the center of the table was a large pumpkin for Decorative Purposes. we all ate and ate and ate. . . .

[At] Prayer Meeting we opened service by singing "Count your Blessings" and then Mr. Shetler ask most of us what Blessings we were thankful for. I told him That "The camp which we are priviledged to enjoy was one of our Greatest Blessings." I would rather be with you at home, but I'd also rather be here than in another kind of camp preparing to Kill fellow man instead of helping him. what this whole world needs is more fear of God in their hearts. also we had sentence Prayers. I expect there were 20 or more Prayed sentence Prayers My Prayer was that I was thankful that God was Present in our midst. I like the services here fine and try to take a small part in them. I think God is blessing me for everyone here treats me like a brother and as good as if I belonged to the Mennonite Church.

Included in this letter, in addition to one of his customary platform descrip-tions of food, is a material element that created a sense of place from Ben's time at camp. He carefully wrapped the chicken wishbone in a paper napkin from the meal. This wishbone made it through the mail to Miriam, and it was still in the envelope when I opened it nearly seventy-five years later. I will admit I was pretty grossed out at first to find a bone in a letter, but after reading the contents of the letter, I understood why it was there and saw the romance of it (even though it is still pretty gross).

The *Turnpike Echo* from December 8, 1942, talked about the meal that the campers had for Thanksgiving:

The Sideling Hill Camp has been richly blessed with many donations during this Thanksgiving season. We had the privilege of having our Thanksgiving dinner donated to us by the Crown Hill Mennonite Congregation of Ohio of which Bro. Enos Hartzler has charge. The feast was held on Wednesday evening, and included lots of delicious roast chicken, filling, dressing, dried corn, peas, celery, pickles, cranberry relish, peaches, layer cakes, cupcakes, mince pie, and last but not least, candy. The tables were beautifully decorated with large pumpkins surrounded by apples, oranges, and grapefruit. The dining hall was appropriately decorated with pine boughs, oak leaves, and crowfoot, which made it appear very inviting for the special occasion. The dietitian and the kitchen boys worked hard all through the day to prepare the dinner.[2]

I imagine that the holiday feast at Sideling Hill was similar to what many families would have put together, even as rations limited what they could cook. Poultry was not rationed, but there was a scarcity of turkeys, since most were sent to the soldiers overseas, so chickens were more common on war-era tables at home. I think, too, that the cooks at the camp must have saved their rations of sugar for months to create cakes, pies, and candy.

Thanksgiving was not such an event for Miriam. She had her Thanksgiving meal with her family the previous Sunday afternoon.

[November 22, 1942]
We had what I considered a good dinner. It was our Thanksgiving dinner. We had chicken, rabbit, mashed potatoes, gravy, noodles, lettuce, baked beans (Kesler special) pickles, cheese, cranberries, butterscotch cookies, buns and—pumpkin pie with whipped cream on it. Don't hardly seem like enough does it ha! Your Mimmie missed you dreadfully today I couldn't hardly stand it not to be able to give you a kiss & a ^big hug when nobody is looking. I just couldn't stand it so when the rest were eating I went down to the shanty & gave vent to my feelings but that doesn't help ^too much. Doesn't it?

On Thanksgiving Day, November 26, Miriam wrote,

Hi Honey! And I can just hear you say. "Lo! Honey!" Darling I wish I could. This is "Thanksgiving" day. But it's so hard for me to find very many things to be thankful for since you are away cause you are what I always did things for & planned for. And if we can't be together to enjoy the holidays I don't have any amount of happiness at all. Then too I am so disappointed that I can't do what I want to (with all my heart) on Christmas. I want to be with you. But with things the way they are I can't even get any presents. It nearly drives me frantic some times to not have you ^to help with so many perplexities to contend with.

That day the Holdermans invited Miriam to join their family for Thanksgiving dinner at a relative's house. Miriam opted not to go because she would not know anyone and because she wanted to be alone so she could write a very long letter to Ben. In the afternoon she visited Ben's parents.

Your mother let me read all of your letters and honey I think you used very good judgement when you wrote to them & I tried not to say anything about anything else either. I was glad they didn't begin on talking about the house. I went over to the house. But it brought ^back so many memories that as soon as I found out everything was OK I came back. They wanted to bring me. But I said, "No, I enjoyed the walk!" & I meant it too. It did me good to get out in the fresh air. It was the first time I had a chance to be alone & get out & go for a walk since you left.

It had been nearly three weeks since Ben had left, and this was Miriam's first chance to be alone and get out for a walk. The changes to her life and lifestyle were not as obvious as Ben's, but here we can see one aspect of the changes. By first moving back home with her family and then moving in with the Holdermans, Miriam was never a free agent as she had been in her own home.

The last thing to note about Thanksgiving is that whereas Ben described the abundant meal he indulged in for Thanksgiving, on November 29, Miriam told Ben that she did not eat much at all: "I've been wondering what you had for dinner Thanksgiving Day. A turkey? I didn't. I had a dish of jello, a couple cookies, 3 olives & a glass of chocolate milk. a cup of coffee for breakfast & a dish of ice cream for supper." Clearly, the separation impacted each of their eating habits differently.

More than Thanksgiving, Christmas proved to be very, very difficult for both Ben and Miriam. The entire month of December they each mentioned their preparations for the holiday, the gifts they were making, the surprises they were keeping secret, and the ongoing lament that their first Christmas together as husband and wife would be spent hundreds of miles apart. Although they did express their grief at being apart, they each tried to keep the other's spirits up. On December 16, Miriam wrote, "We'll just have to keep on remembering that in about 20 more days half of the time will be gone. (The time when you left & the time when you'll return)."

They tried to re-create the holiday spirit and celebration in their letters. In Ben's letter from December 20, he included an envelope that said "please don't open this envelope till X-mas Morn." He had sent a box of Christmas gifts he had built in the camp's woodworking shop for Miriam and her family. The envelope contained a list of what gifts went to each person. The note read:

Book Wrack—Dad
Pot holder, Candle Holders, Pin Cushion—Mother
Book ends—Dale
Key—Verda
Letter Box—Barbara
Wall shelf—Grany

Judy—(horse)—Charlie
Lamp and Glass Carrier—Miriam
<u>Horse shoe Motto (my Wipe)</u>
                              Ha Ha
Pin Cushion—Catherine
Key—Viola
MERRY XMAS
TO
ALL

One sweet aspect of the above list is that Ben referred to Miriam as his "wipe" because that is what her young brother Charlie called her when he would write pretend letters to Ben or Miriam. Charlie was not yet able to pronounce the "f" sound, so "wipe" was the closest he could get. Ben and Miriam used the term often in their letters to impart both affection and humor.

On Christmas Eve, Ben wrote:

We worked all day today Planted trees this forenoon and hauled wood in afternoon. We quit at 3:00. We gave Mr English, our Boss, his Xmas gift we got for him last night. He opened it. And This morn. Thanked us for it. It was a $6.50 Brief case. at supper this eve. Clarence Hooley Presented a Bible Concordance, to Mr. Shelter, (by the way he is only 30) a Box of Linnen stationary to the Nurse, and a Parker Pen to the Dietician. on behalf of all the Campees. They were very pleased and surprised.

We had an Xmas service in the Chapel this eve. there were three speakers. Roy Miller asst. Director opened services with Devotional reading, Clarence Hooley read a Chapter pertaining to Christ's Birth. Luke 2: and Mr Edwin Weave spoke Conserning Xmas in other lands and how it was observed. Very interesting.

Honey I'm Just Bubling over with Curiosity as to what is in those Packages. What say I go to bed and dream about them. O.K. alright. I'll say good night now Darling I hope you have as Merry an Xmas as is Possible considering the Dreadful fact that I won't be with you. Oh How I wish I Could and we could spend it in our own home Darling Just <u>you</u> and <u>I</u>.

Oh Honey I have some sweet happy thoughts sometimes but that's as far as it goes. Soon tho' Darling we'll make them all come true. Sweetheart I Love you with every oz. of me and I am Pretty heavy you ought to know (I betcha) Oh Honey Isn't it great to be loved by some one who appreciates your love in return? I'll say it is.

Good night now My Sweet
<u>Your Ben</u>
I love you

<u>Merry Xmas</u>
Here's a kiss for <u>you</u>

The next day Ben wrote a lengthy letter about the goings-on at the camp on Christmas Day.

Sideling Hill Camp
Well Tannery, Pa
Dec. 25, 1942
Merry Xmas Honey;

Another Xmas day has come and gone Darling But it wasn't near as nice as last year. Oh, Honey I longed for you this morn. When I awoke I just layed and tho't how nice it would be if we were laying together in stead of so far apart. I Just had to think about happy times we've had and oh, Darling I long for them to return. It seems an endless eternity since we were together, Honey. Well I'll start where I left off last nite After I wrote your letter I moved Andy Eichers bed and hid it then I Put my own on the floor so when he came in he would not blame me. Well he Came in and found it so when he asked if I did it I told him well what do you think look at my bed I left it like it was Put so I waylayed suspicion we had a lot of fun about it and he still don't know who it was that hid his bed. This morn when I woke up it was 25 after 8:00 so I told the other fellows I was going to stay in bed till 9:00 so most of them did too. about 10:00 I opened my Presents. I was sure blessed with more than my share it seems. I'll have enough sweetness to last me a Month.

Maybe youd like to know what was in my other Packages. Ruth sent me a small fruit cake, Miriam and Albert sent me a box of Cherry flips. I think you know what was in the other two Packages. I sure appreciated the kids pictures they're sure swell children and I love all of them That flash light will sure come in handy I'll use it tonight when I go to bed I'm sitting in the Dining Hall writing tonight it's after 10:00 last night there were no bells. I sure appreciate the overalls Dad and Mother sent. the ones I have are still all-together but they're Pretty thin. . . . Well we were to have chicken for dinner but the Place where it was coming from got quarren-tined in with the small pox so we did with out. We had a good dinner tho! Boiled ham took place of Chicken we had potatoes, corn, cranberry sauce, Sweet Potatoes (fried) cake, Pineapple Dessert. Cherry Pie alamode (ice cream on top) All in all I ate too much I felt miserable for an hour or more after ward. I didn't finish my Pineapple Dessert as good as it was. The Camp staff served dinner and the Shetler boys helped wait on tables Oh, yes. They also Brought a Basket of oranges this morn. I took their Picture. There really smart cute little boys. Mr. Shetler has a girl too also a Baby girl. quite a start for only 30 (eh!) Well

I loafed around most of the day A few fellows went on hikes But it was sloppy so I stayed in. this eve.

The *Turnpike Echo* also wrote about the Christmas meal and quarantined community in the January 5, 1943 issue:

> The kitchen boys received word on the evening before Christmas that they need not report for duty the following morning. Some of us were wondering if we would have no Christmas dinner or just what kind of dinner it would be if we did get one.
>
> The [next] thing we heard was that there would be no breakfast served, but that oranges would be served to the barracks. . . . Well, we awoke bright and early the next morning (about 9:00) to see Bro. Shetler's two young sons with their basket of oranges. When we came to the Mess Hall at eleven o'clock for our dinner we found a splendid meal on the long table through the center of the Hall. We found also that our Director was there with his clean white apron ready to serve. He and his family with the staff were responsible for the long night that the cooks enjoyed.
>
> We were sorry that the folks from Belleville were unable to bring the dinner they had planned and we sympathize with them in the sickness that has brought a quarantine to their community and anxiety to many homes.[3]

That same issue of the *Turnpike Echo* listed the secular program that the campers enjoyed on December 26. There was "Instrumental Music arranged by Ben Kesler," a "Reading [by] Ben Kesler," and another "Instrumental Music arranged by Ben Kesler." In the first instrumental arrangement, "John H. Hochstetler with a guitar and Ben Kesler with a violin played 'What a friend We Have in Jesus.'" In the second arrangement, "Lewis Delegrange and Ben Kesler played on one guitar 'You are My Sunshine.' . . . Finally all four of the men played 'Jingle Bells' and 'Wabash Cannon Ball.'"[4]

Miriam's Christmas was spent with her immediate family and was a much quieter affair.

Christmas Even.
5:15
Hello my Darling;

Oh honey! I've got so much to tell you. But oh how I wish you could have been here to enjoy it all; yourself. There was something lacking all day. And that something was "you"! my precious. We all missed you so much. But I missed you the most. But they have all tried to help make the day bearable for each other and especially for me.

Charley is just "galloping" Judy [the broom-handle horse] around the table.
He is so proud of it cause "Bennie" made it for him.

We were all wonderfully blest with gifts. . . .

I'd like to go out right away and buy a shade for the lamp but it would be
just something else to store so I'll wait until we can take ^them to "our home" and
then we'll have the joy of fixing things all over again together.

Well maybe I'll finally get around to telling you what I got for Christmas.
Dail and Charles gave me a pair of silk stockings, the girls gave me a pair of pants
(I mean "bloomers") and a garter belt to hold up my stockings. I don't really need
a corset since I am thinner. I bet that will be good news to you. Cause you never
liked them anyway. ha!

Granny gave me a pair of house slippers. They're a pretty blue with blue
rosettes on the toes of them. . . .

And—the folks got me a swell new dress and I happen to know how much they
paid for it. $4.98. I don't think they should have spent so much. It is blue. Nearly
the same color as my spring coat. It is made about like my green one (the one I got
last summer) It is a swell one. I'll bring it along when I come and then you can see it.

We had a turkey dinner. The breast of the turkey weighed a pound & a half.
how would that be for just one piece of meat. Besides Turkey we had mashed potatoes, gravy, cold slaw (Kesler brand) spiced peaches, date cake and ice cream. I
made the date cakes. I made three of them, a big one, middle-sized one and a little
one (Sounds like the three bears, don't it? ha!) Then I fixed ice cream and we're
going to have some for supper to and also date cake and cold turkey (Oh yes, we
had dressing too.) . . . I have been munching hard-tack and peanuts and grapes.

Both Ben and Miriam did a pretty good job pretending that their experiences
on Christmas Day were enjoyable, that they upheld the traditions of their families, and that it was just another day apart. But it was not just another day apart
for them; the holiday made their distance seem just that much farther. Both spent
the majority of their letter on Christmas Day telling of all the "fun" they had, the
gifts, the food, and the traditions. And both, toward the end of their letters, gave in
and expressed how frustrated and sad and lonely they actually were. Miriam wrote:

Oh well shoot! what's the use of pretending I enjoyed the day. Cause I
didn't; every minute I was thinking of you and longing and wishing and oh—my
heart just aches down deep inside of me and I want to come flying into your
arms and hear you tell me you love me and want me. Cause I feel so unwanted.
I know the folks love me & the kids too; but "Nobody else can take you place!"
and there love is nothing in comparison with what yours means to me. You are
all I have and ever want. Darling I just can't write any more now. I'll try to write
Sunday Eve. and tell you all the news.

But I'll have these pages all blurred and the writing will swim away. So I'll just go to bed (on our davenport) and try to go to sleep. Any way I'll cover up so nobody can hear me cry. It just feels as though something were tearing loose down inside around my heart. ˙

Night honey. Sleep tight.

I'll go now & try to dream about you. Your lonesome wife;

"Miriam"

Ben's letter is almost a mirror of Miriam's:

You are my only hope of a home Darling without you my dreams of home could never come true some sweet happy sometime we can again enjoy the pleasure of home life and I'm Praying that God will speed the day. Honey I'm getting so anxious to see you. I look at your Picture and there we stand the happiest Moment in our lives and here I am far away from the one I dearly love. I Just have to quit thinking or I'd have to go away and bawl. I've quit hugging my pillow. I Just get that much lonelier for you so it's best if I leave it alone. . . . Darling I love you and no Matter how many miles we're separated it will remain the same.

I'll say good night now Honey
Darling My heart aches for Your
Love I wish I could fly to your
arms and there rest Content.
Nite Honey

Your Hubby

Pardon this letter it sounds kinda blue;
But I can't help it, I want <u>you</u>. only <u>you</u>
Are you going to make any new years Resolutions? I don't know what I'd Resolve to do unless it would be to be more loving if I can be and to always be true and faithful to the Darling I Love, honor, Cherish, respect, and adore. Honey those words are ment for only you. You are my only Sweetheart oh my <u>Darling</u>

<u>I Love You</u>

The parallel of their letters at Christmas was not repeated at New Year's. On New Year's Eve the camp boys did put on a bit of a celebration and had some fun. Ben wrote:

Good Morning Darling I is up and at it again. This is the first Morn. of The new year and we sure had a good time bringing it in.

Last eve we had our party after I had written part of this letter I signed off and

Lewis and I (I call him Long Louy) went over to the kitchen and popped a dishpan full of corn and made three pitchers of Lemonade. ~~Whe~~ We got Heber good to give us the Lemons and sugar. He works in kitchen and had the storm room key. We took it over to the social room and started our Party. There were 15 of us, we played cross questions and silly answers first, then Fruit Basket turn over, Pleased and displeased, Wink um then at 11:30 we had our Lemonade and Popcorn (Refreshments) Just before 12:00 we all got over to the Mess hall and got ready to ring the Bell so Just at the minute we rang the Bell and also the fire gong and hollored to beat everything. I had a flare I found along the turnpike and we lit it and we all danced around it. Just like a Bunch of kids. But we had a lot of fun I bet everyone woke up If they didn't it wasn't because we didn't make enough noise Theron Christopher and Ray Hersberger Blowed their car horns. Ray has his car here and Theron Blowed John Ramsyers car horn. Well all in all we had a good time.

Miriam's New Year's experience was much less celebratory. In fact, Miriam's celebration was not a celebration at all because she worked straight through it for the Holdermans, who seemed to have added insult to injury by underpaying her for that week. "To-day was New Year's Day and I 'shore' started it out right. Up to my neck in work. And to-night Everett gave me my pay for this week. It was <u>ten</u> dollars. And after all I have done this week and beside that I have to stay to-morrow. (Saturday) and work and I wont even have time to go up town. Cause I have to stay right here."

To again show the difference in their holiday experiences, it is interesting to note that Ben received a total of fifty cards for Christmas from various friends and family. Miriam received fifteen. Much like the histories written of the war experience, more attention was paid to the men who were away than to those who were left behind. It makes sense that this was the case, given that the entire nation was dedicated to supporting the "men overseas" and sending their love and admiration to keep spirits up. Such a focus on those who were away was mirrored in the CPS program, though for both military wives and families and CPS wives and families, life at home was often bitter, difficult, and miserable.

Both Ben and Miriam did their best to describe the events of their Thanksgiving, Christmas, and New Year's holidays, to maintain that space of intimacy and togetherness of the platform. Both also lamented openly how miserable they were and that the conduit of their letters were simply not enough to quiet their yearnings. It is both sweet and sad to read how they managed and got along without one another. We see both the brave face they put forward to outsiders and the anguish they shared with only one another. The desperation to be together was more evident during the holidays than any other time, and that desperation provided the impetus for their decision to transfer even further from home to work in a mental hospital, of all places, just so they could be together.

CHAPTER 9

Transition to Rhode Island

[I am] altogether willing that we should work in a mental hospital if you can get the chance go and then let me know and then I'll come at once.

MIRIAM, JANUARY 10, 1943

T HIS CHAPTER TRACES THE DECISION-MAKING PROCESS BEN AND MIR-
iam went through in transitioning to mental hospital work. Even as their
letters detail their anguish at being separated and their desperation to be together,
they also have elements of hope that they would find a way to be together sooner
rather than later. This hope, in part, stems from the fact that the government
approved CPS men working in hospitals and mental institutions to alleviate the
worst wartime staffing issues in the nation. Nonresistant CPS men were able and
willing to work in hospitals and mental institutions because these were jobs that
were not connected to military service. The other major staffing issue the nation
faced was in farming and food production. Some CPS men subsequently worked
on farms, but doing so was a gray area theologically, given that the food may
have been destined to feed military troops. Their overall desire to help mankind
won over any objections the churches felt about food production as part of the
war machine. In the same way, Ben's desire to do work that was of actual use to
mankind, more so than burning brush or digging holes, along with his desperate
desire to be with his wife, won him over to the sobering prospect of working with
the mentally ill.

Just as letter writing proved a difficult way to conduct financial business, it
proved complicated and difficult in making such a big decision as moving across
the country to work in something as off-putting as a mental hospital. The risks
involved in the move were many. Would Miriam actually be able to join Ben, or
would he transfer an additional five hundred miles away from her? How would
they ensure that she arrived safely when they barely knew where they would be
going? CPS provided no list of what to bring for wives, so what should she pack
and what should she leave behind? How would they coordinate her moving and
the myriad details when there was a lag of three to five days between letters?
Would mental hospital work be as bad as they assumed? Would the scary and
potentially dangerous environment be worth it just to be together? Before being
able to answer any of the logistical questions, the simple, yet not simple at all,
decision whether or not to go had to be made.

The first letter to mention transferring to hospital work was actually from Miriam. On November 16, 1942, barely a week after Ben had been in service, she wrote, "Say honey do you remember that minister that was at the bus & talked to us about working in a hospital in New Jersey & said he knew of a couple who were doing that. . . . But I don't see how any one could stand it to work in a mental hospital." This passing comment did not take hold as an actual possibility for almost another month.

In the November 28 edition of the *Turnpike Echo*, a brief notice announced that

Friday, November 20, a telegram was received in the mail stating: "Request Telegraphic reply to National Service Board Office giving number of campers interested going to mental hospitals. Reply does not mean any final commitment but we need preliminary indication number men probably available— Henry A. Fast"

This would indicate that the field of detached service, especially in mental hospitals is opening up fast. Recent accounts in newspapers indicate that a number of mental hospitals in Ohio will soon be opened to Civilian Public Service Men.[1]

Ben did not write to Miriam of the possibility of being transferred to a hospital to work until December 9:

Good evening Sweetheart:
 I'll come in and talk a little while If I may. I just got back from Prayer meeting. After Prayer Meeting we had a talk given by a Mr. Layman who is Director of the M.C.C. He gave a good talk then opened up the way for questions. It was real interesting. There is to be detached service on farms, in Mental Hospitals, and General Hospitals. And He explained about it. I wouldn't mind General Hospital work If I could get close to Home. But I'd have to have your opinion before I do anything different. If I could get in a General Hospital we could Probably live together if we couldn't I wouldn't have to go. Mr. Layman said in Both Kind of Hospitals that they are so short on help that they will hire any one nearly so I'm sure you could get work, either nursing or cooking. Maybe that dosen't strike you. If not we'll forget it.

Miriam responded to the idea on December 13:

Yes I like the idea of working in a hospital (But not a mental hospital) You find out all you can about it and perhaps around the first (or middle) of February I could come out and we could try it. Of course that will all depend on whether or not they will let us be together after working hours in our own room. And by

I mean by "being together" you know how! . . . You be sure to tell me everything you find out about the . . . General Hospital. That proposition sounds swell to me and I'll be so anxious to hear from you and know what you have found out. Just think what it would mean to us even if we only could see one another once a week & if we could be together every day that would be heaven. Oh wouldn't that be wonderful! . . . Not only do I think it would be a good idea to work in the hospital so that we could be together but also I think that if there was a "call" then for men to be shipped over seas that if you were engaged in caring for the sick in our own country they wouldn't send you across as soon as they would if were where you are now.

Clearly, Miriam was open to the idea of hospital work, though at first the idea of working in a mental hospital did not appeal. I find it interesting that a month into Ben's time in CPS, they were still concerned that the government would go back on its word and force him to go to war. Perhaps if Ben were engaged in work in critically understaffed locations, helping mankind, he would not be forced to that fate.

Miriam continued to write that she was open to hospital work, and eventually she even declared that she would work in a mental hospital if it meant they could be together. On December 17, she stated, "I think I'd almost go anywhere if I thought I could be with you." Again, on Christmas Day, Miriam wrote, "I wonder whether you didn't understand or over looked what I wrote about two weeks ago. I asked you if you wouldn't like hospital work. I'd be glad to come out and stay. . . . Honey can we please go to a hospital to work? I'll even go to a mental hospital if only I can be with you. I don't think I can bear it all to be away from you much longer." And though Miriam was pretty clear in her letters that she was open to the work, even work in a mental hospital, Ben somehow did not receive that message and still was not certain of her feelings.

Over the course of the next two months Ben repeated in almost every letter how much he wanted to get into hospital work so they could be together. It is hard not to feel exasperated with his repetition of the possibility of hospital work and his inability to read and understand that Miriam was, yes, willing.

[December 30, 1942]
Honey I don't know about this Detached service question. There are no calls right now for Mental hospital workers and the General Hospital work has not opened up as yet. As soon as I know anything at all Definate I will be sure to let you. know. I sure do above all else want to be where I can be with you. And I'd sacrifice a whole lot for that Privilege If you'd like to work in Mental Hospital work. the first chance I get I'll sign up I don't know if that would be so advisable or not. But if we could be together I'd stand anything.

[January 6, 1943]
We may have to take Mental Hospital work But I'd be willing if you would. Here's something I learned this eve. The General hospital ^work is or has nearly fallen thru. The M.C.C. wants to use the money for Post war relief and the Government wants it put in the treasure so until there is an agreement made General hospital work will not be available. If I get a chance to go to Mental Hospital should I take it then have you come there?"

[January 7, 1943]
Colonel McClean of Selective Service was here this eve. and gave us a lection on Detached service he said that Mental Hospital work was all the would be available at the Present time and would afford oppurtunities in Perhaps a month or so. after the cold wether is over. Well it's food for tho't anyway.

It is also difficult to understand how Ben could misread Miriam's responses when she wrote on January 10, 1943, that she was "altogether willing that we should work in a mental hospital if you can get the chance go and then let me know and then I'll come at once." For some reason, Ben struggled to make this critical decision with only letters between them. They managed the sale of their home and other critical financial issues via letter, but the prospect of moving across the country, with or without Miriam at first, left him indecisive. The reasons for this are many. Perhaps Miriam found making firm decisions easier than Ben as an aspect of their personalities. Perhaps the weight of the decision made Ben feel unstable—he was in a situation that probably felt far removed from reality, was told what to do at every moment of the day, and rarely had decisions to make. And perhaps the conduit and platform of letter writing simply did not suffice for this particular decision.

We can only speculate as to why the conduit and platform fell short in this instance. In most other instances where letter writing was not ideal, even the situation with their complicated finances, Ben and Miriam were cohesive in their overall opinions and goals. Letter writing was a complicated and sometimes inexact way of communicating, but the conduit and platform were maintained between them because they were a united front against the frustrations caused by his parents and in their desire to sell the house. This could have been because they had discussed it thoroughly before Ben left, so they were able to rely on that prior agreement when the mode of letter writing complicated things. In this case, it seems the prospect of going to work in a mental hospital was not one they had discussed previously, or at least not one they had discussed much. They had no prior agreement or unified view on the matter and only had the letters to foster that discussion. We see here the limitations of conduit and platform for Ben and Miriam. The letters can and did do so very much for them and their relationship, their communication, and their lives. But that capacity was somewhat stretched beyond its capabilities in this case.

Another aspect that may have hindered the conduit and platform was the relative squeamishness that people felt about discussing mental illness. The stereotypes about mental health, the stigmas, the jokes, and the avoidance of the topic are something that are a part of our modern world. Those reactions are not new, and perhaps Ben and Miriam struggled against them as they made their decision. Further, alongside the stigmas and jokes was at least a vague notion of what might go on in a mental institution—at a minimum it would be a large number of "crazy" people in one place. Moreover, these "lunatic asylums" had not been represented as safe and comfortable places in the news reports and literary interpretations over the preceding one hundred years. Indeed, Ben and Miriam's fears of mental illness and institutions were founded on generations of beliefs. It is no wonder that even their conduit and platform struggled to be maintained against such history and stigma.

Eventually Ben did at least fill out a questionnaire about what kind of work he would like to do for CPS. In a letter from January 15, 1943, he wrote, "I Put Hospital service down either Mental or General." Mennonite Central Committee (MCC) Archives provided me with copies of Ben's service record. In these records was the questionnaire that Ben filled out and it too was dated January 15, 1943. Ben typed his responses rather than handwrote them. He noted his reason for choosing CPS: "I am opposed to Military Service and believe it wrong to take life." The survey asked if he had any family obligations that would limit his work to a certain area of the country. Ben replied, "Yes. I am married and my parents are aged considerably. I would prefer to work in Western Ohio or Indiana." The survey then asked if he was interested in detached service opportunities. Ben wrote, "I'm interested mostly in hospital work."

Later that month, the opportunities for transfer to mental hospital work started to become reality.

[January 25, 1943]
I reckon I'd better tell you the latest. There is Mental Hospital work opening up in ~~Conneticut~~ ^Providence, Rhode Island. and Mr. Shetler said this eve. when I talked with him, that Probably a fellow from the hospital would be here next week and tell us about it. If the Proposition sounds favorable and There would be an opportunity of your being able to come with me, would you be willing? It is . . . about 900 [miles] from home But if we were together what would it matter? We'd have each other and then we could take a trip home sometime together, do things for each other and together That's the Part I like about it. from all reports, The fellows who went to mental hospitals say they wouldn't want to come back to camp, so there must be something to it That isn't so bad. I had

Mr. Shetler Put my name on the list for mental hospital work But I don't have to take it unless I ~~don't~~ want to. I've told all I know so you think it over, and what ever you descide, That's what I'll do.

[January 28, 1943]

I've got some news Darling, The fellow is to be here tomorrow to interview us who are interested in Hospital work. There was a man here this eve. who spoke to us at supper time, he told us a few things and The man who comes tomorrow will explain all about the nature of the work, and if we can have our wives there etc. I'm Pretty sure it can be arranged. I wish I had your opinion about it, but so far I haven't heard from you concerning it. Maybe I'll get word tomorrow. I think it all may Prove to be answer to our Prayers But we shall see. This Mr. Mosler who talked to us this eve. said that all the boys had to be in camp for 90 days before they could leave for hospital service. I will have been here 90 days the 4th of next month that's only 7 days so I could qualify along that line I'm sure. he also stated that it would be about 2 mo. till another hospital opens up and that one will be in Mass. so if we want to get in a hospital, Perhaps we'd better take the oportunity while we have the chance. I believe I would like it. I'll find out all about it tomorrow and tell you.

In spite of the fact that letters from Miriam over the last month clearly stated her willingness, Ben continued to feel unsure of her feelings on the matter. The opportunity to transfer came quickly, and the decision had to be made in a matter of days. Letter writing simply did not suffice for the immediacy of the need. Additionally, it was more than just the lag time of the postal system at play in this instance. Ben did not know that Miriam was at her grandparents' home and her Grandpa Carpenter was dying. Grandpa died on the January 26, right as Ben desperately waited for word.

On the January 29 Ben wrote,

That guy was here this eve. telling about the camp at Rd. Island. he told all about it how the work is done, and that our wives could be with us. It could be arranged for both to be off duty on the same day. They give one day a week and we could have our room together. But I didn't sign up. You'l wonder why. I don't know except that last night and today I Prayed that if It was God's will that I should sign up that He would so direct me. After the talk was over I didn't feel as tho' I wanted to sign up so I didn't. . . .

Darling that is the only way we'll have of getting together before the Duration is over so It will be up to you whether I go to a mental hospital or not. I hope you won't think hard of me for not signing up this time, if you thought it would be O.K. because I was waiting for word from you that I never got. If you descide you'l go, I'll take the next opportunity. Darling I want to be with you so much but I don't want to do anything you wouldn't want me to, so give me a definite answer as to what you think. then I'll Plan to that effect. . . .

P.S. Lewis had a notion to sign up but he didn't because he didn't hear from his wife either. Honey I think it would be O.K. But I don't know, at this hospital in Rd. Island The women get $50.<u>00</u> Per Mo. to start with. And a $2½ raise Per quarter until they reach $70.00 That really wouldn't be so bad.

It is somewhat difficult to explain the intensity of the letters through this week. Miriam's letters were filled with anxiety, frustration, and grief at the drama at home. Ben's letters were filled with anxiety, frustration, and desperation at a decision that had the potential to change their lives completely for the duration of the war. And neither would receive the letters until after the drama of the two situations had largely passed. Nowhere else in the letters was it so clear that they lived separate lives as in this week. The conduit and platform of the letters does such a good job of framing their relationship, making that space and place that meant so much to them as a couple, that they seem a cohesive whole. This week, they were clearly existing separately and both felt that separation in painful ways and, in contrast to the holidays, practical ways as well.

After Ben's lengthy description of the opportunity and why he opted this time not to sign up, he repeated this explanation and most of the rest of the information over the following days, almost word for word. I think that Ben was not only afraid of making a decision without her explicit input, he was also afraid if he signed up and was shipped to Rhode Island, he would be that much farther from her for any furlough days he accrued. I also think he was afraid to hope for being together in Rhode Island for the rest of his time in CPS. When two people are as connected as Ben and Miriam, a hope like that would be devastating if it did not come to pass.

On the first of February, Ben finally received Miriam's emphatic "yes!" to sign up for the transfer. She had paid extra for airmail in the hopes he would get it in time. Ben's letter in response was bereft though he tried to speak hopefully of the future.

[February 1, 1943]
I got your air mail letter today but it's to late now to sign up for Rd. Island now. But now I'll know what to do the next time a favorable opportunity presents itself. from the way they talked it won't be so-long. Perhaps. I don't know how soon tho' that our camp will get another chance. It may be a few weeks or a couple months. when ever it is, I'll come home before we go. Well Darling Don't worry. If I could have known what you thought; Probably I would have signed up fri. In fact I know I would have because a chance that we can be together

is what I'm wanting. I would like This hospital work I'm sure because There I know I would be doing some good while here, we aren't doing anything which I would consider Important. we were shoveling snow again today.

Ben's letters over the next few days were very, very short in comparison to his usual. He apologized repeatedly for not signing up for Rhode Island. On February 8, 1943, he wrote,

In my thoughts, heart and mind I've thought about us a lot today and I wished many times that we were going to a hospital soon. The releases came thru for the other fellows who signed up for Rd. Island today. Warren Meyers and Paul Yoder backed out. they are not going But when the list was made out they chose two alternates to take in case some one did back out or the release wasn't approved. I wish we were going, But we'll have to wait till the next chance.

And so they waited for another opportunity for hospital work. The letters returned to the closeness, and their space and place were reestablished, but not even two weeks later, Ben was faced with another decision: when and if he should take a furlough. CPS men earned two and a half days of furlough for every month of work.[2] At this point, Ben had earned eight days of furlough, and he would have twelve by April. He and Miriam had discussed his furlough options before he left home. They had planned that he would come home in April for their first anniversary, but knowing that he had days available and the means to go home proved to be a great temptation. On the one hand, he wanted to have a full twelve days at home with her at one time. On the other hand, he could take six now and six in April instead. The letters followed the same pattern as the previous ones pertaining to the decision of hospital work; there were questions and missing or delayed answers. Ben initially decided that he would not take furlough in February because he had not heard from Miriam, but eventually, he decided that taking the split furlough option was the best. On February 19, Ben wrote,

here I be and I'll soon be there. I got your letter Just in time so I'm leaving tomorrow eve. and am coming home to you. Oh darling the closer the time comes the more enthusiastic I get. . . . So Hurray! I'm on the way tomorrow eve. . . . I will Probably get home before you get this letter But I Just must write in order to maintain my "Perfect record." I haven't missed an evening yet Honey, and I am so glad of it.

At this point, there is a significant break in the letters.

Miriam's letters after he returned to camp indicate that while home, Ben was very ill, though that did not stop him and Miriam from the intimate reunion they had planned for months. The archive contains a series of postcards as Ben traveled from Goshen back to Pennsylvania (figs. 9–11).

> Sat. 10:00 A.M.
>
> Honey, I'm still going away from you. I got this card in Toledo and am writing now as I ride. It's a terrible feeling to know I'm going when a few hours ago we were so close—Bye Now.
>
> Your Ben

> Hello Darling;
>
> I'm in Pittsburg waiting for my bus I just sent you a telegram There is sure lots of People traveling today I took taxi from Depot to Bus stations. Throat no worries
>
> Love Ben

Ben wrote about how he felt as he traveled back to camp, away from his love. I think the leaving was harder this time than the first time because he knew what he was leaving and what he was headed toward. CPS service had lost the mystery, and the lonely nights ahead were all too real. "I had a feeling of Loneliness and emptiness when I left. I was leaving the most Precious Person in the world and

FIGURE 9. The front of an undated postcard sent by Ben on his travels from camp back to Goshen, Indiana, in early 1943, sent from the same location that he apparently called home: "This is where I made the Phone Call. It looks Pretty on the Card But it really isn't so pretty now."

FIGURE 10. A postcard sent by Ben from Toledo, Ohio, in 1943 on his return trip to the camp, describing the "terrible feeling" of parting from Miriam.

FIGURE 11. A postcard Ben sent from Pittsburgh, Pennsylvania, on his return trip to CPS service in 1943. Ben assures Miriam his health is on the mend: "Throat no worries."

the one I love above everything on this earth It was a terrible sensation." He traveled through Toledo and Cleveland in Ohio, then Pittsburgh, Pennsylvania, via trains. Then from Pittsburgh to the camp he traveled on a crowded bus that was choked by heavy smoke. Finally, on February 28, "it was about 12:20 when I got down to camp so I am O.K. and won't get an AWOL." This letter also contained significant information for Ben and Miriam's future. At the start of the letter, Ben wrote, "I reckon I will have to wait a few weeks. Maybe not tho'. I've got some good news to tell you. I'll keep you guessing a while yet. I'll tell you in this letter tho. So Keep your Shirt on <u>haha</u>." Toward the end of the letter, Ben wrote,

> Well Honey you've had lots of Patience enduring the Suspense so now I'll tell you the good news. Mr. Joe Byler was here last eve and today. wanting more men for Hospitals. Lewis signed my name But didn't sign his. . . . If he don't change his mind he intends to call his wife next Sun. So I'll call you too. Be sure to be at home next Sun. afternoon. we'll call at 3:00 our time that would be 2:00 your time. Next Sun afternoon at 2:00 March 7. . . .
>
> Mr. Byler tho't our release would come in about 2 wks. So I may come before April. He also said he thought it would be best to go to the hospital first and then get the wives to come later. He said If they go right away that they wouldn't get as good a Job as if they waited a little. I'll explain more fully when I come. But I don't know whether we'll do that or not. I'd like to take you right with me then I'd be sure you were there.

In the early weeks of March, Ben and Miriam did indeed have their phone conversation, enabling the immediate response Ben needed to make the decision to transfer. They began preparations immediately for his transfer and, more significantly, for Miriam to join him in Rhode Island. Ben's letters definitely took on a bright and excited note from mid-March on. He also planned for one last brief furlough back to Goshen, since he would lose his accrued furlough days with the transfer.

> [March 8, 1943]
> Well Honey, got every thing Packed? No, well we'll get things fixed up. I think I will bring my trunk and big suitcase along and then we'll have something to bring your things back in. I'll tell you something you can get for me if you want to <u>Whhhat?</u> Well, get me two Pair of Pajamas (large) I think <u>haha</u> get two piece ones like the ones I have. Maybe you won't want to be embarrassed by buying them If you don't get them I will when I come home.

Some of the details of the transfer and the transition simply are not present. This lack of detail is an aspect of family history writing methodology. Often when researching and building a small history, the missing pieces make it difficult to see the full picture We are often left with more questions than answers. Here, we can know a bit about what he was told to expect from one of his last letters in 1943 from March 15.

O.K. well, I've got some news that isn't so good so I better tell it now and get it over with. Mr. Hearnley the Director told me this eve. That he got a letter from the Hospital Supt. and He said that when we come to the Hospital we should not bring our wives with us right away. He said we should get settled then make arrangements for our wives ^to come. Mr. Hearnley thought it would be 3 or 4 days maybe a week before arrangements ^would be made for our wives to come. Here is my Plan. when I come home we'll come back together and go to Rd. Island together. The Hospital is about 5 miles from Providence, Rd. Island. so If you are agreed we'll find a room for you or hotel room and you can stay till arrangements can be made to come on to the Hospital. I ask him if there is any Possibility That you would not be able [to] work in the Hospital. He said No, they wanted women so he seemed to think all would be alright. what has Probably happened is: that one of the fellows who took their wife right along didn't get along very good. I mean to say, the wife maybe couldn't do the work or something went wrong. so they don't want to take any chances. . . . if I had to work in that hospital and you couldn't be with me I'll say not. I don't know what I'd do if such would be the case. I guess there's nothing we could do. I hope that we'll get along O.K. If I thought we couldn't be together I'd take my name off the list. I'll find out more about it and act accordingly. If I find you can't be with me I'll stay here and if you can we'll go. The whole thing has me a little worried. our Transfers haven't come yet from Washington and I don't think I should come home unless I come out before [*sic*] they come. I will call Sun. aft. at 2:00 if I don't come Sat. I hope they come this week and everything will be O.K.

Ben's last letter from Sideling Hill was on March 16, 1943. He gave no indication of whether he had received his transfer from Washington, DC, whether he was going on furlough that Saturday (March 20), or whether Miriam would join him immediately in Rhode Island or wait a week. It is a somewhat dissatisfying ending to his time at that camp, boring as the work must have been. Here, letters simply are not enough to help us envision exactly what went on in his mind, her mind, and their lives. Archival work records from Sideling Hill show that Ben was "p" or "worked on project site" on Saturday, March 20. Then he was marked as "f" or "on furlough" on March 21 through March 24. Once again, on March 25, Ben was marked "p," indicating that he returned to Sideling Hill and worked for a single day. Then on Friday, March 26, his status was marked "t" for transferred. The work reports for that same month in Rhode Island showed Ben as "AR" on March 26, meaning "Arrived."

Miriam's last letter to Ben at Sideling Hill was March 17. "Hi! Sweetheart! Here's your Mimmie once again. And I think this will be the last time I'll write to you. Now don't look like that? No honey I hope it will be the last time we'll ever need to write to one another and that instead we'll be able to talk to one another instead of writing for the rest of our lives." Letters were a lifeline for their relation-ship. Without the conduit of their love expressed over the miles, and without the platform they built for their relationship, they would have been in a much dif-ferent place in their relationship after five months apart. Yet, Miriam hoped they never had to write letters again. As much as those letters were a lifeline over those five months, they still did not replace being together and living life together. I can imagine that they were so sick of letters by this point they could have happily disposed of them thinking "I never have to do this again!" Nevertheless, Miriam saved every letter. One might ask why she did so if the letters reminded her of a painful time apart. I believe she saved them because, despite being a reminder of painful times, they were a written record of their love developing over time. The emotional work they did to maintain and build their relationship is visible in the letters, something that is not usually available to a couple who are together. The letters served as a journal or diary of their relationship as much as a conduit and platform.

In that last letter, Miriam speculated on the upcoming travel, "Honey I think it would be a good idea to send our trunk via of express. What do you think? Then we would only have the suitcase." At the end of her last letter she said, "I [am] waiting for you so hurry honey! Your little sweetheart Mimmie. . . . I'm not going to give you a kiss to night Instead you'll have to [come] home & get it." We can only speculate exactly what the events of this week were. The fact that no let-ters from Ben exist after March 16 could be an indication of how hurried things were for them. Perhaps he mailed letters as usual through March 20, his last day before furlough, but as Miriam traveled with him back to camp and on to Rhode Island, she never received them.

On February 19, 1943, before his first furlough, Ben wrote, "I'm bringing all my letters home because I don't have hardly any Place to keep them and I don't want to run the risk of any one reading Your precious messages of Love which are meant Just for me and me only." Neither Ben nor Miriam missed even one day of letter writing for the entire time they were apart. They both acknowledged their connection through the letters and wanted to preserve them as the platform they were, so Ben brought his pile of Miriam's letters back to her for safekeeping. Given that they both stopped writing letters on the same date in March, I suspect they agreed on that date when they were last together or in their phone conversa-tion. Whatever the facts, Miriam did indeed keep those special letters she wrote to Ben, and his letters to her, for her entire life.

CHAPTER 10

Archives, Family History, and the Personal

Oh honey I don't care whether we go to a mental hospital or the end of the earth as long as I can be with you.

MIRIAM, MARCH 6, 1943

T HE REMAINING CHAPTERS PRESENTED MORE CHALLENGES FOR ME IN tracing Ben and Miriam's story than the previous ones. Though the majority of Ben's time in service was spent at the Rhode Island State Hospital for Mental Diseases (more commonly referred to as the State Hospital) in Howard, Rhode Island, I had the least information upon which to build a history. First, for most of the three years Ben spent at the State Hospital, Miriam was there with him, working in the hospital. As indicated previously, Ben took this transfer mainly so that he and Miriam could be together. Thus, they were not writing letters back and forth, sent across the country in order to maintain their relationship. In fact, only one collection of letters exists during their years at the State Hospital, from November 30, 1944, through January 30, 1945. Miriam was pregnant with their first child, and instead of bearing this child in a state mental hospital, the excited and eager couple opted to send her home to Indiana to have their baby. The composition of these letters presented a second challenge to re-creating their story. The collection is comprised entirely of Ben's letters to Miriam. Apparently, only Ben's letters survived.

So the following chapters differ greatly from previous chapters. I could not rely on Ben and Miriam to tell their own story as I did throughout the rest of the book. Instead, to create a sort of patchwork story, I combine excerpts from Ben's letters, a few friends' letters, historical records, and primary data from three different archives (the Mennonite Central Committee Archive in Akron, Pennsylvania; the Rhode Island Historical Society Archives in Providence; and the Cranston Historical Society in Cranston, Rhode Island), news reports from several Rhode Island newspapers, and as many scholarly sources as I could find. This patchwork, instead of telling a somewhat linear story, gives small bits of the whole, vignettes if you will, that together craft a complete, if "patchy," picture. This patchwork, in turn, reveals several aspects of family history writing (FHW) methodology that may not have been as clear in previous chapters: the flexibility and fluidity of the methodology, the changes it makes to our understanding of archival research, and the ways it challenges our notions of the personal and researcher positionality.

I discuss in chapter 2 that FHW methodology is distinct from genealogy, which carries with it a pejorative "hobbyist" connotation. The assumption is that genealogy research is done in someone's spare time, often by retirees who do not use an authentic historical or academic approach. It focuses on the amassing of names and dates and often carries with it a nostalgia or a "longing for a home that no longer exists,"[1] and it is often romanticized. Instead, the patchwork created by weaving together warp and weft—the official records and the familial histories, the archival data from Rhode Island and the archived love letters in my campus office—is a broader representation of Ben and Miriam's story. Of course, there still may be a sense of nostalgia or romanticism, but that is mitigated by the inclusion of those official records and archival data.[2] FHW methodology, like other forms of qualitative and archival research methodologies, offers a triangulation of data as it verifies and validates the letters with broader archival data and vice versa.

But the fluidity of the methodology is an answer to the very practical question, "what happens while doing archival or FHW research when someone hits a dead end?" Students doing family history projects in my undergraduate and graduate seminars struggle with this issue from day one. The information available about small-h histories is often limited or seemingly tangential. While they may be able to find the names and dates for the genealogical family tree, when they try to dig deeper, to really understand their ancestors as human beings, and when they try to write their story in a coherent way for outsiders, they must use the "available means of persuasion" and the available data sources. These sources do not usually match what they want or expect to find. For example, a student might easily find names and dates on ancestry.com. They might find census records or marriage licenses and other official documentation. These are fine details, but they do not offer that personal information that would enable them to connect to their ancestor and tell their story. The details are "fine, I guess, but it's so boring" they might say. So to move forward they look for personal details. But few inherit an archive of four hundred love letters as I did. Instead, they have to get creative. Suppose they see in the census records that their great-great-uncle worked for General Electric (GE) at the turn of the century, so if they spend time researching GE in 1910, they eventually find information about the work done at the Fort Wayne plant and the workers. This large-H historical data leads to finding work records for Uncle Joe, and they find a host of images. It is not necessarily directly about Uncle Joe, but it is more interesting and engaging than just the names and dates. This large-H historical information may eventually, serendipitously, lead them to something much more interesting and personal about Uncle Joe's specific story.

Kirsch and Rohan's edited collection *Beyond the Archives* offers essays on the "how" of doing archival research. Because archival research seems disinterested, objective, and "just the facts," this text stands apart as positioning it, instead, as subjective, experimental, and nuanced. It "teaches the value of attending to how our family, social, and cultural history is intertwined with more traditional notions of history and culture. It helps us understand and explore the fissures of historical narrative, the places at the margins where voices have been suppressed, silenced, or ignored. Furthermore, these essays show that researching family archives and local stories can and does lead to sustained scholarly work."[3] Further, Kirsch and Rohan point out that "family history cannot be extricated from public history because individual lives shape and are shaped by the times."[4] Through FHW, the "privatized" histories can and do have an impact on the wider historical trends. Too often research of archives and material culture has focused on the contributions of white, male, and wealthy individuals as having large impacts on the world. The small, the low, the marginalized, often female, people and artifacts have been ignored. These items, both written and physical objects, reveal more about the in-betweens, the mundane moments, that are significant only to those involved.

Family history research and writing attends "to facets of the research process that might easily be marginalized and rarely mentioned because they seem merely intuitive, coincidental, or serendipitous."[5] One could say that the fact I, out of all my relatives, received that lumpy cardboard box of letters was serendipitous. Perhaps, but what I have chosen to do with that box is what sets family history apart from genealogy. Genealogy would have me sort the letters, read them, maybe reproduce them so that others in the family could read them. It might lead me to do some nominal research on Civilian Public Service (CPS) even. But to delve into the contents of the letters, to invest in telling Ben and Miriam's story to a broader audience beyond the family, to investigate how their story shaped the world around them and how the larger historical events shaped their letters, that is FHW methodology.

Kirsch and Rohan reiterate that "the most serious, committed, excellent historical research comes from choosing a subject to which we are personally drawn, whether through family artifacts, a chance encounter, a local news story, or some other fascination. . . . The personal connection can make all the difference in our scholarly pursuit."[6] JoAnn Campbell remarks that the writer of a historical account "is never a disinterested, objective observer of fact but always a selector of objects and interpreter of tales, [and so] the writing of history requires recognizing the location of the teller, the impetus of her investigation, and her vested interest in the tale."[7] FHW stands at a nexus of more traditional forms of historical research, memoir, qualitative research, and genealogy and is a form of personal, life writing. It would be impossible for me, the researcher, to remain objective because, for one, no historian can truly be objective, but more to the point, I am a member of this family. My lived experience is woven into theirs now; who I am as a person is shaped by who Ben and Miriam were *and is in the process of being shaped* by telling their story.

Wendy Sharer notes the risks of revealing personal feelings or emotions or the vested interest one might have in her archival work. She asks, "How can I turn this tale of my research as lived process into something 'intellectual' and something 'significant' for other scholars to read?"[8] She points out that her most significant research project originated "within the emotion-laden family."[9] She suggests that "rather than turning away from or hesitating to reveal how research is connected with lived, and often affective, experiences, researchers should seek out these experiences and make them known in a spirit of enthusiasm."[10] Seeking out experiences that alter ourselves as researchers greatly shifts the researcher's positionality. As the researcher, I am, of course, both insider and outsider. Much like the autoethnography methodology employed in my previous work, I am both the researcher who is distanced from the story and observing it as an outsider, and I am the researched, a member of the family, an insider to what I am discussing.[11]

As I sought to reconstruct Ben and Miriam's extraordinary, ordinary story, in a patchwork of official and personal details, I found that the story had to make sense to me first, as both an outsider and an insider, before I could communicate it to others. Thus, this chapter offers a piece of the larger story of mental hospitals in Rhode Island and the nation so that we can better understand the context in which Ben and Miriam worked. Without this seemingly tangential, large-H historical information, their immediate story would be less impactful and less complete. And without this chapter, I would have been able to more easily maintain the more comfortable position of etic, the outsider, in my writing. I could more easily talk about *them* rather than *we*, in discussing the deplorable conditions of mental hospitals. Instead, I sought out the experiences that altered my ways of thinking, digging in and allowing myself to understand the historical conditions of the hospital, to feel the weight of the conditions in my chest and the weight of Ben and Miriam's involvement. I invested my emotions, and thereby Ben and Miriam's emotions, and my emic perspective in the research. It is odd that in this case the large-H, impersonal history of mental hospitals was a practice in maintaining my insider status and emotional commitment to the story.

As representative of the methodological explanation above, this chapter presents two very different perspectives that may seem distant or tangential to Ben and Miriam's story: my own perspective as I visited the State Hospital in January 2017 and the 150 years of historical accounts of the State Hospital that preceded Ben and Miriam's arrival in 1943. Together these perspectives provide bookends for Ben and Miriam's experiences both in terms of chronology and in historical perspective. They contextualize Ben and Miriam's story and four years of small-h history within a much, much larger context. These bookends also illustrate that the impact of their small-h history is ongoing.

I took a tour of the State Hospital campus in early January 2017. It is not hard to find, there in Cranston, Rhode Island, as it is huge. I mostly went up and down Howard Street to see the main buildings that were part of the State Hospital in the 1940s. They are imposing, hard-edged brick, sterile, institutional, and other than parking lots, they appear vastly the same as the pictures of them in the 1940s. I was uncertain which buildings Ben and Miriam would have worked in. The main building seems to be the Rhode Island State Mental Advocacy Building, and it is the one that faces Howard directly. It is also the one that every historical archive has an image of when talking about the State Hospital, so I had to assume that it was central. Across the street and a parking lot are two three-story buildings side by side. These identical buildings are not as large as the main building, so I think, based on specifications I had read the previous day at the Rhode Island Historical Society Archives, they might have been the men's and women's dormitory buildings.

My visit was on a blindingly sunny day. It was clear, and the lack of snow was a blessing for this research trip. It was also so cold my teeth hurt. I bumbled my way along in my rental car. I had grown used to the waving arms motioning me to get out of the way. I found eastern drivers to be as abrupt as the researchers I met had been generous and friendly. I knew the East Coast attitude had to show up someplace. I parked in one of the many parking lots that line Howard Street. The one closest to the main building was open so I maneuvered my Toyota Corolla into a spot.

I got out to take pictures and walked around a little. The place did not feel particularly like a *mental hospital*. It was almost like a college campus except that the buildings were farther apart and there was ample parking. When I really studied the main construction (figs. 12 and 13), however, it was sobering. This building,

FIGURE 12. Medical Building, Rhode Island State Hospital for Mental Diseases, CPS Camp #85, 1944. Courtesy of Mennonite Central Committee Collection, Mennonite Church USA Archives, Akron, Pennsylvania.

FIGURE 13. Rhode Island State Hospital for Mental Diseases, 2017.

this imposing, stoic, buttoned-up-tightly brick structure must have been much more terrifyingly huge and imposing to Ben and Miriam. Aged twenty-one and seventeen, almost nine hundred miles from home in March 1943, the experience of arrival itself would have lurched the most confident of young hearts. That day, in the cold, bright January sunshine, in my rented Corolla, it was still heart lurching. I did not want to go inside (indeed I could not, but that is a fact aside). I did not want to linger here, except that I recognized that I was unlikely to return to Rhode Island anytime in the near future.

While I did not exactly hurry, I was brisk about the business of snapping photographs. I took enough photos from my limited perspective on the sidewalks to satisfy myself. I worried that I did not take that one *right* photo though. You know, the one that will unlock some mystery as I continued to write, or one that Ben will specifically talk about in his letters. But I was uncomfortable with the cold and with only the vaguest knowledge of what occurred in these buildings so many years ago. The atrocities committed in the name of silencing or controlling a troubled mind, the violence, the filth. Whatever it was that Ben and men like him walked into as they sought to somehow help, I can only imagine how these men of conscience had to work to love the seemingly unlovable, to refuse violence when all other doctors and attendants recommended it. To clean walls, beds, floors, and people with the knowledge that they would be soiled again within the hour.

As I took my photos of those institutional creations, I felt their weight in my chest. I felt the depth of worry and care for those inside whom I could not help. I mentally hugged my grandfather and grandmother for their bravery, integrity, and charitable work ethic. And I got in my rented Corolla to return to the land of the living.

What I saw of the State Hospital in 2017 was a far cry from its inauspicious beginnings. Records of the treatment of the mentally ill in Rhode Island date to a letter written by Roger Williams, founder of the colony, on November 11, 1650, when he described a woman, Mrs. Weston, as having "distempers" and as being a "distracted woman."[12] In most places in that era, the care of a mentally ill person was left to the family, friends, or the community. "But as early as 1725 a law was enacted whereby the towns of Rode Island on the mainland were empowered to build a house of corrections for vagrants 'and to keep mad persons in.'"[13]

The nineteenth century led to more explicit public efforts to manage the mentally ill, if not necessarily to care for them. In 1843, a man named Nicholas Brown bequeathed $30,000 in his will "toward the erection or the endowment of an insane or lunatic hospital or retreat for the insane, to be located in Providence or vicinity."[14] These funds were essentially seed money that eventually, in 1847, led to Rhode Island's first state asylum, Butler Hospital for the Insane. This facility was like many of the nineteenth century, and because so many of the patients and their families were wealthy, they "began to demand a standard of living in construction and material comforts equal to their own well-appointed homes."[15] Butler thus developed a strong base of donations and updates for huge bay windows, a conservatory, hanging plants, and singing birds. Unfortunately, because of donations and updates, those with financial means dictated who was welcome in the hospital and who was not. The facility eventually stopped admitting foreign-born and first-generation Americans, as well as those too poor to pay for admission. Instead of well-appointed rooms and care, "there was only a bed, or sometimes just a stone floor, for those who could not pay. The dual system was to last into the 1980s."[16]

In the mid to late nineteenth century, the state General Assembly met and decided to create a public mental institution to account for the disparity of care received at Butler. "In January 1869, the General Assembly authorized building a state institution and appointed a committee to find a farm suitable for the purpose, not less than 200 acres and with the sale price of not more than $25,000. In May, the committee reported its purchase of the William A. Howard farm in Cranston."[17] Thus, "the maimed in body, the unfortunate in mind, the offenders against the law—all are located at Howard."[18] These institutions were under the control of the Board of State Charities and Corrections.

The Howard farm was located, like many institutions, away from more populated areas (the correlation to CPS camps being located in out-of-the-way locales is worth noting). "For the most part, state hospitals of that period were isolated from the communities in which they were located. Fences usually surrounded the cluster of buildings that comprised the patients' quarters. Even more insidious was the invisible wall of fear and ignorance that kept these institutions hidden from public concern and awareness."[19]

The original state asylum consisted of two one-story wooden buildings with a third building added "to house violent patients."[20] The lunatic asylum on Blackwell's Island, New York, served as a model for the buildings.[21] Yet, DeSilva notes that Blackwell's Island was "considered at the time the worst insane asylum in America."[22] As a model for the new facility, the committee chose the asylum on Blackwell's Island in New York City not *because* of the quality of care there but, rather, *in spite* of it. David Rochefort notes that the wooden buildings cost a mere $22,000 to construct.[23] While the Blackwell's Island asylum had gained some infamy for its decrepit and unhealthful conditions, it nonetheless offered a compelling example of how to provide public care for the mentally ill at a cut-rate price: the New York facility spent only $2.12 a week per patient, the lowest cost anywhere in the nation.[24] Cost was the key attribute of the facilities that the Board of State Charities and Corrections focused upon.

Toward the turn of the century, other buildings were added. These were "brick, the architecture of a simple colonial style and portions of the new buildings were of fireproof construction. These new buildings comprise a congregate dining hall, with a seating capacity for 800 . . . , a service building, boiler house, and one ward building."[25] These buildings were a vast improvement, but before they were built, conditions at the asylum were deplorable indeed. In 1943, just as Ben and Miriam began their time at Howard, Henry A. Jones, the resident physician of the State Institutions, published a memoir. In *The Dark Days of Social Welfare at the State Institutions at Howard, Rhode Island*, Jones writes of the experiences he had at the turn of the twentieth century when he first arrived at Howard. He notes that "while many of the other states of the Union were progressing to a higher social order in the treatment of the insane, the prisoners, the feeble-minded and the poor, Rhode Island, in those dark days, was singularly backward."[26]

Howard was and is an entire campus of state-funded institutions; in the years leading up to the CPS unit, in addition to the Hospital for Mental Diseases, the state-run facilities included a State Prison, a State Workhouse and House of Corrections, a State Infirmary (originally the State Almshouse), Reform Schools, a State Home for Children, and the Exeter School for the Feeble-Minded, according to a 1930 report to the Public Welfare Administration.[27] In its earlier years, criminals headed for the prison and mentally ill "inmates" headed for the mental hospital were treated in the exact same manner, though many would argue that the mentally ill inmates were treated far worse than prisoners.

Mentally ill inmates were treated little better than cattle. Jones's memoir begins: "'Howard! Howard!'—What memories the name awakens; memories of the ball and chain, the . . . prisoners with closely cropped heads, and dirty gray uniforms; the lockstep, the downcast of head that showed, by its baleful and furtive glance, the seething mental condition of the mind that had not found itself and was tortured by the expressions, 'Justice', which was, to the wretched prisoners, a mockery, and it's very sound and echoed to them of 'Man's inhumanity to man.'"[28] Jones reminisces about his first glimpse of Howard as the train pulled into the station. While he discusses more the individuals headed for Howard prison, he does give an account of "one poor female, who, clanking her shackled wrist as one would a bracelet, screamed out some unintelligible language which showed she was insane." Later, Jones notes that while the sheriff took most of the people to the prison, "the officer with his other prisoners and the shouting, gesticulating insane woman wended their way up the hill to the 'Asylum for the Insane', there to unshackle her from the others and himself, leaving her there without any history of her past, and with only her name and apparent age and her reason for being there upon committing her to that Institution."[29]

He later notes that when prisoners and new asylum inmates arrived, they were all shackled together, in spite of the fact that superintendents tried to have this altered. New asylum inmates typically came with no history, nothing more than their name. "Attempts to glean a history of the case from the admitting officer usually failed. They knew only the name on the admittance slip. There was no social worker with a case history, no stenographer to take notes, no typist; the history gleaned from the patient was often disputed in its entirety when friends or relatives visited them."[30]

At the turn of the century, during Jones's "dark days," the asylum had a capacity of 600 but held 715 patients, and all were housed in the original three wooden structures built almost forty years earlier. Building new buildings and improving the existing facilities was long overdue. Dr. George Keane, the superintendent at that time, wrote in his annual report: "Food for the 715 patients is all cooked at the workhouse and house of correction and each meal is transported in food carts fully one quarter of a mile in all weathers before it reaches many of the dining rooms,' he said in asking for construction of the kitchen."[31]

Two 1914 reports published by the Rhode Island Board of Control and Supply offer a bit of insight to the development of the State Hospital campus. These two sets of specifications show that new buildings were going up, even as the wooden structures were still in continual use. The first is *Specifications for a Kitchen and Service Building*, so apparently Dr. Keane's request for improvements was met, though several years later. In it are detailed (and by detailed, I mean very, very detailed) descriptions of every aspect of the proposed building to be erected. There are paragraph descriptions of the excavation, flooring, masonry, pipes, fixtures, door frames, lighting, heating, and everything else one can imagine. There are no images, sadly, or diagrams.[32]

The second 1914 report is a *Specifications for a Men's Ward*. "Specifications of material to be furnished and labor to be performed in the erection of a three-story brick building, to be known as a Men's Ward, corridors connecting said building with the adjacent building, and other work for the State Hospital at Howard, R.I."[33] The paragraph descriptions are almost identical to those of the kitchen, with the addition of a more extensive section on lavatories ("forty vitreous China lavatories 20" x 18"), bath tubs ("ten porcelain enamelled"), urinals ("eleven Class A white porcelain"), water closets ("twenty-eight extra heavy vitreous porcelain syphon jet W.Cs. with integral porcelain seats"), and six fountains.[34]

These newly constructed buildings were a great source of pride to Jones. He writes:

> The Asylum for the Insane, now the State Hospital for Mental Diseases, is the largest of the group of institutions at Howard. This institution occupies, at present, the largest share of public interest. Time was when this was not the case. Those days I shall now attempt to portray, so that the student of psychiatry or other interested person may be holding compare the mighty surge upward that this institution is making, and how it has emerged from the so-called "sheeppen", as it was termed by visiting psychiatrists from other mental hospitals, to the place of prominence it now holds.[35]

Jones had a very lofty opinion of the progress that had been made at Howard in the forty years he had been there. He continually contrasts the early years with the much more "enlightened" methods used in 1942. He notes that in the early years, patients were given medical treatment that was "without doubt, the best at that time. A weekly bath was the main attempt at hydrotherapy. The patients were uniformed mostly in prison grey."[36] But attendants, who came to work at the asylum from "older and more modern institutions, . . . brought with them the arts of subduing patients without bruising or 'marking them up.' Towel strangling, rubber hose beating and other refinements of cruelty were surreptitiously used."[37] Contrasted with these archaic methods, he writes, "How different, now! There, upon that puny battleground, which is yet so great to the welfare of the bodies and the minds, yea, even the souls of thousands, rises a modern City of Healing. There it stands, resplendent in the sunshine. There it raises its beautiful walls that were the aspirations and dreams of the builders of long ago. . . . There is an oasis of healing, equipped with all that medicine can devise. . . . The State Hospital for Mental Diseases crowns the hill, and cannot be hidden."[38]

Clearly Jones believed strongly in the vast improvements made at the State Hospital since the turn of the century. New dorms to house employees of the

State Hospital were finally constructed in 1936, for example. But his "City of Healing" that is "resplendent in the sunshine" stands in stark contrast to other reports of the State Hospital in those years. Some things had improved over the rough wooden structures, but internally, the workings of the hospital were not as different as he would like everyone to believe.

The belief that conditions in the mental hospital had improved to high standards of care seemed to be a common one among state employees. In a 1930 report to the Public Welfare Administration by Katherine Burt, she states that "the history of the care of the insane in Rhode Island is the story of the development from haphazard, inadequate care of 'lunatics' because they were a danger to the community, to a highly organized state institution, headed by a prominent psychiatrist with a staff of experts."[39] This public perception of improved conditions stretched outside the state and on into history as well. In one of the most recent books regarding CPS's involvement in mental hospitals, *Acts of Conscience*, Steven Taylor notes that "the institutions, and wards within individual institutions, were not all the same. Some, such as Howard State Hospital in Rhode Island, had relatively modern facilities."[40] He later notes that while the Cleveland hospital "had a reputation of being one of the worst mental hospitals. . . . Howard was probably one of the better ones."[41] The facilities at Howard were newer by the time COs arrived to work, but the treatment and care of patients was basically the same across all mental hospitals. I think that "relative" is an important factor in this description of Howard. Relatively better when describing horrible, inhumane conditions does not mean good.

The truth is that conditions at Howard and *all* mental hospitals at that time were deplorable, and in most cases, these conditions continued to be deplorable for decades. Finally, in the 1970s and 1980s, Rhode Island returned to the problematic idea of community-based care that had been present nearly three hundred years earlier when the state was founded. Now, instead of the mentally ill living in a facility, they live on their own, dependent upon governmental financial support, or they are in prison. In a personal interview with Dr. Sandra Enos, a sociologist at a local university in Rhode Island, she noted that we have, essentially, replaced one sort of institution with another. Instead of being in a mental institution, many, many mentally ill patients are now in prison. One is left to wonder if we will keep repeating the same mistakes we have been making for hundreds of years.

CHAPTER 11

Conditions of the State Hospital in 1943

I sure do above all else want to be where I can be with you. And I'd sacrifice a whole lot for that Privilege If you'd like to work in Mental Hospital work.

BEN, DECEMBER 30, 1942

I have did a lot of thinking about <u>everything</u> lately. I am altogether willing that we should work in a mental hospital.

MIRIAM, JANUARY 3, 1943

Honey here's my honest opinion; I feel that I could be of more service to man-kind and do more good in an Institution of that Kind and That will be the only opportunity for us to get together for any length of time whatever until after the Duration.

BEN, JANUARY 31, 1943

WHEN BEN AND MIRIAM AND OTHER CIVILIAN PUBLIC SERVICE (CPS) workers arrived at the State Hospital, they entered in the midst of the "great changes" discussed in chapter 10. It was March 1943. Henry Jones was finishing his memoir and lauding the "City on a Hill . . . resplendent in the sunshine," but reports of the goings-on internally were unchanged from prior accounts of deplorable care. The fact that a CPS camp was created at the hospital speaks to those deplorable conditions, made far worse by a critically low staff. In fact, to say the staff was critically low is a gross understatement. Leslie Eisan reveals the extent of the national mental hospital labor crisis by offering excerpts from letters to the National Service Board (NSBRO) requesting conscientious objector help throughout the nation:

"Our personnel needs are acute and growing worse daily. We are short today 165 attendants out of a normal complement of 225."

"We are working with less than half our proper force and are definitely below the level of safe coverage."

"At present the demand for admission is so great, and the available help so short that the pressure upon us is severe."

"We are 150 attendants short out of 256. The situation is dangerous."

"Our institution has become severely affected by the war effort in the selective
service, so much so that we have already thought of the possibility of having to
close up half our main building."[1]

The Rhode Island State Hospital for Mental Diseases (State Hospital) had a
population at that time of 2,801 patients, "many of them disturbed cases requiring extra care."[2] A 1971 Legislative Commission Study Report to the General
Assembly called *The Howard Reservation* states that "estimates on patient bed requirements have varied over the years and projected needs have sometimes been
seriously less that accurate. In the 40's and early 50's the State Hospital and the
State Infirmary . . . had a combined bed capacity of approximately 4000."[3] The
report indicates the *bed capacity* of both the mental hospital and the infirmary,
not the actual population; overcrowding was a serious issue, particularly in the
mental hospital. The 1940 Census records state that the State Hospital for Mental
Diseases in Cranston had a population of 3,258.[4] My guess is that that number
included employees. DeSilva's 1981 article notes that at its peak, the hospital had
3,000 patients, so this is the era that such a number must have been reached.[5]

The State Hospital superintendent in 1943, Dr. Ross, described it "'as tough
a situation as I've ever run into in the 35 years I've been in this field.'"[6] To show
how short staffed they were, Dr. Ross pointed to the conditions in the building
for disturbed women patients. "There are 300 patients in the six wards in this building, which in pre-war times had a complement from 25 to 30 attendants. . . . 'We've
had as low as six attendants in this building and never more than eight in recent
months,' Dr. Ross said."[7] He described the situation as gravely serious and reiterated the dangerously understaffed conditions by stating, "'I doubt if anybody on
the outside realizes what we're up against. . . . In all my years in this kind of work
I've never been as uneasy as I am now.'"[8] He pointed out that while he had many
plans for improvements and innovations in the hospital he admitted in the interview that he was "largely 'marking time' because of the serious help situation."[9]

While conditions at Rhode Island State Hospital were severe, they were indicative of a larger, systemic problem across all mental institutions. In *Turning
Point*, Alex Sareyan writes, "In some institutions, the situation was so severe that
only one attendant would be on duty to oversee entire buildings housing as many
as 500 patients. . . . To comprehend fully the enormity of the personnel problem
during that period, compare it with the current [1990s] day situation at state
hospitals, where there is roughly one attendant for every two or three patients. In
many such facilities the attendant staff outnumbers the patient census."[10]

It was into this difficult, dangerous situation that Ben and Miriam, ages
twenty-one and seventeen, ventured. What did Ben and Miriam see and experience in their first days of work at the State Hospital? We cannot know their
unique perspective on the sights that greeted them, but we can piece together

personal reports of conditions at the State Hospital and other mental hospitals throughout the country. "Paul L Goering recalls his first impression of Howard State Hospital in Rhode Island: 'My initial reaction was one of shock. I didn't realize and couldn't believe that these conditions would exist in our country.'"[11] According to the CPS records, Paul Goering worked at four different camps in his three years of CPS.[12] His third location was the Howard State Hospital, and his fourth was Cleveland State Hospital. Campers at other institutions described their initial reactions as depressing and shocking, and many could not believe the government treated human beings like this.[13]

CPS men at the State Hospital took it upon themselves to compile a written history of "experiences never to be forgotten," which they titled *The Seagull*. Melvin Gingerich says that "the three-year history of CPS Unit No. 85 at Howard, Rhode Island, is ably told in *The Seagull*, a 62-page mimeographed book produced by the members of the unit. The unit opened in February 1943, when twenty-five men selected by Dr. Regan, assistant superintendent of the Rhode Island State Hospital for Mental Diseases, arrived at Howard from the Sideling Hill camp."[14] Note that Gingerich considers the history of the Howard Unit to be "ably told in *The Seagull*." I found the text to be only somewhat helpful in understanding exactly what the men did there for three years, what a day was like being a ward attendant, what they ate, what they wore, what trials they faced, and so on. This sixty-two-page unpublished volume contains a variety of information, but unfortunately, only a small fraction of it pertains to the daily work done by CPSers and the realities of the mental patients housed within Howard's walls. Instead, much of the focus is on religious life, sports, the controversies caused by a "Relief Unit" and the "Girl's Unit" assigned by the Mennonite Church at different points in CPS's three years of service to the State Hospital.

Aside from five pages of description, little else is said about the daily lives of those working in the mental hospital. From this account, it almost seems as if this were a vacation or summer camp experience. The rhetorical choices of the authors of this document seem to want readers to remember only the positives of the experience, to craft a story that is considerably shinier and more pleasant than what other reports indicate. Still, some key pieces of information present in the opening pages of *The Seagull* help us understand a bit about the conditions that existed upon their arrival. The existing staff was not quite sure what to do with the new workers, so many were guarded as if they were prisoners.[15] They were originally regarded with suspicion and mistrust, since none had heard of conscientious objectors (COs) or Mennonites ever before. The original group arrived in mid-February; Ben arrived in the second group several weeks later, and presumably Miriam arrived a week or so after that.

The author of this section of *The Seagull* writes: "Most of us had probably never even seen a mental institution up to this time. We saw many buildings here, both large and small with roads and walks running octopus style. The hospital is located in the country right off the main highway. Most of the buildings are fairly new looking, and the general aspect of the place resembled a large university campus."[16] It is worth noting how my impressions in January 2017 of a college campus–like arrangement of buildings were similar to the very first of the CPS men's. This contrasts starkly to Jones's account of his arrival at the turn of the century when prison and mental hospital "inmates" were all chained together and delivered like cattle.

The newness of the buildings did provide a bit of reassurance to the men at first look. The men were to be housed in building A-3, which was on the top floor of the A building, "where the senile women patients are housed."[17] The floor was set up like a dormitory with eighteen beds in it. Though the newness of the buildings was reassuring, the odor and sounds inside the building were quite the opposite. "The odor of the building is not too pleasant and the shrieks and 'hollering' of the patients can be heard much of the time. Also, in the basement of the building are the laboratories with their peculiar medical smell. The rabbits used for experimentation were also housed in the basement which did not add any merit to the odor of the place."[18]

One of the key advantages of taking on a position at a mental hospital, and the specific one that compelled Ben and Miriam to move, was that married couples could be together. At Howard, some effort was made to accommodate these married couples, particularly since women ward attendants were in even more critically short supply. "The married couples as they came were placed in the Night Watch Cottage, an entire cottage with 18 rooms strictly reserved for married people. Each couple had only one room, which was nothing very elaborate. . . . I think the living quarters on the whole were a disappointment to all."[19]

Similarly, at first blush the food at the hospital seemed as good as that of the Sideling Hill Camp. "But much to their regret they soon found out that one easily tires of the limited variety of steam cooked food."[20] Ben later described the food at the State Hospital as "another Howard Special." On December 1, 1944, he wrote, "They'll have chowder or something fishy for Supper so I didn't go."

Upon their arrival in February, the first cohort of CPS boys were shown around the campus. The tour started off in the better wards, but "when we finally came to the Pinel Building, we were told to stick close together and keep our eyes open because the patients in this building were very dangerous."[21] Interestingly, this first group was the "only privileged to be shown through all the wards as the rest of the group . . . had to find things out pretty much for themselves."[22] Even though this introduction to the first wave of CPSers lacked much in terms of helping them acclimate, when Ben arrived two weeks later, he and all others who arrived thereafter were left to figure things out on their own.

The practice of men beginning work in mental hospitals the day they arrived with little to no training was common. "Most of these men found themselves thrust into wards occupied by active or physically-ill patients—with little or no instruction or guidance in what to do except for hurried directions or comments from supervisors sometimes less educated and less humanitarian than they," write Clark and Burgess in a *Psychiatric Quarterly Supplement* article in 1948, only a few years after the close of the CPS program.[23] Accounts confirming this common practice came from a variety of CPS men. For example, in the first camp that opened under Mennonite supervision on August 19, 1942, "nineteen men . . . arrived at the state hospital grounds. Within an hour the men were put to work. . . . No instructions were given to the men on the wards except that they were presented keys, were warned to watch out for the patients as they could not be trusted and were told to lock every door they went through."[24] *The Seagull* reports that, unsurprisingly, "when the men finally reached their respective places of work they were almost at a complete loss as to what to do. They were thrown in with a group of mental patients, and it took the very best in them to initiate themselves to this entirely new experience."[25] For those whose place of work was the Pinel Building, filled with the most violent and dangerous patients, "initiating" themselves meant always watching their keys and their person.

Toward the end of *The Seagull*, several COs wrote retrospective accounts of their time as ward attendants. These accounts add a bit of context to the opening chapter's descriptions of those first weeks. A man named Leatherman writes,

> When the opportunity came for me to transfer to Howard, I began to think quite seriously as to whether I should actually follow through with the transfer. In my mind were harbored so many confused and erroneous thoughts which everyone seems to have regarding the mental patient. Could I possibly adjust myself to working with the "insane" and, as I thought at the time, with people who were "mad", and were to be feared as wild animals. It was my misconception of mental illness, which is the popular conception, that was soon to be changed by first hand experience.
>
> As was the case with most men assigned to CPS units, my work on the ward began almost immediately without any orientation. I had to adjust myself to the work, rid myself of some preconceived notions, and grasp the one central truth that <u>patients are people</u>. Each patient and [sic] emotions and ideas, likes and dislikes, hopes and fears—just like the rest of we humans. . . . Becoming adjusted to the abnormal personality without any previous training and experience was indeed the difficulty of the assignment.
>
> To be an attendant in a mental hospital, especially in a time of acute personnel shortage, is to be many things to many men. One often had to serve as a combination nurse, housekeeper, watchman, companion, counsellor, errand boy, and general handyman. . . .

Doctors and nurses may tend to deny it, but attendants do play a very significant role in therapy. . . . The doctors and nurses would come and go, but day
after day we were in constant contact with those in our charge. The attendant
is the most tangible and continuing contact with the world of sanity and reality
that a patient can have.[26]

Interestingly, official reports from Rhode Island hospital administrators tell a
very different story of employee life at the State Hospital. For example, in a memo
to the US Public Health Services on October 29, 1943, Miss Mary E. Corcoran,
RN, states that "food is of good quality, abundant, and there is suitable variety.
Butter is served at each meal and employees may have milk as a beverage. The
dining room is neat and well cared for. . . . Rooms are comfortably furnished and
attractive. An orientation course of teaching was given to the men when they
came on February, 1943."[27] Note that this "course of teaching" was given only
one time in February to the first group of men. However, "no amount of training
could have prepared the CO's for what most would see, hear, and smell when they
first stepped onto the wards of the mental hospitals. . . . Conditions in the wards
stood in stark contrast to the stately exteriors of the buildings and manicured
grounds of the institutions."[28]

Ben, like most other COs, received no instruction when he arrived in Rhode
Island, nor was he informed of the conditions he was walking into. As previously
noted, the first camp work report from Howard, Rhode Island, shows Ben as
"AR" on March 26. Then, he is marked "D," "on duty," for the next five days
of March. This basically means that Ben had a four-day whirlwind trip home to
help Miriam get things together for the move, a final day of work at Sideling Hill,
a single day of transportation from Sideling Hill to the State Hospital in Rhode
Island, and then he was immediately on duty in a mental hospital for which he
received virtually no training.

When Ben had arrived at Sideling Hill the previous November, camp records
indicate that he was "C" or in "conditioning" for the first four days. If you recall,
he received a physical and shots for typhoid and did a lot of sitting around or
cleaning within the camp. It was a slow and inauspicious beginning. It seems
that his time at the State Hospital began in a very different fashion from his time
at Sideling Hill. In fact, there is no code for "conditioning" or training at the
hospital in the work reports. The descriptions for the codes were on duty (D), in
hands of civil authorities (CA), on leave (L), arrived (AR), in hospital (H), sick
in quarters (SQ), absent sick (AS), transferred (T), vacation (V), absent without
leave (AWOL), in travel status (TS), camp administrative duty (A), and refused
to work (RTW).[29] Already at the beginning of his time at the State Hospital, Ben
faced a much different and much more rigid set of expectations.

Conditions at the State Hospital clearly were critical when the COs arrived early in 1943. Many of the men chose to transfer to hospital work because they felt that it was a more direct service to mankind, more so than digging ditches or planting bittersweet. Some men came with aspirations of making a positive impact or change within a difficult, troubled system, but they were faced with a system much larger and more problematic than they had imagined. In an interview, former CO Paul Goering described Howard:

> They were modern buildings with modern equipment. The concept of treatment were not very modern. They certainly didn't have the staff to carry them out. So there seemed to be very little treatment. It was custodial care. This was the depressing thing. . . . We were not encouraged and in some cases not allowed to take initiatives to do things for the patients. The charge man where I worked lined the chairs up around the perimeter of the room and wanted it quiet. . . . He didn't like it when I brought a radio in and got patients to sing. He said, "You're stirring them up. Don't do that." Of course, I'd do it when he was off, when he was away and he didn't like it that I'd do those things.[30]

COs were appalled at the conditions upon their arrival at the State Hospital, but they were discouraged from making positive changes at every turn because of the short staffing and because of outdated treatment models. Jones's memoir that contrasts the dark days at the turn of the century with the modernity of the 1940s system reflects a moment in time of changing viewpoints about the care of the mentally ill (though there have been many such moments over time). In an unpublished 1941 master's of social work thesis at Brown University titled "A Study of Mentally Ill Criminals at the State Hospital for Mental Diseases, Howard, Rhode Island, October 1941," Phyllis Brown offers a glimpse into a duality of perspectives. Her thesis compares "matched pairs" of patients; for every criminally insane person in the disturbed ward (presumably the Pinel Building), she found another patient in the mental hospital with a similar background, nationality, age, education, and so on, in order to determine any causative reasons for criminality. She notes that while there were more than 2,700 patients in the State Hospital toward the end of October 1941, there were only 27 in the Criminally Insane Building.[31] Alcohol and drug addiction were mainstays of the criminally insane, and the most common diagnosis was schizophrenia. "A certain, rather small, percent of those who are feebleminded (idiots, imbeciles, or morons) may become psychotic."[32] Of those 27 men, "10 were diagnosed schizophrenic and 7 as psychosis with psychopathic personality," which was a distribution not usual in the general hospital population.[33]

What is noteworthy in her thesis is that we can see both "sides" of the mental healthcare situation at that time. On the one hand, she defines those with mental illness, the "idiots, imbeciles, or morons," in ways that seem limiting and prejudiced: "All civilization may be divided, hypothetically, into two groups: normal and abnormal. Normal individuals, in general, are those we accept as being like us. . . . If the abnormal should become normal according to our present classification, we should reclassify, raising our standards so that we might keep with us always the normal and the abnormal."[34]

On the other hand, she points out that those who are "abnormal" by this classification system might become that way because of any chronic condition, even a toothache, that changes a person's behavior to be outside the norm. "Therefore, illness of any kind, physical or mental, may be included as a factor in maladjustment. . . . Although much has been accomplished since 1900 in educating the public to accept mental illness as they would any physical illness, the general population is still reluctant to accept former mental patients into the community."[35] Similarly, Brown seems perfectly tolerant of treatments and practices in use at the time, which have since been greatly debated, while at the same time she expresses progressive ideals about the overall care of the mentally ill in the United States. For example, she discusses one man who "has been violent, frequently needing restraint. After he chewed off a portion of his finger two years ago, he was given electro-shock therapy in an attempt to make him less of a behavior problem."[36] At that time, electroshock therapy was given to patients without anesthesia or muscle relaxants, leading to full convulsive seizures, dislocation of bones, and retrograde amnesia. Because these early treatment methods produced such serious side effects, the treatment was eventually criticized as a form of abuse (though, with informed consent, the treatment exists today and proves helpful to some patients).

Even as Brown writes plainly and uncritically about the procedure, she questions the social and legal situations that enable the criminally insane and mentally ill to be mistreated in general. Brown makes note of the fact that "the American people sincerely believe that their laws have been made for the benefit of all American citizens, for the offenders as well as the communities. Yet, much time and money is spent on proving a person guilty and practically none is spent on his treatment."[37] She completes her thesis by advocating for change: "The public has to be made to realize what could be accomplished with more appropriations for the care of prisoners and patients in mental hospitals. The public has to be shown what an increase in the number of individuals with better or specialized training could do for these maladjusted individuals. It is a hard-hearted public which has to be convinced, people who stalled at being influenced by Pearl Harbor and necessary, well-planned propaganda."[38] Given that the "hard-hearted public" was wholly focused on the war effort, making significant changes to the existing system was almost impossible without financial and staffing support. According to *The Seagull*, over time, the practices of how to treat patients improved, and as patients' trust of the attendants increased, patient behavior improved. These facts seemed to anger the state employees. Some of those employees were ashamed and changed their ways, but most of them quit or were fired for drunkenness.[39] Yet the turnover of staff was not entirely positive. The fact remained that the State Hospital was severely, critically understaffed.

Still, efforts were made to improve conditions and treatment options. The superintendent, Dr. Ross, made many positive changes during 1943. Selig Greenberg interviewed Dr. Ross and wrote a favorable article about the CPS men in the *Providence Evening Bulletin*. This article educated the local public a bit about the Mennonites and the CPS program, the issues faced by the State Hospital during the war era, and the benefit CPS men and their wives were to the hospital. "With the coming of Dr. Ross as superintendent, conditions in the hospital improved rapidly. He was impressed with the work of the CPS unit and did much to help them. Other men were added to the unit."[40] Unfortunately, the fact that Dr. Ross made many positive changes meant he did not last long as superintendent because city and state lawmakers did not appreciate his candor and ambition to make changes that might cost more money (recall that keeping costs as low as possible was the main goal throughout the history of the hospital).

The article states that as of November 1943, there were fifty CPS men and eleven wives working at the State Hospital, and another twenty-five were due to arrive soon. "'I don't know,' Dr. Ross said, 'what we would have done without them. I only wish we could get a lot more of them.'" In spite of the seemingly large numbers of CPS men, Dr. Ross noted that the hospital was still critically understaffed and to bring the personnel requirements up to anywhere near normal, "about 100 more attendants would be needed."[41] But funding to make improvements in the care and to increase the pay in order to attract more workers did not exist because of the war. While the eleven CO wives were paid at the regular, albeit poor, wages, CPS men received "an allowance of $15 a month out of which they have to buy their own work clothes."[42] I actually question Greenberg's report that the men earned $15 a month because Ben told Miriam he would earn only $2.50 per month when they were making the decision to move to Rhode Island.

Thus, because of severely limited staff and lawmakers unwilling to funnel more financial support into the State Hospital, the vast majority of the work COs did in mental hospitals was custodial and keeping patients as content as they could. "The large majority of the conscientious objectors in the mental hospital units worked as Ward attendants, caring directly for the needs of the patients. . . . The working day was generally quite long especially for the attendants, many of whom worked shifts of 60 or more hours per week. Coupled with the long days on the wards where the trying conditions of handling patients unable to care for themselves in any way and the seeming lack of hope for their restoration to full health."[43]

CPS official work reports indicated that a work week consisted of seventy and a half hours of work. Shifts seem to be eleven hours and forty-five minutes, if the calculation of seventy and a half hours is precise. So, basically, Ben and other CPS men worked twelve-hour shifts six days a week. Looking at a randomly selected work reports from December 1943, Ben worked six days, off for one, seven days, then off for one, five days then off for two, six days on then off again.[44]

A Maryland hospital report to the Brethren Service Committee describes the duties of an attendant. "'The work of award attendant varies[;] generally speaking his job involves: complete Ward housekeeping—sweeping, mopping, waxing and polishing floors, bed making and taking care of patients' clothes. He supervises and assists the patients in eating, bathing, dressing, and undressing. He might be an aid in giving various treatments such as dressings, injections, electric shock and hydrotherapy. He may accompany patients on walks outdoors, to the weekly movie, or monthly patients' dance. Attendants work with patients of the same sex.'"[45] Ben's letters are filled with brief descriptions of exactly this kind of work.

[December 2, 1944]
We kept busy all Morning in the ward. We washed the Day Room and Waxed the floor. Gunden went on an errand for Mr. Shaw then went for Pine-oil & wax. This after-noon I made a trip to the Making Room for a Package for a Patient also took up the census Report.

[December 3, 1944]
It's 5 after 6:00 (our time) so I'll go to work. . . . We dressed some of the Patients a little extra and waxed the corridor.

[December 9, 1944]
This Morning I waxed our Corridor That's about all we did except regular routine work. ^and shaving our Patients" This afternoon I took charge of the front door letting in Visitors There weren't so many but one come in for our Ward after 4:00 We fed our Patients early and were undressing them for bed when the Visitor come in of course It was a woman Visitor she stayed till after 4:30 P.M.

[December 29, 1944]
This Morn. We bathed our Patients then trimmed their finger & toe nails I'm always glad when that job is finished.

[January 2, 1945]
I got up in Plenty of time this morn. was the first one on duty.
We sure Put in a good mornings work This Morn. I went to first meal and while the Boys (Bill & Ralph) were at breakfast I started taking all the beds out of the Dormitories then got ready and scrubbed them. The three of us worked all Morn. We scrubbed the 3 dorms. and the long Corridor. We got the Dorms waxed and Polished but didn't get the Hall way done.
This afternoon we were supposed to have Movies on our ward. They're

starting having them twice a week here now. on Tues. & Fridays. We Put blankets on the windows to shut out the light and I had them all up when we got a call that the machine was broke, so we took Patients up to the Harrington Hall. Bosler, Martin, Mr Shaw & Myself took them—the Pictures was a Pretty new Picture with an old setting "Johney Come Lately."

[January 10, 1945]
Hello Sweetheart;

I'm checking this eve. This is one extra day I'll have toward my vacation as I'm working on my day off.

we really worked too what I mean. This Morn. we (Jim Bosler, Ralph Gunder, & I) mopped and waxed and Polished the 3 dormitories then sprayed all our Pillows and Mattresses and then Mopped & waxed & Polished the Hallway. It was Just 11:00 when we finished time for me to go to dinner.

This afternoon I got things ready for visitors we had only 2 so I sat in the office and dosed for nearly an hour this P.M. Mr. Shaw is off Wed afternoons and Thurs. you know.

[January 23, 1945]
we had Movies on our ward. "Jungle Siren" was the name a (Lovey Dovey) Picture. we had the mess all cleaned up tho now and the Patients are getting their beds made. . . . This Morning we waxed the corridor and washed our light fixtures. Mr Shaw called and said our wards were to be inspected. wanted all the doors open so we had everything in good shape Dr. Brehrendt & Dr. Patterson tripped and Just walked in and out. Dr. Brehrendt did say tho' our day room looked clean and Sunny.

Ben's descriptions of his day are routine, somewhat limited explanations of work he and Miriam know well. He did not spend a lot of time describing the drudgery of washing and waxing corridors because there was no need for Miriam to know exactly what he was talking about. A more candid and thorough explanation of custodial work exists in a newsletter called *Viewpoint* from CPS Unit #51 at Western State Hospital in Fort Steilacoom, Washington.

Custodial care is the main job of the average attendant in a mental hospital. With the exception of those persons who administer medications or who do work of a specialized nature, the principal requirement for a good attendant is one that includes a genuine underlying concern for the people with whom he will spend the day. Some patients can, within the routine of the hospital, pretty well take care of themselves. A few are able to give excellent assistance in taking care of the more helpless. But it is the attendant's responsibility to see that things run smoothly. The "up-patients" must be gotten out of bed and dressed.

All must be washed and combed, and fed. They must be kept warm and have exercise. They should be kept from feeling locked up. They must feel that there are friendly people around them. They should be kept happy, but they must not be pampered.

One of the major and most distasteful parts of custodial care comes under the heading of bed-changing. Bed-patients abound in hospitals for mental care. Many of them are incontinent and must be changed often. The proverbial "patience of Job" and a firm determination are valuable assets to the attendant assigned to the sickening odor and picturesque unpleasantries of an incontinent ward. . . .

Custodial care includes everything. It is not the glamorous or exciting part of an attendant's job. Events do occur, however, to lend interest to the regular routine. Sometimes the patient must be prompted and urged eat in spite of the fact that he is firmly convinced that he has no stomach. The job is a little more difficult if he thinks you are trying to poison him. He must be bathed even during the times when he is sure that the attendant is set on drowning him, or that the tub is full of crocodiles. When he is in the most disturbed condition the patient will continue to grow whiskers and when he eyes you from the bathroom wielding a gleaming straight-edge razor it may be fairly difficult to convince him that the razor is to cut the beard and not his throat. But even more trying on the nerves of the average attendant than the patients with delusions and hallucinations which are fairly pronounced, is the one with whom and about whom you seem to be able to do nothing.[46]

A common practice to provide some semblance of being able to assist all patients was to employ more able patients "to fill the void for attendant personnel. In most instances, these were individuals whose mental illness was in a state of remission and for whom discharge was not a viable option as they had no families to accept responsibility for them."[47] Ben mentioned one such situation:

[December 19, 1945]
We got another one in this afternoon from the M Building. He is a good worker and seems to be O.K. He is feeble minded, went only to the 4th grade in school, can just write his name that's all. Mr. Shaw said he wrecked a train when he was 21 and was to Exeter school, from there he was sent to the M. Building. He is now 33 and says he was in that Building 11 years. He talks very good sense, and isn't too bad looking a guy he weighs about 140 or 145 I'd say. He'll make an excellent worker. Dr. Patterson is trying him out to see how he'll get along.

But even employing some patients as workers simply was not enough to make up for the overall lack of staff.

Miriam's work history at the State Hospital is less complete than Ben's. For Ben I have his letters, references to him in work reports to CPS and the government, and details in his conscription records. But for Miriam, there is precious little to show what job or jobs she performed, how much she was paid, or any other details of her employment. Alex Sareyan writes that wives of COs (or "COWs" as they were jokingly called) were fully invested in the workings of CPS mental hospital units. They joined in all the same activities, events, and experiences as the men. They also

had to put up with the same "slings and arrows" that their husbands initially faced from coworkers or persons in the community who are hostile to their pacifist positions. In time, most of these ill feelings became muted or disappeared entirely. For some, it was a truly difficult experience. But the wives had one thing going for them. They were not subject to the whims and regulations of Selective Service. They were free agents and could come and go as they pleased. They were entitled to the same employment conditions as regular employees of the hospital. And they often brought with them an array of special skills, ranging from medicine, the behavioral sciences, and nursing to teaching and secretarial services. However, because the most serious staff shortages were on the wards, they were usually assigned to attendant duty.[48]

We have no way of knowing for sure what work Miriam did, but it was likely either working as an attendant or in the kitchens.

But one notable piece of information exists. Early in my research for this book, I found the most complete and maintained CPS website (http://civilianpublicservice .org), which was an invaluable resource. It set me on a path toward the most respected histories of CPS, the locations of various units, and the archives that would prove most useful in reconstructing Ben and Miriam's story. Imagine my surprise to find on their page of Camp #85 at Howard, Rhode Island, *an image of my grandmother* serving food (fig. 14).

I called my mom right away to have her show my dad. Dad's immediate response was "Why, that's Mom!" The caption to the image online simply says: "On the back is written 'Jacobs, female Ward service, one of the wives.'" I contacted the curators of the website, excited to help them put a piece of a puzzle together. I thought that this would enable them to honor a specific woman who served, instead of naming her merely "one of the wives." Instead, I was met with resistance to updating their information. The woman in the picture was referred to as "Mrs. Jacobs" because the name Jacobs was noted on the back. Instead of seeing "Jacobs" as the photographer, they assumed he was her husband. I sent them a copy of Ben and Miriam's wedding photograph, and images of her employment records there. They agreed that there was certainly a likeness in the images, but they were not convinced enough to update the information.

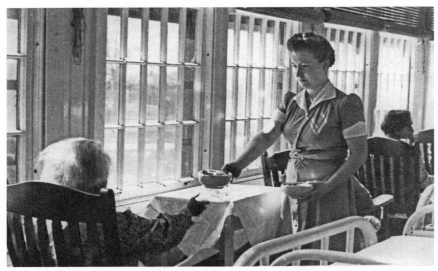

FIGURE 14. Miriam serving food at CPS Camp #85 in Rhode Island. Photograph from civilianpublicservice.org. Courtesy of Mennonite Church Archives, Bethel College, North Newton, Kansas.

I, however, remain certain that the image above is a captured moment of my grandmother working at the State Hospital. Merle Jacobs was the photographer, and he was known in CPS Camp #85 as such. *The Seagull* actually documents Merle's adventures in photography:

> Speaking of photography, it is not uncommon to see fellows in rather unusual positions trying to get a candid shot. One day a call came into the main office that a patient had crawled down into a manhole between two of the buildings. The chauffeur rushed the chief supervisor to the scene followed by a doctor. All were much excited as they all suspected that it was a suicide case. Much to their surprise when they reached the manhole who should crawl out of it but Merle Jacobs, a unit member, with his camera. In rather excited voice he told the supervisor and the doctor that he was only hiding in there to get a closeup picture of some seagulls. This incident proved amusing to everyone. Merle was a very good photographer, and he was always on the go, as all who knew him well will remember.[49]

Clearly, Merle Jacobs's photography was a well-known aspect of life at the State Hospital. The inscription on the back of the photograph lists him as the photographer, and if it was his wife pictured, why would it say "one of the wives" instead of her actual name? I may not be able to convince the curators of the website, but I can at least honor my grandmother and her work here.

One of the most challenging parts of being a ward attendant for nonresistant COs was remaining consistent, kind, and nonviolent in their care of patients, even when patients were at their worst. Al Benglan's article in *Viewpoint* again gives us a sense of what this was like: "The constant small irritation of never know-ing what your patients will do manages to set many an attendant on edge to the extent that civil response to the patient becomes very difficult. Routine becomes set and patterns to keep patients in order rather than keep them happy become the line of least resistance and the accepted custom. To the pacifists the situation offers a challenge."[50] Violence from patients was a reality of day-to-day work. For hired attendants (those not COs), returned violence to patients was a common, accepted, even expected practice. The huge number of patients, the limited number of attendants, and the limited resources available meant that for most attendants, keeping patients quiet and in order were their main goals. To do this, beatings, locking patients up, restraints with wristers and even chains were employed. While violent practices were common, the COs were given a set of rules when they first arrived and asked to sign it. The rules included an agreement "never to strike, injure, tease, or swear at patients" (fig. 15).[51]

Signing the document and making such a promise was done easily for men whose foundational beliefs were in opposition to all forms of violence, but main-taining that promise and that commitment to nonviolence was not so easily done, particularly when faced with violence directed at them on a daily basis. For exam-ple, on January 21, 1945, a Quaker CO named Sawyer who worked at Byberry, wrote, "'In the last two weeks, one of my coworkers has had his jaw splintered when a newly admitted patient attacked him. The teeth on one side of his jaw may have to be pulled. . . . I, too, was another victim of violence when a patient hit me in the mouth. There was some bleeding, but fortunately, it was only a minor injury. One of the serious disadvantages under which we work is that if we are seriously injured or incapacitated, none of us in the CPS unit is covered by insurance or Workmen's Compensation.'"[52] Ben wrote of several instances of violence in the ward.

[December 7, 1945]
I was on Pinel 3 this Morn. and as is always the case was on 5 this after-noon^(Thurs). I had to break up a fight first since I've been over there in the P. M.'s.

[December 28, 1945]
This Noon while Bill was gone to dinner I got a call from the Dx Building. The lady talking . . . said well we need some help over here some of the Patients were fighting I told her There was only one ~~Patie~~ attendant on each ward. But

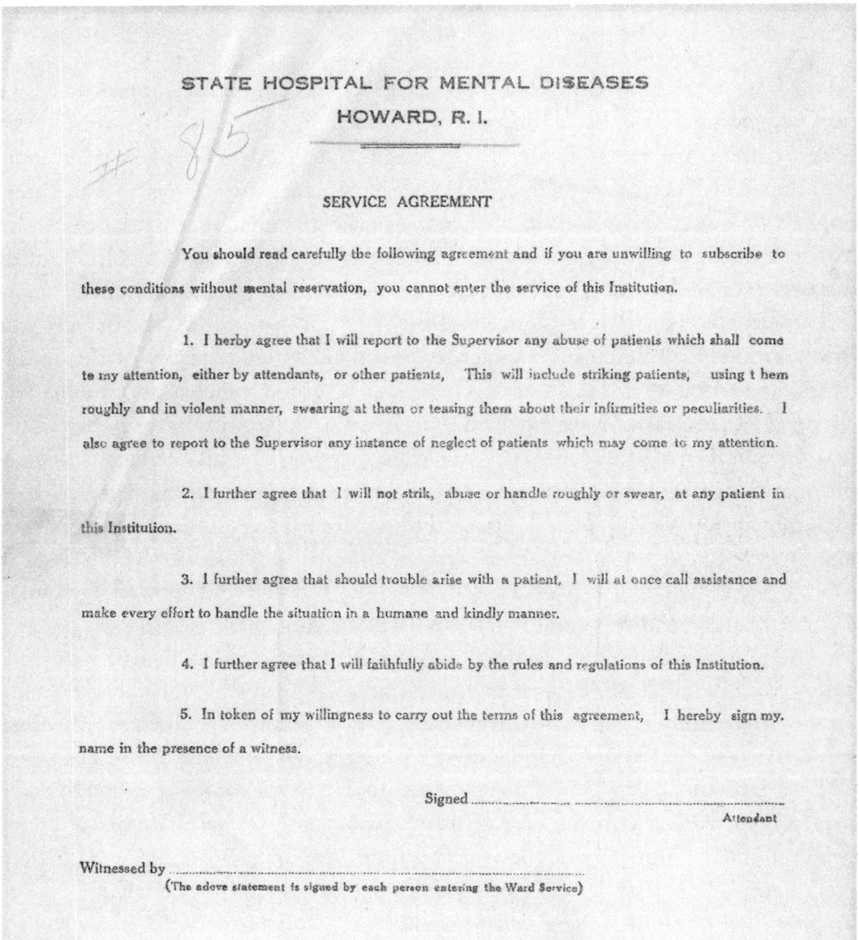

STATE HOSPITAL FOR MENTAL DISEASES

HOWARD, R. I.

SERVICE AGREEMENT

You should read carefully the following agreement and if you are unwilling to subscribe to these conditions without mental reservation, you cannot enter the service of this Institution.

1. I herby agree that I will report to the Supervisor any abuse of patients which shall come to my attention, either by attendants, or other patients. This will include striking patients, using t hem roughly and in violent manner, swearing at them or teasing them about their infirmities or peculiarities. I also agree to report to the Supervisor any instance of neglect of patients which may come to my attention.

2. I further agree that I will not strik, abuse or handle roughly or swear, at any patient in this Institution.

3. I further agree that should trouble arise with a patient, I will at once call assistance and make every effort to handle the situation in a humane and kindly manner.

4. I further agree that I will faithfully abide by the rules and regulations of this Institution.

5. In token of my willingness to carry out the terms of this agreement, I hereby sign my. name in the presence of a witness.

Signed...
Attendant

Witnessed by..
(The above statement is signed by each person entering the Ward Service)

Date................................

500-12-11-41

FIGURE 15. Medical treatment agreement signed by COs working at the Rhode Island State Hospital for Mental Diseases. Courtesy of Mennonite Central Committee Collection, Akron, Pennsylvania.

would try to get over. I called John Hoffman and told him to have Kistle watch his ward also Pinel 2.—Georing was on 5 so I had him keep and eye on 3 and John and I went over. We went up stairs and asked what was the matter The attendant a large heavy set woman said everything was O.K. now. She had the Patient in the room that was causing all the trouble she was disgusted at the operator Calling us. She said she called downstairs for one of the girls to come up and help her but the operator instead rang the G Build. and we went over. So it was a false alarm.

CO ward attendants were faced with a difficult problem. "The difficulty centered around the extent to which nonviolent techniques could be used in handling mentally unbalanced patients, and as to how far the use of physical force could be reconciled with a thoroughgoing pacifist philosophy."[53] Some COs felt that force was unnecessary and would cause psychological harm to a patient. Others argued that in some instances, force was the only option available when restraining patients. Generally, there was a distinction made between the use of force in restraint rather than as a measure of punishment; basically, some felt that there was a difference between force and violence.[54]

But the problem was that they entered a system in which the regular employees used physical punishment often and freely, often going beyond keeping order. *The Seagull* recalls how the employees described daily ward work to them when they first arrived:

> The state employees who already work on the wards told the C.P.S. fellows all kinds of horrible stories of what these patients would do to you. They said you should never let a patient get behind you, and that the only way to get along with the patients was to make them fear you. You must prove to them that you are not afraid of them, and that you can whip them, or they will whip you. There were all sorts of cautions and warnings. I think that perhaps these state employees saw how they were scaring the boys, and it was a source of delight to them. But I also believe that the state employees believed in what they told us because that is the way they dealt with the patients. They beat and knocked the patients around for no reason at all, and it was their definite policy to make the patients fear them. Many of the terrible examples of mistreatments of patients I saw I would hesitate to write here. They are not fit to be told.[55]

At that time there were no other models for how to care for mentally ill patients, and there were very few workers to keep order over sometimes hundreds of patients. So some simply mirrored what they saw regular employees doing. But others stuck closely to their nonviolent beliefs and over time changes came from those beliefs. For one thing, violence was no longer seen as acceptable. Ben writes of an example in January:

[January 29, 1945]
Shaw saw Hamilton beating up a Patient this afternoon so told him to leave, later Shaw told me "I Just did something I hated to do." I said, "what's that," I

asked—"Fired Hamilton" he told me. Then explained how the Patient looked. That Patient was John Gleavey Do you remember about the Gleaveys. Margaret the sister? John is a Catatonic case and won't do anything don't even move unless someone moves him. Jack told Shaw tho' Johnnie struck at him.

Further, CPS workers across the country who worked in mental hospitals began a series of publications and collective efforts to instruct on nonviolent patient care, and those publications and efforts had lasting impact. First was the Mental Hygiene Program. Leslie Eisan quotes from one of their many publications to show how the men had three interrelated goals:

> We seek to improve the quality of our own work.
> We seek to help public institutions. . . .
> We seek to promote a deeper public understanding of institutional needs and problems.
> In an attempt to make a contribution . . . we have united our efforts in the Mental Hygiene Program of Civilian Public Service.[56]

The Mental Hygiene Program begun by CPS workers eventually became the National Mental Health Foundation. In 1950 it merged with the National Committee for Mental Hygiene and the American Psychiatric Foundation to become the National Association for Mental Health. Second was the *Attendant*, "a monthly publication with ideas, attitudes and methods which are directly related to work in mental hospitals and training schools."[57] The Quaker CO Sawyer wrote on August 29, 1944: "'One of the significant developments that has emerged from the presence of our unit here at Byberry is the publication of a periodical called *The Attendant*. It's a modest publication which features constructive suggestions for handling mental patients. The articles for it are being provided by men in various CPS units throughout the country.'"[58] Eventually the *Attendant* became the *Psychiatric Aide*, but in spite of its good quality and the sincerity of those who launched it, the publication ended before 1950.

And third, CPSers across the country worked to create a series of orientation handbooks including "*Handbook for Psychiatric Aides*, a *Handbook of Restraint*, a *Handbook of Activity Therapy*, a *Handbook for Training School Attendants*, and a *Recreation Handbook for Training Schools*."[59] The Mennonite Central Committee Archives had copies of a few of these publications. In particular, the *Handbook of Restraint* offers a perspective on the sincerity of the COs and their commitment to nonviolence:

> There is only a very small percentage of patients who are ever violent and dangerous, and . . . most of these are only disturbed on rather rare occasions. . . . The

problem of handling disturbed patients arises because certain types of mental illness leads inevitably to violent and continual action. Patients who are overactive, who want to kill themselves, who want to harm others, who want to break things up can not help themselves. These reactions are as much a part of their mental illness as sniffling is a part of a cold in the nose. . . .

Faced with patients who are this way, not through any fault of their own but simply because they are sick, you, as a psychiatric aide, can do three things for them: 1) you can try to remove the incentives which force the patients to react in these unhealthful ways; 2) you can offer constructive ways in which they can expend their energies instead of destructive ways; and 3) you can restrain them physically so that they are unable to do the things which they ought not to do.

Obviously, it is best to do the first thing. . . . But sometimes, when the aide fails in his job, or the hospital facilities are inadequate, or it is just too late to use any other method, the third way of treatment has to be used.[60]

Finally, we can get a sense of the work Ben and Miriam did as ward attendants in the letters they received from friends. The earliest dated letters of their time in Rhode Island are actually to Miriam from two of her friends, Maxine and Dorothy. Maxine wrote to Miriam on September 29, 1944, at Howard. Maxine clearly knew where Miriam worked and what kind of work that involved. She wrote,

Miriam, how are you making it with your patients? I just about know what you are going through because we are having the same thing here at our house. Grandma Jarbae (Mamas mother) is staying with us now. She has lost her mind. And oh goodness!!! Sometime, she has mama up a <u>dozen</u> and <u>more</u> times ^at night. She won't sleep at night. She does her sleeping in the day time. Sleeping pills don't have now more effect on her than a moon does good in sunshine. She is always thinking that some body is sick or dead. Then she thinks she sees her brother go by. And he has been dead for years. She gets mad spells and slams dishes around, talks ugly and makes ugly faces and just carries on. Sometimes when she gets mad she gets her cane and tries to <u>bean</u> some of us. Ha. When she gets mad she gets strong. And it is just about more than Mama can do to handle her. None of our relatives will have her so we keep her. I sure wish lots of times that she was in a place like were where you work. If she was she would probably drive the nurses crazy.

Maxine's comments about her grandmother, and her wish that her grandmother could be committed somewhere, were a common sentiment. None of Maxine's other relatives were willing to take care of the woman. In the early years of the twentieth century, "mental institutions housed growing numbers of elderly whose own children were unable or unwilling to care for them."[61] In many families, everyone capable of caring for an aging parent or grandparent was employed, and therefore, no one was at home to provide care.[62] The number of elderly people in mental institutions continued to grow. In the Department of Social Welfare's *Annual Report* in 1949, for example, 33 percent of the patients admitted were over sixty-five, whereas only 12 percent of the state's total population was in that age group.[63]

The second letter to Miriam, dated November 5, 1944, was from a woman named Dorothy. It was only a few weeks before Miriam would head home to Indiana. Based on the contents of the letter and a bit of investigation, it seems that Dorothy was the wife of another CPS man named Leonard E. Gerber.[64] Leonard also served at Sideling Hill with Ben, so at this point in 1944, they would have worked together for two years. Dorothy, then, was also one of the "CPS wives" who worked in the hospital, so her letter gives some insights, and perhaps some gossip, on the work she and Miriam did. She begins with "it's a month now that I came home. Feel just fine. Wonder sometimes why I have to be home. But a kick in the tummy reminds me." Apparently, Dorothy was pregnant, and, like the decision Miriam and Ben would make later that month, had opted to have her baby at home.

Dorothy then wrote as if responding to Miriam's previous letter. "So Susan helps on bath day. Can imagine the relief that Florence is gone, is to you. Does Rebecca help as she always did? At least Hilma will leave you alone so long as she 'snooz' Doesn't Solimanda have ^any thing to say about you and the coming baby?" We can surmise that Florence was another ward attendant who gave Miriam some trouble and had now left; hopefully, Hilma, another trouble-maker perhaps, would leave her alone too. Someone named Susan helped out and perhaps Rebecca. Solimanda, possibly another attendant, apparently had not wished Miriam well regarding the baby. I suspect that this is just typical gossip between friends about coworkers, but it does give a tiny glimpse into the workings of the hospital. Clearly, bath day required a great deal of effort and multiple hands.

Another letter in the archive, dated November 21, was from Stan and Mary Ann Martin. They wrote from Springfield State Hospital, in Sykesville, Maryland. There was a mental hospital CPS camp there that the Brethren Service Committee ran (whereas the camp at Howard was run by the Mennonites).[65] Stan and Mary Ann both worked at the hospital in a situation similar to Ben and Miriam's. It seems that their connection was based on their similar Christian denomination and not on having met while in service. They wrote, "We're getting along fine or at least as well as we could ever expect too until we get home again. We're at least together which means an awfully lot." Stan noted that he would never want to "go back to camp again," so it seems that he also worked in soil conservation prior to moving to the hospital unit.

Stan wrote quite a bit about their day-to-day lives, and his discussion is likely similar to the duties that Ben and Miriam had at the State Hospital in Rhode Island.

> Mary Ann is still on the ward hoping for an office job. She put in her application when we first came here and took her state Civil Service examination about two months ago. She received a very high score—first in this county, so she should get a chance when there is an opening. As for me, I left the ward about a month ago and am in the kitchen now. I certainly like it fine too—much better than ward work. Especially since I have much shorter hours. I go in at 6:00 A.M. the same as usual and usually am off from 1:00 to 4:00 and then off again ^at 6:00 or when I get last hours, I get off at 3:00 which is surely fine. Was off about 2:45 to-day. I took a bunch of patients down to the slaughter house to pick turkeys today—149 of them. Patients and attendants both have turkey on Thanksgiving day. I helped the butchers clean out the insides. Took us all forenoon and until about 2:30 this afternoon. It wasn't a hard job at all but the hardest days work I've had since being in the kitchen. I have a bunch of patients who I look after, that do all the work. My main job is ^in the prepara-tion room down stairs where we prepare all the vegetables for the cooks. It is my responsibility to see that they are there on time and in the right amounts. The patients get along fine without me though as they have been doing it for so long. I just told them this morning before I left what we were to have and that's all I saw of them. Then too, I have to relieve in the cafeteria (I'll be there tomorrow), patients dining room and kitchen. I sure like it better than the ward as there isn't the commotion and fights and what I like best is that I'm not around sick patients. We are living here at the Epileptic Colony Service Building now and Mary Ann works here. The Building she works in is just across the driveway and she eats here in this building so usually comes up to our room at mealtime. I guess we have it about as well here as we could ever expect to get it being drafted C.O.'s.

Note that part of Stan's work in the kitchen was to monitor patients who worked. It is interesting to hear why Stan was so thankful to be away from in the wards. For ward attendants, the hours were worse, the work was harder, there were fights and commotion, and there were sick patients. These were the realities of the job that Ben did. In fact, given that he was in the Pinel Building, which housed the violent and deranged patients, his job was that much more difficult.

One last aspect of ward work was going after patients who ran away. Ben described one incident in great detail, and I have added a few paragraph breaks to make this description of another "perfect day" at Howard easier to read. Here "Moron" refers to Ben's supervisor who apparently was not always on top of things:

[December 13, 1945]

Well, well, it's now 9:15 and I just returned from going after a Patient. (The end of a Perfect Day) . . . I hurried to the Nite Watch and Just got changed into one of my Uniforms when Moron Blew his Horn. I wanted to change my shoes But didn't have time. so we went after the guy. We went to the E. Greenwhich Jail, they told us the Patient had eloped from the Hospital and went home last nite. The Pats [patient's] Mother told the Police, but before they could get a cop over there he had left. So this eve. he came home for supper and she called again so the police notified the Hospital and we went down.

When we got there the Patients had left the house and was roaming the streets the Police were looking for him but couldn't locate him. John called the Hospital and Moses told him, we should come on back. Just as we left the Police told us that last nite someone saw him in apenoog. So we drove slow—by home, and sure enough in apenoog we saw him on the street. We called him over to the car and asked him his name and where his home—etc. But he wouldn't answer any questions, But asked us who we were.

So when we started to get him he ran, said he was going to the Police. Gross or I didn't know the Patient but John tho't he recognized him. We were worried tho' for a little for fear we might not have the right guy. But we did The cops there questioned him and he had some paper with his name on them. The Police questioned us too, so we had them call the Hospital, so when we finally got things straight the Police told the Patient to come along back. He didn't want to of course but didn't cause any trouble. John and I each took his arms and led him.

When we got back Moses said take him to Pinel-2 so we went down. Gross hadn't been in the G-Bldg. So we showed him around. Old Tom Dimuccio had the entire lower floor. Young and Richards were upstairs. Whee! Such excitement I fear It's too hard on my High Blood Pressure. Anyhow it breaks the Monotony. John Put the car in the Garage then said let's go to the Medical Kitchen and get something to eat But it was too far for me to go up and back in the cold, so I come on down to the room.

Thus, we can see the challenges faced by COs who worked in mental hospitals across the nation. Some histories, particularly from those with firsthand experience of the CPS program such as Alex Sareyan in *Turning Point*, applaud the efforts of COs and point to the successes they had while working within the hospitals. Others offer a more objective perspective, such as Steven Taylor's *Acts of Conscience*. From both firsthand experiences and more objective outsider perspectives, what is evident is the sincerity of the majority of COs who worked in mental hospitals. They did their best to make changes while they were there, and many made efforts to effect long-term changes.

What we also see in this chapter is that when doing family history research, the quantity and quality of sources is a significant issue. This is not to suggest that personal accounts of life at the State Hospital are somehow suspect as "valid" the way that large-H histories might question them. Instead what I want to point out is that when broadly accepting sources that are not as "mainstream" as academic historians, the family history researcher still must pay attention to the source, the verifiability, and the positionality of the writer. We still include threads that are less verifiable, but we acknowledge that the source is family lore, for example. Here we see the written history of the State Hospital, as told by the COs who authored *The Seagull*, as perhaps shinier than the reality of the situation. It reads as if they wanted their readers to see their experiences in the best light possible, fearing that to write more frankly of their time there would be seen as complaining or ungrateful for the opportunity to be working in CPS and not going to war. But their caution means that seventy-five years later, when compiling Ben and Miriam's story, the account conflicts somewhat with what Ben wrote in his letters. Making sense of disparate threads is an aspect of FHW that is more pronounced than in other forms of historical writing. FHW methodology brings the tension between "fact" and "memory" to the foreground.

CHAPTER 12

Daily Life at the State Hospital

MRS. BEN KESLER left us this past Wednesday. Ben accompanied her to New York and then came sadly back to spend the winter in bachelorhood. Mrs. Kesler expects to be back in the spring.

NEWSETTE, DECEMBER 1, 1944

As indicated in the previous chapters, only one collection of letters exists during Ben and Miriam's time at the State Hospital in Rhode Island, letters from Ben to Miriam from November 30, 1944, through January 30, 1945. There are also a few letters from friends that offer more context for what their daily lives were like living and working at a mental hospital. Whereas the previous chapters about their time at the State Hospital focused on their work as ward attendants and the hospital itself, this chapter explores the daily life aspects of their time by focusing on the married couple's cottage, the food they ate, what they did when they were not working, and amusing or dramatic moments they captured in their letters. To supplement the contents of their letters, the unit newsletter provides additional context, such as the quote opening this chapter. Like many CPS units, the State Hospital CPS unit developed its own newsletter publication, this one printed every week (the Sideling Hill *Turnpike Echo* was printed every two weeks). The *Newsette*, similar to most newsletter publications in CPS, offered bits of the goings-on throughout the unit, details about sporting events or upcoming speakers, and often a short essay written by the director or another CO.

With family history writing methodology, the weaving of data strands is again apparent in this chapter. Together, the letters from Ben to Miriam, as well as the letters from friends and the *Newsette* provide enough information to understand some of what their lives were like. What is noteworthy here is the smallness, the inconsequential details of their lives, preserved in their letters. In large-H histories, less attention is paid to such small details. I think we miss a lot of what our predecessors have to teach us by focusing only on their public lives. Much of this book is about their private lives, certainly, but this chapter offers a counterpoint to the two preceding chapters, which focus more on their "public" ward attendant selves.

As was their custom, Ben's letters typically included a description of what he ate. As discussed in chapters 1 and 4, food was an aspect of platform in that it was a physical representation of their love and devotion. Sometimes, this manifested in sending literal material artifacts in letters. Other times, this manifested in elaborate discussions of what they ate each day. Food was comfortable, easy. It enabled them to feel as if they were closer, and it provided comfort that their bodies were well enough—even if the distance taxed their emotional and mental well-being. Apparently, the cafeteria food was not always what Ben would have wished.

[December 4, 1944]
We [had] another round of those good old Howard Meal specials today.
   Griddle Cakes with some of that "reclaimed Motor oil for syrup" as Joe Hog. Calls it
   For Breakfast.
   Those little . . . sausages, tomatoes and onion soup for dinner. I had my share of tomatoes tho'.
   And for supper we had our Dinner all combined into one dish. Ground sausages, Tomatoes and onion flavor with Macaroni. I got around mine O. K. but you should have heard Joe Hog gripe. He said they threw what was left of the dinner to the Pigs at the Piggery and they turned their noses up at it so had to bring it back for us. It sure takes a lot to satisfy Him. He can find fault with nearly anything.

When the food was good, he ate his fill:

[December 6, 1944]
What do you suppose we had for supper, wrong the first time—Ham and Eggs. And believe me I had my share. I sat down with Jim Lonnigon and Harley Smucker. Jim has just been in a minute when I sat down so and Harley was finished. Jim Had Harley go back and get himself another Plate of Ham and eggs then soon as Harley was back He went up—himself and got another Plate full and gave me all the Ham on it and one egg then I went up and got myself another serving of Ham and eggs. Boy we were full and How. I had 5 eggs altogether and I must have ate nearly a Pound of Ham. also had 2 cups of Cocoa, 2 cookies, 2 dishes of beets and a couple slices of Bread maybe you think we didn't eat.

[December 30, 1944]
I Just got back from supper and Boy what a supper. We had beans as usual But had breakfast also. John Martin and I were the first ones thru the line he asked for 1 Weiner & Beans, I asked for 2 weiners and just a very little beans I Put on Plenty tomatoe sauce tho' for desert we had Peaches. On the way thru John & I each smuggled 3 dishes, Brenman & Geroring each got two. Then later I went

up and got 3 more one for John, & Breneman then when those were gone John got 3 more one for Paul Georing one for me & one for himself. We had only 16 dishes of Peaches between the 4 of us. John & I each had 2 cups of cocoa also. To top it off then when we were going back thru the kitchen John & I each got a tangerine. That makes up for the supper I didn't eat last nite. I'm telling you I sure feel full.

As often as he ate well, Ben skipped meals. Sometimes, he skipped because the food was unappetizing. Other times, he skipped in order to sleep longer.

[December 8, 1944]
We had Mackerel for Dinner boiled Potatoes & String Beans. I skipped all that and had two Pieces of chocolate Pie and 3 cups of grape fruit Juice. that was my Dinner this eve. I didn't go to supper.

[January 17, 1945]
I feel O.K. I'm eating the last one of the cookies you sent me, for X-mas, now. It is a little brittle but It's Pretty good considering I didn't see the inside of our cafeteria today.

[January 22, 1945]
This Morn. I slept another hour instead of breakfast. we had french toast, and apple sauce so I Just said "apple sauce" and went down to sleep a while.
This noon we had ham, cabbage, and Potatoes with cake for Dessert, grape fruit Juice too. I had 5 little cups of Juice. Aren't I a Pig? That made up for my breakfast.

Unsurprisingly, Ben started losing weight after Miriam left as his eating was so inconsistent. On December 10 he noted, "Heres a little News Flash tho Darling: I love you with the whole of me. I'm pretty big to altho' I've lost 4 lbs since you left. I weight 198 now."

Ben also continued to do woodworking and other hobbies and wrote about those things in his letters home. In an early letter to them both from Miriam's Aunt Rozelda, she compared Ben to her late husband: "But Ben my hubbie was not so good at knitting and crocheting as you are." Apparently, Ben was so bored when not working that Miriam taught him to knit and crochet to help fill the hours.

The fact was that Ben and Miriam were terribly bored in Rhode Island. Certainly, they worked very long hours in the hospital, but it was the after-hours time that weighed heaviest upon them. There was precious little to do, they had no means of transportation to go elsewhere, no money to spend, and not enough time to do much anyway. They had but one room to call their own, so cleaning and homemaking was minimal, and they did not do their own cooking. As he had in Sideling Hill, Ben spent a great deal of his free time in the woodworking shop creating everything from clocks to wooden games to pieces of furniture. The woodworking shop was "located in the room directly opposite the guinea pigs and rabbits" according to the *Newsette*. Particularly in this set of letters, when Miriam went home to have the baby, he spent even more time there. For one, it was lonelier in their empty room at the cottage, and two, he was busy making a crib for the new little one.

[December 4, 1944]
Last eve. after I wrote I started to look over my furniture Plans. I drew the Plans of the Play. Pen over. Same dimensions but hinges similar to the ones we saw on the one in the City Hall Hardware store. I may make the chest before I do the Crib Mr. Hiesey is going to get Plywood and white Pine now and Hardwood a little later.

[January 17, 1945]
Tonite I want to get the boards all tongue and grooved for all the ends of the 2 desks, Then fit my gates on the crib. That'll Probably take up all my time. I hope I don't have luck with my screws like Leonard did. (I'm going to say something naughty—looks like Leonard and I both had the same <u>luck</u> with one of our <u>screws</u> wow!) Bad little boy now ain't I?<u>ha</u>.

Acquiring wood seems to have been one of the biggest challenges Ben and the other woodworkers faced in order to complete their projects. Finances were tight, and good lumber was difficult to find because it was in short supply. While lumber was not rationed, the supply dwindled as loggers were conscripted and sent to war; this created lumber shortages in the military as well as on the home front.[1] Ben spoke often of traveling to see about wood, digging through piles of rubbish to see if there was quality wood buried there, and even putting ads in the newspaper to find scrap to buy.

[December 12, 1944]
Jake Hen and Mr. Hiesey were in town today again this afternoon it was; but still nothing in the line of hard wood. I'm going to try to find some scraps of oak for framing if nothing else then use some-thing softer for the rest. I'll use Plywood for the Pannels on the ends of the crib.

[December 14, 1944]
I just got back from a wild goose chase after some lumber. . . . Henry Stall & Katie took, Jake, Dick Kistle, Leonard and myself over to a Place where there was some cherry wood advertized. Jake tho't we might be able to use it. But It was too thin and besides He wanted 50¢ Per sq. ft. for it. we went to another

place that answered an Ad. that Jake Put in the Paper. A lady called Jake and told him she had some carved Mahogony so we went there. Jake and Dick went in I told them it's Probably some old maid that has a couple Bed rails for sale. When they back to the car They were laughing and we couldn't imagine what about. But sure enough some old lady had a high backed bed for sale. Jake said when she showed them He tho't of what I said and couldn't keep from laughing. He said He didn't burst right out, but couldn't help laughing a little to save his neck. So then we come home.

[December 16, 1944]
I helped Leonard up out the Posts for his Crib He found a 2X10 Maple board about 12' long in the C Basement. It sure works up nice. I think he'll have enough to make his crib framing. He's Putting solid Panel ends in his. He says he Knows of another Maple Piece but it has been laying in the Water a while.

In addition to woodworking, Ben did indeed have Miriam teach him how to knit, crochet, and sew. The *Newsette* reported on this fact in its very first issue on October 27, 1944: "Our reporter says there is nothing of special interest from the Cottage. Things are as usual with the girls knitting and the fellows playing monopoly. However, we must not forget Ben Kesler. We understand he has made, and is making, some knitted clothing which will come in very handy before long."[2] That Ben did some kind of needle craft is one of the few stories I knew about their early lives when I was growing up. Oddly, I never knew that they were in Rhode Island or why, I was just amused along with the rest of the family to know that Ben used to knit and crochet out of boredom (although I ended up marrying a man who knits, does counted cross stitch, and quilts far, far better than I do). Ben's sewing seems to have been mostly utilitarian as he mentioned sewing up a rip in his clothing while Miriam was away. Woodworking was the pastime and skill that stuck, and most of my family's homes have at least one piece of furniture, a clock, or a wooden game that Ben crafted at some point in his life.

The sewing machine that they had was crammed into their small room in the Night Watch Cottage. Each CPS couple was allotted a single room to themselves. In a December 20, 1944, letter, Ben mentioned that in their room there was a bed, "two chests of drawers, a sewing machine and a trunk." This was a lot to pack into a single room. They also did some of their own laundry out of this room, so there were usually clothes drying on lines strung by the radiator.

Living in the cottage was cramped, and the walls, apparently, were fairly thin, so Ben's letters were filled with stories and gossip about the other couples and sex. Sex was a common enough topic that Ben and Miriam wrote about throughout their time apart. For example, in December 1942, when Ben was still at Sideling Hill, Miriam wrote,

[December 14, 1942]

Honey just send the folks & my things all in one package and send it up there. That's what we did about your package. You mustn't open it until Christmas Day. Will you? I wish somebody would ship me in a big box to you & then you could open it up & find me wouldn't that be swell. We would really celebrate Christmas. I bet-cha! You just wait a wee bit longer and then—Oh boy! We'll exercise that piggy & kitty. We'll be all tuckered out (Was that a T or a F). I'm getting naughty or somepin' so I better sign off for to-night. Your one & only loving wife.

Throughout their letters, Ben and Miriam referred to sexual intimacy some-times directly and sometimes with euphemisms. Here was one of the first in-stances of more overt talk along with jokes and eyebrow waggles. While references to intimacy were regularly a part of their letters, this example demonstrates how severely limiting letter writing was to their relationship, particularly as newly-weds. The platform created with the materiality of letters was simply not a sub-stitute for sex, and while they joked about it, lamented about it, and earnestly discussed their desires, I imagine that both writing and reading such letters left them more frustrated than anything else.

The letters from the State Hospital included stories of sex and discussions of other CO couples, as well as jokes and comments on their own sex life. For example,

[December 2, 1944]

woops, I just heard from our Giggle Colony across the hall. Sounds like the Shanks are in full swing this eve. ha.

I got out my fiddle and Played a little this eve. before I started writing so maybe the neighbors don't appreciate that too much either, 'spose?

Well Honey I think I better get my laundry Put up and go to bed. I tried sleeping with your letter in the Pocket of my nite shirt but it's getting wrinkled so I may have to Put it under my Pillow. Oh Honey it tells so much. I'm glad you wrote it. It's the best thing I have while were apart. IT came from your heart that's why I cherish it so.

As is their custom, Ben joked about their own sex life in similar ways, such as in a December 10, 1944, letter: "The radiator was on all day and boy is this room Hot. (not as much tho' ^as if you were here I-betcha)." In another example, Ben discussed neighbors and his own commitment to Miriam:

[December 11, 1944]

Gossip has it that stoltzfue has been stepping out on his wife. Now isn't that a good Amishman? Only been Married a little over a Month they say he took that

Clair Brown out to dinner. He says It wasn't a date. That Miss Brown wanted to ask him about his wedding. Bob Strubon was with them so maybe things were on the level. But Him Bosler told me today they've been making excuses. Well Honey I'm sure It'll be awful warm day in Jan. before you hear anything about me like that. Darling I'm being a good boy. Honest Sweetheart I wouldn't no more think of being untrue, than I would cut off my right arm. I love you so much Honey sometimes I Just almost choke up I don't have an outlet for my Love. You're sure going to have to take lots of Loving Hugging, & Kissing once we're together again.

Similarly, Ben wrote of his commitment to Miriam through an amusing story:

[January 5, 1945]
I found a note from Betty Hoffman under our door when I came in it said "some time between Now & 7:00 in the Morn." She wanted your address so I wrote it on the Paper and Just now slid it under her door. (Imagine me corresponding by Notes to a Married woman. wow! what scandal) haha.

Some weeks later, Ben again wrote of the Stoltzfuses in an amusing "newsflash" of gossip:

[January 12, 1945]
FLASH: Mr & Mrs Stoltzfus think there's no use wearing out the carpet between their twin beds so they got rid of one—Now isn't that some new Item? No Kidding ol' Stoltzfus said "what's the use of having two beds, we only use one" so they took the one out and put it in the basement. It has given Rise to quite a bit of funny remarks. I didn't Know it till John Hoffman <u>was</u> telling me today.

On January 28, Miriam's friend reiterated this bit of gossip in a letter:

Ammon Stoltzfus' wife is here. they live in room 2—there room <u>had</u> two beds. He requested one to be removed it made the room to crowded. As a result the two of them ~~slept~~ sleep in one twin bed!
It's quite a problem here: More couples signed to come—no place to put them, night watch & service Bldg. full.

Ben's letters also told amusing stories, particularly about sex and discussions with friends.

[December 11, 1944]
Bill got to talking about intercourse this afternoon. He says He and Mim only ∧(They can't yet now) ~~do~~ ∧did it once a week. He says "We're both Passionate" Wow! I

didn't say one thing, but I tho't a Plenty. He asked about us so I told Him in an evasive way "The Doctor say 2 or 3 times a week isn't too much" He says I know. But I don't feel too good when I do it often. I'll Bet Mrs. Rathmon wants more than that Don't you. Maybe that's why she was so. You know how, last summer with the fellows.

[December 26, 1944]
Bill told me his doctor told them that they must wait about 6 to 8 weeks after the baby arrived before they could practice intercourse. He said after the Mother has had her first normal Period after she stops flowing. Some women the Dr. said are much longer than that with their first Period. Bill has been drinking quite a bit of Egg Nog everyday that is brought over for the Patients who don't eat well. So I was Kiddin' him told him he's trying to build himself up so he'll be able to take it when he can do business again.

[January 15, 1945]
Jim Bosler & I were talking this afternoon about sex relations. He says he don't know too much but he knows Lib.—isn't very Passionate or emotional. (wonder how he knows?) I tried to Pump him a little, but he wouldn't talk. ᴴᵃ.

I chose to include details about Ben and Miriam's sex life and their comments about others for a few reasons, though I debated this choice quite a lot. It is intimate information (pun intended), and something that were they still alive, I worry they would prefer to have left out of their story. Family history writing has to pay attention to what gets included and what does not get included in a different way than other qualitative methodologies because the main participants are usually no longer living. What is included can have ramifications on the wider family, and I was concerned about that.

I opted to keep this information included in part because my parents tell me Ben and Miriam were not shy about their enjoyment of each other, so why should I keep out such details, and in part because this information demonstrates the depth of their commitment and love for one another. Additionally, outsiders to conservative Christian communities often assume that members of the community are "prudes" because they dress modestly, avoid alcohol and drugs, and speak differently. But they are just people with the same desires and hormones as anyone.

Space in the Night Watch Cottage was at a premium, and with Miriam gone home to have the baby, some of the hospital administrators and the CPS director Mr. Hiesey pressured Ben to vacate their room for another couple that was soon to be arriving.

[December 20, 1944]
I don't know what kind of a letter I'll be able to write tonite, I'm mad as a hornet. I just got a call from Hiesey and he says I've got some bad news for you. He says There's two new couples coming and he wants me to move out of our room. He said he talked to Mr. Hagon and Dr. Regon and They asked him to ask me to move; said They didn't want too but had to find some Place for the Couples. . . . So I asks him how about when you come up He said I think you should have the room back, so I says where will the ones in our room go He says we'll have to find a Place for Them. I says why don't you do that now and save a lot of moving. . . . He suggested giving me a room in the Male Dorm. But it would be only a single bed. and no Place for a couple. He said don't be in a hurry about it, I'll see what I can do. (you know his line) I told him well I don't like it and to tell Hagon and Regon so, But if there was no other alternitive I'd have to I guess.

Ben pushed back at the directive and protested the move, stating that Miriam would be returning with their baby in a matter of months. If he moved to make room for the new couples, where would they live once Miriam returned? He argued that it made more sense to find an alternative spot for the newcomers than to have him move so much. In the end, Mr. Hiesey and the hospital administrators agreed with him.

[January 4, 1945]
I got to work at 10 till 6:00 this Morn. and to my surprise Mr. Hiesey was there. He had been talking to Theron a little bit when he all of a sudden said "about your room, you'l be able to keep it." He said Doctor Regon told him if The wife was gone only 4 mo. a couple could keep their room. He said also so said Hiesey "That'll ~~keep~~ take care of the Kesler case." so now never fear we can Keep our room. If at the end of 4 mo. you wouldn't have come back yet, I think they'd let us have it for a few extra weeks any way.

The issue of space continued for the couples of the Night Watch Cottage. From what I can tell, there were to be about four different women having babies around the same time. The difficulty was what to do with the children when the women worked their shifts at the hospital. It was out of the question that they not work, as the reason they were able to be housed there was predicated on their employment. One couple opted simply to leave their newborn child at home with relatives:

[January 10, 1945]
about Bill & Mim. I think it's more her Idea than his that the baby be left behind if it is. seems like they are so willing to Part with it. ever since they knew

it was coming they've been trying to find out somewhere where they can Put it or have someone keep it for them instead of trying to figure out a way to Keep it with them. I think Bill would like to have it near at least but he did say He didn't want his wife working all day and taking care of the baby at nite. That's alright I agree but did he ever think that he could help out caring for it? I know I would. The thing is. They don't want to be tied down to much it seems to me. I hope I'm wrong. (enough ~~eritzeng~~ critizing).

As leaving children behind was not even a consideration for Ben and other couples, they began searching for a solution.

[December 22, 1944]
Leonard and I were discussing the Prospects of taking care of the children when our wives come back. We talked back and forth and exchanged Ideas. He said he tho't we might get a room here at the hospital and one of the wives (if us & Rothamon) could take care of the children while the others worked to support all three babies and the one who takes care of them.

Their proposed solution was met with opposition from both hospital administrators and CPS director Hiesey.

[January 19, 1945]
This noon I saw Leonard and he'd be in favor doing whatever he can but he says Hiesey said Dr. Regon Just isn't interested bothering with trying to find a way to care for the children. He told Hiesey it isn't expense thats holding back fixing a Nursery He said the state would Pay for it. what I think it is although he didn't say so in so many words is He's Just a little afraid to favor us for Political reasons. If he made it too easy ^for us the opposing Party would use that to get him out of here.

Leonard said He don't think we should tell Hiesey about it but go directly to Regon about the matter and tell him if something can't be arranged about Keeping our wives here, We aren't interested in staying. He tho't if we told Hiesey, He might mess things up a bit or else Regon might think we were Kinda ganging up on a Threat of some Kind and would resent it. I think That may be a good Idea. I also tho't if I talk to Him I'd mention the fact that if I couldn't work something out I'd try to get a transfer to a Hospital that had a nursery. Not that I really would but what do you think of the Idea. Marlboro has one and then we'd be only half the distance we are now from home. There are a lot of angles to think about I guess.

The men also discussed renting a house to use as a nursery.

[January 19, 1945]

Bill says Merle and He were talking about renting a house and getting some used furniture for it then one wife taking care of the house & babys while the others worked. I don't think much of that Plan first thing we'd get too much money in furniture, Pay electric Bill, water, rent by good for whoever took care of the children and Then there would be no satisfactory way to have some one nights with the babys. I don't Know but I think we'll get something thru the Hospital yet. That would be the Ideal set up. Then Too if you breast feed our baby that won't work you trying to work and leaving the baby somewhere. I think we'd better Plan something on our own hoots ~~then maybe~~ and let the others do as they will.

We cannot know for sure how the problem was resolved. I suspect that some combination of care was figured out. Since female ward workers were in such short supply, the hospital administrators would likely have done what they could to keep the women there. I do know that Miriam returned to Rhode Island once the baby, my Uncle Jim, was born and that she returned to Goshen in 1946 to have their second child, my Aunt Connie.

Apart from spending their time making babies, woodworking, and knitting, Ben and Miriam may have taken part in some of the recreational and educational opportunities put together by the CPS program and discussed in the *Newsette*. There was a basketball league that took place at the Baptist Church gym in Cranston, a bowling league (the location is never named), several different Bible studies, sermons and prayer meetings, a lending library, choral and musical practices and performances, and special social events for holidays. Ben described one social gathering, a small party held to celebrate the new year.

[December 31, 1944–January 1, 1945]

The New Year is Now 1 hour and 25 minutes old. I watched the New Year in and the old one out with the croud down stairs. The girls cleaned the Basement and hung Bed spreads around from the top of the basement about 3' from the wall. It hid all our suit cases Then we all took chairs down and card tables. Some of the kids went to church, there is a Minister here, Hafstetter I think and stayed longer than they Planed we didn't start till 9:00 oclock. Leonard and I were one couple. We Played 3 games Then had refreshments. Just before Refreshments tho we were singing some Norm Townsend was siting beside me and said we should Play a few numbers. So we come up and got the Boys and Guitar He Plays the Guitar very good. better than I. so we went down stairs. We started Playing as we started down the steps we were Playing Jingle Bells. At Midnite we all had to Pop our Paper Cups on the floor to make Noise. Norman had a (22) and he shot 3 times up in the air.

For refreshments we had cookies Ice cream Potatoe chips, and orange Juice with a touch of Cinnamon. It was good. We had a swell time all together. I sure missed you tho Honey. All the others had their wives there nearly But I didn't let my inward feelings show on the outside.

We Played Music again then after the Party was over. Right after 12:00 we were lead in Prayer by Jim Shank.

Ben's name was not listed in any of the sports pages of the *Newsette*, and I think it fair to say he did not participate in those activities. One other pastime that Ben developed was writing song lyrics. Apparently, he had some successes in selling his music, though not at first.

[December 3, 1944]
I forgot last eve. to mention I got a letter from Ruth Larkin Editor of the Haven Press. She has selected 2 out of the 6 Lyrics I sent in, to Put in her book. To get them Printed in tho' I must buy 3 copies of the Book. The 3 copies will cost 15$\frac{00}{}$ the reason they're so high is, extra copies will be made to give to music houses, libraries, movie producers etc. the two she chose were "I'm headin for the Ozarks" and "what will we be to Him". I don't know what I'll do about it. It's just a money making scheme I think still I'd like to try sometime.

He wrote on January 13, 1945, that he received a card "from Los Angles (Beverly Hills Calif) They want to compose music for my songs and Print them free so I guess I'll write I can't do anymore than lose a stamp $\underline{ha}$." Through January he continued to correspond with the "song co." as he referred to it. The letters end before we find out exactly what happened to his lyrics.

As ever, Ben continued to fill his time with letters home to his Mimmie. The letters in this series are a mirror of those he had written from Sideling Hill. They have the same basic pattern of salutation, establishing their shared platform and space, and end with that same conduit flow of love and endearments over the miles. These letters differ a bit in their content and tone, however. There is a sense of steadiness to the letters, of stability and routine, established by having been married several years and having been together in the same location and having experienced the same things. There was less to describe about the place and his work because Miriam knew all about it. Instead the letters looked ahead to their baby, making plans and waiting with anticipation.

[December 24, 1944]
Darling I appreciate your letters so much because I know what an effort It must be to write them, with your tummy. Keeping you away from the table. Are your arms long enough to reach? (ha) Oh Honey I have the most adorable wife in the world and that's barring none.

CHAPTER 13

Finances and More Conflicts

B EN AND MIRIAM'S SMALL HISTORY RETURNS TO FINANCES AND CON-
flicts with family in their years at the State Hospital. As I discuss in chapter 7, communicating on such things through letter writing, which depends on
the postal service for responses, and discussions involving multiple parties proved
a problematic enterprise. While they were preparing for the arrival of their first
child, Ben and Miriam had to rely on the often-opinionated Benjamin Sr. as not
just their parent but their pastor and head of their denomination and on church
official voices from two different denominations. Cluttering the issue was the
more official correspondence that passed between church officials, often getting
delayed, lost, or forgotten in bureaucratic holdups.

Here we can see how a small history offers something that a large-H history
may not: the ways that a single individual negotiated between personal need,
familial obligations and expectations, and official and bureaucratic factors. Entire
histories of the US Postal Service have been compiled, and the Smithsonian's
National Postal Museum is dedicated to the study, preservation, and presentation
of postal historical items. Certainly, their vast collections contain letters written
to and from various parties on day-to-day as well as larger issues. The collection I
have does this, but we can also clearly see the movements Ben made between the
different parties, the holdups, and the frustrations. Through these letters we see
the reality of being a conscientious objector (CO) with dependents, the results of
the government's decision to not pay COs, and that the Civilian Public Service
(CPS) program was an imperfect solution for COs.

As I discuss in chapter 7, Ben and other COs were not paid for their work,
and dependents were not paid the stipend other conscripted men's families received. When they were apart, this meant that Miriam found work as a live-in
hired girl with the Holdermans, sold her and Ben's house, and found other work
as she was able. Ben transferred to the State Hospital mostly so Miriam could join
him, but finances still played a role. They would be together, but Miriam also
would be paid for her work there. Since room and board were part of the deal
with the unit, Miriam's salary helped them stay afloat with needed purchases of
clothing, medical or dental treatments, and toiletries. The addition to their family
meant that she would not be able to work as much, and they would have an additional person to take care of, greatly stretching their limited financial resources.

When Ben wrote to Miriam of the opportunity on January 30, 1943, he described how it would work to have both of them working there and what they would earn. "The wife gets $50⁰⁰ per Mo. to start with and 2½ raises Per quarter until they reach $70⁰⁰ ∧The men get 2½ per Mo. also." I believe he meant that she would get a $2.50 raise per quarter until she earned $70. This also meant that Ben was paid $2.50 per month, which is hardly enough to consider pay. The low wages for regular employees at the State Hospital only contributed to the critically low staffing issues, making their jobs that much more difficult. If we assume these numbers are correct, Miriam was making about $65 a month by the time she returned to Goshen. The loss of this income, small though it was, was critical for their growing family.

To offer some context for Miriam's income, consider that the federal minimum wage in 1944 was $.30 per hour.[1] If Miriam worked a 40-hour work week, she would earn $12 a week or $48 per month. But Miriam was likely working at least 10-hour shifts, 6 days a week, which would be $72 per month if she was paid hourly without overtime pay. Further, the median annual salary for women in 1945 was $980, which is about $82 per month.[2] According to the US Department of Labor's *Occupational Outlook Handbook*, "the basic annual beginning salary for hospital attendant jobs under civil service in 1947 was $1,954," which would be $162 a month.[3] (I assume this last salary was for male employees, as women made about $.62 for every dollar men earned, which would translate to $100.44 per month.) Most salary quotes above included daily meals as did Ben and Miriam's positions.

Based on these data, Miriam and other CO wives earned well below the national minimum wage while also trying to support their husbands (and possibly children). Some might point out that the COs did not have to pay for housing, such as it was. Rhode Island's median gross rent in the 1940s, which includes estimated costs for utilities, was twenty-eight dollars per month for a renter-occupied unit with only one bedroom, one bathroom, a sitting room, a kitchen, and perhaps a den or parlor.[4] Ben and Miriam had a single, small bedroom to call their own. A generous estimate of the cost of renting a single room would be fourteen dollars per month. If we add Miriam's sixty-five dollar salary and this fourteen-dollar "housing stipend," her total monthly earnings would have been seventy-nine dollars, which would have been barely minimum wage. And that money needed to stretch to support two people's medical and dental needs, clothing, shoes, toiletries, and sundry other items. It also needed to cover the costs of Miriam's return home, any expenses related to the delivery of the baby, as well as fund Ben's visit home while on leave. Once those expenses were paid, they would then have a baby and the loss of Miriam's income to contend with. Truly, they needed financial assistance.

Ben tried to find additional paying work to fill his hours while Miriam was gone, and he also began to petition for monetary support from the sponsoring churches. CPS often allowed for men to work offsite after-hours because they knew the desperate financial situation of COs and their families. Further, when specific financial needs arose, the historic peace churches tried to meet those needs. So Ben's letters to Miriam at this time were filled with his efforts to procure additional money. The archive also has copies of the letters Ben sent to various church officials asking for assistance and their responses.

After Miriam left, Ben sent her a letter on December 5, 1944, telling her that he had begun looking for paying work for his off-hours, specifically Wednesdays. After finishing an overnight shift at the State Hospital, Ben went to Providence by "thumbing a ride" with a "lone sailor driving a 37 Packard." Once there, he asked about work at City Hall Hardware but was told they employ only full-time help. He asked at the outlet store, and "the lady there told me to wait again till Miss Newcome come in, said she'd be in, in an hour. . . . I went back to the outlet only to learn there are no openings for Wed." He tried the Boston store, where there was no part-time work, then Shephard's, which had part-time work but wanted him to work a little every day. He tried a laundry in Cranston that had a sign "men wanted" in the window, but they were not interested in someone who could only work one day a week. "In Cherry and Webb I was told they employ only Lady Help, Then I walked over to Montgomery wards and they needed no one at this time so I got on a Bus for Home. . . . I got home at 5:15 so I guess I ain't supposed to get a job."

Ben decided to see about working in the hospital's sundry shop, which sold various items to patients and employees. "Maybe I'll see if Mrs. Kenny Could use me in the afternoon. I may look a little more for a job, I don't exactly know where tho'," he mused. He finally found a bit of success with the sundry shop.

[December 6, 1944]
I asked Mrs. Kenny if she needed any help for this afternoon so she told me to come in about a quarter till 1:00. . . . About 20 till one I went up to the store. I got along Just fine the first customer I had were John and Betty Hoffman. John was getting a ward order for one of—his Patients.

About 4:00 Mrs. Kenny told me at 5:30 I could go to supper so at that time I left she gave me 2 Bucks for the afternoon and told me to come back this eve. But wants me next week so maybe I'd better be satisfied with this so close at home. If I worked in the stores in Prov. and had to Pay fare each time I wouldn't be much better off. Mrs. Kenny wants me to try to get my day changed one week and run the store for her she says she'd like to take a day off occasionally. I don't know if I could or not. Depends on How good a mood Mr. Shaw is in.

Ben knew that he could make more if he worked in a shop in Providence, but he would have to pay bus fare both ways to get to the job. Given his limited availability, finding work there already proved nearly impossible, so he settled into working for Mrs. Kenney whenever he could.

> [December 13, 1944]
> I worked for Mrs. Kenney this afternoon again. I went up about 20 till 1:00 and was there only about 15 mins. when a fellow come in that visits his Brother in Pinel-1. He hasn't been here since I was there. So I talked with him a little, waited on him, told him I was just helping Mrs. Kenney out on my day off so when he Paid me he also gave me 2 dollars. He said here's a little Xmas Present for you, so that was O.K. wasn't it. If I'd have been in the building tho' I wouldn't have seen him and would have missed out. So with the 2 Bucks Mrs. Kenney gave me, the 2 Bucks I got from him and 5.00 from gross for the coats I netted $9.00 all told not bad for one day eh? I may help Mrs. Kenney out next sat after-noon.

Because working for Mrs. Kenney worked out, Ben did his best to be put on a schedule that would enable him to work for her more frequently. If he could time his overnight shifts, what he calls a "P.M.," he could get more time in the store. The trouble was that his immediate supervisor, Mr. Shaw, was not always kind and not always consistent in how he handled scheduling and other staffing issues.

> [December 19, 1944]
> I asked him today to have P.M. on Sat. so I could help Mrs. Kenney. I told him That's about the only way I have of making a little extra dough so he said he'd look on the schedule for ~~Thurs~~^Sat. and see if he could arrange it. about 10 minutes later he called and said it would be O.K. so I'll get two days work again this week.

Ben was truly thankful that Mr. Shaw gave him a schedule that permitted him to work. Ben continued in his letter on December 19 with explanations of the work he would be doing in the sundry shop.

> Last eve. Mrs. Kenney told Norm Townsend she wanted to see me, so this noon I went down. She wants me to open up the store in the morning at 9:00 and be there all day. She wants to do some shopping also spend a little time with her sister who has arrived. She had her nephew there this afternoon. so at 8:30 I'll go over she has a Patient go in early and clean up, get coffee started etc. He has a key to the back door so he'll be there and she told me she'd hide the key behind the silverware box for the front door. She put 50\underline{^{00}}$ and a bag of change in the back I'll have to Pay the Baking Co, Ice cream man, also Rd. Island Banking Co. ~~Where~~ she expects to get some Crackers cookies etc. tomorrow.

So I'll be some business man. I told her this eve. When I stopped in to get the details straight I'd do the best I could. One thing sure even tho' the job doesn't Pay like some others It's handy and convenient and I can work nearly any time I'm off. If I had a job in the city I couldn't just go in and work any old time. Seems as tho' God is just directing our lives for the best.

I am uncertain how much money Ben made working for Mrs. Kenney, but every little bit helped them. The other significant effort Ben made to help their finances was to petition the sponsoring churches about getting some assistance for their additional dependent. The challenge to his particular situation was not that there was no money available for such assistance. Each of the historical peace churches paid out additional funds for circumstances such as Ben and Miriam's. The difficulty was that he was a Dunkard Brethren man working in a Mennonite-sponsored camp. He was never an outcast, as their beliefs were so similar that he even led prayer meetings and spoke on occasion, but when it came to individual financial support, church membership mattered.

Further, while there was money to help out those COs in financial crisis, it was limited. Sibley and Jacob note that "public funds were not made available either to pay the c.o.'s for their work or to meet the bulk of the operating and maintenance expenses. This saddled an untold financial burden upon that small segment of the community which was sufficiently concerned about freedom of conscience to pay for it."[5] Any money made available to the COs came from donations from members of the peace churches.

In the letters throughout the end of 1944 and 1945, we again can see the limitations of conducting business or financial deals through the postal service. Multiple letters were sent to and from Ben, Miriam, Benjamin Sr., Mennonite Central Committee (MCC), and the head of the Brethren CPS committee, Reverend Flohr. Letters containing virtually the same information crossed each other in the mail, adding confusion, frustration, and stress. What should have been a simple matter ended up taking more than six weeks to figure out.

Ben began his efforts by discussing the matter with the MCC-appointed director of their unit at the State Hospital, Mr. Hiesey.

[December 2, 1944]
I went on over to the E. Bldg and we [Hiesey] discussed the Dependent Problem. I asked him if he'd write for me and tell them we're depending on it, He agreed to do so—so Mon. Morn. He's going to send a letter. He says He can't see why we shouldn't have it.

To his initial relief, Mr. Hiesey supported his petition and sent along the request. Two weeks passed, but Ben heard nothing.

[December 15, 1944]
I spoke to Hiesey today about the dependency and he says he hasn't heard anything. He says He thinks they'll Just answer by sending a Check. He says He
thinks they'll be made Payable to me since I'm the one who's in C.P.S. so if they
are I'll Just enclose them and send them on to you or will send Money orders.
Rothmans get theirs now Bill has received 2-35$\underline{00}$ checks and can you imagine
it they haven't got them yet cashed tho' also have all their expenses Paid too. I'm
glad for them but don't know how they managed it.

It seems that others who had made similar requests to MCC had no trouble in securing additional funds for dependents. Here it seems that the Rothmans already
had their expenses covered but received two thirty-five-dollar checks in addition.
Ben seems bemused at how they accomplished getting that much financial support. A week later, since he still had not received a check or heard a response, Ben
wrote to MCC himself to ask after the matter.

[December 23, 1944]
Mr. Hiesey called me this afternoon and told me he got a letter from M.C.C.
concerning our Dependency. It so happens I mailed a letter to them just this
morn. wondering why I haven't heard. Hiesey read the letter over the Phone to
me. It said our case has been refered to our church and so far haven't had any reply.

In early January 1945, Ben finally heard back from MCC regarding his Dependency Status Report. The letter stated:

[January 4, 1945]
We have recently been in contact with Rev. Lewis B. Flohr of Vienne, Virginia,
who is one of the leading brethren in your group.
    Brother Flohr advises that at the last general conference of your group, pro-
vision has been made of CO dependents. In light of his letter we are forwarding
on to him a copy of your Dependency Status Report so that he can give immediate consideration to your needs.
    If you should have any further question about this matter, I would suggest
that you write directly to Rev. Flohr or to his office.

Essentially, MCC passed the issue on to the Brethren Church, specifically a Reverend Flohr. Because Ben was not Mennonite himself, they felt financial support
for him and his family should come from his own denomination. Ben requested
funds from MCC because he had worked exclusively in Mennonite-run camps.
The frustration he and Miriam felt was pretty strong. They were good enough to
serve in the camps, to preach and teach and participate in Sunday worship, but

not good enough to receive additional dependency funding from a church that was not their own. Yet, I can understand MCC's decision; the Mennonite denomination funded thousands of men, and they had the largest number of CPS men in camps across the country.

While Ben waited to hear from MCC and then from Reverend Flohr, Benjamin Sr., who was the minister of his home church, wrote to Ben on December 26, "We lifted an offering for you, Miriam and Clarence Swihart amonnting to $39.29." It is unclear how much of those funds went to Ben and Miriam, but I know that it was enough to help Ben get home after the birth of the baby and to buy a few essentials.

> [January 3, 1945]
> Then I figured up our financial standings. I left $21.06 in the bank, Paid 35.02 for my ticket, 25¢ for Breakfast, 75¢ for files, rasps, hinges etc. 20¢ for Bus fare and have $23.50 here at home now. So I have my ticket bout and $44.50 to use for our "little darling." The crib is all Paid for except stain, shellac & 2 sheets of sandpaper so I'm standing O.K. Much better than I tho't I could. I figured up this Morn. and counting today I've made $16.00 working in the store. Very little I've spent except for necessities, I'll bet you can say the same too.

Unfortunately, receiving financial support from the larger Brethren Church was not so easy; the church dragged its feet in helping their COs. As both Ben's father, a minister of the church, and the founding father of a branch of the denomination, Benjamin Sr. wrote to Reverend Flohr to ask after the issue:

> [January 2, 1945]
> I wrote Brother Flohr in regard to "dependency" cases; he tells me our C.Os are to look first to the family or families, and the church, and if need requires it, the CPS Com. will assist in such cases. We lifted an offering Dec. 24 for you and Clarence Swihart, not as large as I had hoped but the attendance was reduced that day on account of bad weather. I do not know now what the church may be willing to do more in the case. So we shall wait and see. If you will give me an idea of what you may need, I will see what can be done about it. Any how we shall do our share.

As the founding father of the Dunkard Brethren denomination, an offshoot of the larger Brethren Church, I am surprised at the reletive passivity in this letter. Certainly, Benjamin Sr. wrote to the committee but seemed entirely understanding of their response (which passed the buck to the local church congretations for each CPS man). The Brethren Church seemed much less organized about collecting and distributing funds for their CPS men, in comparison with the

Mennonite Church. Additionally, I suspect that there may have been some hard feelings toward the Keslers, as Benjamin Sr. had led the creation of an offshoot denomination due in part to his criticism of the larger group. Perhaps the larger denomination felt that they were no longer part of the whole.

Benjamin Sr. wrote again on the January 11,

> I am inclosing a letter from Bro. L.B. Flohr. I suggest you write him as indicated by my underscoring. Then let me know what he says about it. Do this now maybe you will hear from him before you come home.
>
> Don't think me unkind, but you can easily spend unnecessarily in a case like this. Esp. in stringent times as this.
>
> I wrote for your birth certificate. It will likely be here soon.
>
> Return Flohr's letter to me. Don't worry. You'll be cared for. Papa.

I imagine that Ben was quite frustrated at his father's admonition not to "spend unnecessarily" and his reminder that they were living in "stringent times." Given that Ben earned only $2.50 a month, had to pay for his own uniforms, and had an expectant wife whose lower-than-minimum-wage earnings were now gone, I would say they knew about stringent times. Later that month, Ben finally responded to his father. He included a copy of what he wrote to Benjamin Sr. in a letter to Miriam:

> [January 21, 1945]
> I told Pop in Their letter That I resented their telling us we were spending money foolishly. Heres exactly what I told him. quote:
>
> [In your letter I resented a little the insinuation that we were spending money foolishly. I'm afraid you don't Understand. We have money enough saved to meet our needs also some laid away in case of emergency during child birth. we also saved money by making nearly all the babys things. Since Miriam has gone all the money I've spent beyond my needs is Bus fare to and from the city. we could do without the Dependency allowance if we have too. But Flohr doesn't need to Know that neither do the members in the church. I've been 2½ years now not earning a cent. And I think I deserve the allowance No Matter if I was wealthy. Don't misunderstand me I'm only telling you this for your information. Not to be critical Neither am I offended. Please do Not think these remarks Unkind] end of quote.
>
> Maybe I said too much Honey But I didn't like the tone of his letter no more than you did so he can think what he pleases.

Ben's response to his father is understandable. He was clearly frustrated that Benjamin Sr. insinuated that he and Miriam were being frivolous. He admitted they did have some savings yet argued that they needed and deserved the stipend. While they could have scraped by on their small savings, the baby and its needs would have left them with nothing else, no emergency fund for medical issues, clothing, dental work, and the baby's needs as it grew. Ben would continue working for CPS, earning no money, and Miriam's work hours would be limited as she had to care for the baby. Without health or life insurance, that small savings they had was their only protection. If they depleted their meager savings, they would have nothing.

Eventually, Reverend Flohr and the larger Brethren Church did agree to help them. On January 24, Ben received a letter and a check from the treasurer of the Brethren Church CPS committee.

> B. E. Kesler Jr.
>   Dear Bro. you will find inclosed check for 25\frac{00}{}$ as pr. see order Bro. L. B. Flohr. I am also sending your wife 25\frac{00}{}$ trust this will tide you over till further orders from Bro. Flohr. Well I hope and pray that this war will <u>come</u> to a close soon. the sooner the better

Later that day, Ben wrote of the good news to Miriam:

> I have good news Flohr is coming across so maybe my letter did a little good. I'm sending you his letter you may show it to Pop if you care too But Keep it. He's sending each of us $25.00 now for Dec. & Jan. and asked where to send the other checks so I'll write and have them mailed directly to you. The one he sends me now I'll Keep till I get home or maybe use a little of it if necessary.

It is uncertain how long Ben and Miriam received the stipend to help with the costs of having a baby, but I am certain that the money was a welcome relief during a very stressful time for them. One clue indicates that the stipend was a limited relief, however. In a single letter saved from March 30, 1945, Miriam's mother, Maureen, wrote, "Sure hope & trust you will be able to find nice work with good pay since the other plan failed." One wonders what the plan was that failed, but we have no way of knowing. Ben's last letter to Miriam was on January 30, 1945. The letters ended abruptly because my Uncle Jim arrived the very next day and Ben immediately left for home to see his new baby boy.

Clearly finances were a true difficulty during their time in CPS, but it is important to understand that for them and many others in the program, CPS afforded them a means to express their faith. They considered this a "testimony by work" that "did not imply merely an escape from war. It meant the right for c.o.'s to practice and declare a 'way of peace and love administering to human need which they hold to be a divine imperative.'"[6] Essentially, the historic peace churches collectively thought that such a testimony would make a bigger impact through service than if they simply preached it. "Work performed in a spirit of friendliness and consideration for human welfare would demonstrate the essential qualities of the 'life which takes away the occasion of war.' It would show what the conscientious objector stood for, as well as what he stood against."[7] The churches were convinced that such a testimony could be made even in the framework of conscription. To do so, many adhered to a philosophy of "going the second mile." Such a stance was based upon the biblical passage of Matthew 5:38–48. In verses 38 to 42, Jesus says: "You have heard that it was said, 'An eye for an eye, and a tooth for a tooth.' But I say to you, do not resist an evil person; but whoever slaps you on your right cheek, turn the other to him also. If anyone wants to sue you and take your shirt, let him have your coat also. Whoever forces you to go one mile, go with him two. Give to him who asks of you, and do not turn away from him who wants to borrow from you."[8] Thus, the government compelled men to serve under conscription. CPS and many of the COs who served embraced the idea that while they may be compelled to serve, they would go the second mile voluntarily by working without pay. In fact, even while being compelled to serve the government, and even while going the second mile by doing so without pay, many men in CPS donated time, their limited funds, and resources to help others.

> Many were eager to help victims of war. . . . [Fasting from food] became a familiar practicing camps, men voluntarily dropping dinner once a week or substituting soup for meat, so as to save money for relief. Penniless as were many of the men in C.P.S., special collections and fundraising projects were frequent. During 1945, Mennonite men personally contributed $15,500 to their church's War Sufferers' Relief Fund; earlier, men from a Friends New England camp raised over $1,000 for Greek relief by fasts, contributions, and a benefit program of music and drama. . . . Several Brethren units organize[d] communitywide relief drives [of] clothing and money and shipped boxes of food, medical supplies, and clothing to Europe.[9]

When he was in Sideling Hill, Ben mentioned giving money for a collection, but at the State Hospital, Ben did not. The letters during his time in Rhode Island fixated on preparations for the coming baby, and I suspect that their financial difficulties weighed more heavily on his mind. At this time Ben and Miriam would have been on the receiving end of what they called "love gifts" or "love offerings," which was probably not a comfortable place to be. Generosity and helping is part of the identity of my family, passed down through the generations, but it is difficult to ask for and accept help when we are the ones in need.

Generosity with time and resources, willingness to serve, and doing so without compensation was a testimony of their faith. But CPS men like my grandfather were certainly not perfect, and their efforts to help were not necessarily uniformly adopted throughout all camps in the United States. Either way, the financial burden of CPS fell on the peace churches and the members of those churches. And the people of those churches gave money, clothing, canned goods, and supplies to support the conscripted men in CPS camps. "All together, the churches and the c.o.'s raised over $7,000,000 to pay the expenses of C.P.S.,"[10] and with donations of canned and dried foods, the peace churches gave to foreign relief efforts as well.

Conclusion

Aᴺᴰ ɴᴏᴡ ᴡᴇ'ᴠᴇ ᴄᴏᴍᴇ ᴛᴏ ᴛʜᴇ ᴇɴᴅ, ᴏʀ *ᴀɴ* ᴇɴᴅ, ᴀᴛ ʟᴇᴀsᴛ. Cɪᴠɪʟɪᴀɴ Public Service (CPS) was certainly not a perfect system, and the conscientious objectors (COs) within the CPS system were certainly not perfect people, as if those even exist. Through Ben and Miriam's letters, through their small, ordinary, and yet extraordinary history, we can see the humanity of two members of this system, their sincerity and their flaws, the good and the bad. I do not think that Ben or Miriam would want to be upheld as an example of virtue, of Christian nonresistance, or even of people doing good in the world. Having such attention paid to them, their beliefs, and their actions probably would have embarrassed them. Neither of them would have wanted to be noticed for living the best lives they knew how to live or to be honored for living those lives. They wanted only to be faithful to God, to Christ, to their church, to their way of life, and to each other.

Yet in 2020, seventy-five years after their CPS story ended, because of the letters they shared, we are able to see them as they were. Their day-to-day lives are exposed to us in ways that they would also probably find embarrassing, but through those letters, we are able to honor a couple who persevered, who expressed their faith in word and in deed, who were faithful to one another, and who served "the least of these" in a mental hospital.[1] As a researcher, I find value in telling their story with as much accuracy and detail as possible. As a granddaughter, I worry that telling their story violates their trust, their memory, or the needs of the larger family. Family history writing (FHW) methodology is at a nexus point of such conflicts. The methodology "bundles" stories and archival work as a "process of constructing a community memory."[2] Grappling with this positionality of the researcher, this conflict of what to tell, what not to tell, the fragility of memory, and the duties to family honor are the subject of this final chapter.

The truth is that few in my family knew much of anything of Ben and Miriam's time in CPS. Most knew that they were COs, that they were in CPS (whatever that was), and that they went to Rhode Island. Without having talked to every member of my family, it is hard to know exactly how much some knew, but I can say for certain that I knew nothing about any of it except that Miriam taught Ben to do needlepoint or something like that at some point. My father has been surprised over and over by the stories I have shared with him as I have written the book, and I suspect that my extended family will read this book with great interest, in fact, because it tells a story that they simply did not know before.

So what of this story? Why did none of us know about it? Clearly events during the war and their experiences apart and together in CPS were significant to Ben and Miriam. These years shaped them, for better or for worse, into different people than when they started, but apparently, they talked little of it upon their return to Indiana after the war ended, or at least they did not talk about it much to their children in the decades after their return. In fact, the letters rarely discussed what would happen after their time in CPS was over. Early on, Ben's letters from Sideling Hill expressed his desire to be at home with Miriam in their little house and his wish that "this terrible war" would just hurry up and be over. As newlyweds living apart, their desire to be together is understandable and explains why they fixated on all the "loving" they would make up for when Ben finished his service. But in the letters from Rhode Island, after more than two years in service, Ben only spoke once expressing what he hoped for after their time was done:

> [January 20, 1945]
> Pop has mentioned several times about the experiences we're having now will quickly Pass and will only seem like a dream. I'm afraid he doesn't realize it is such a great reality. Let that be as it may, I'll still be glad to get back to normal living and try to forget.

By saying that the time will pass quickly and "seem like a dream," Benjamin Sr. was probably trying to comfort Ben and Miriam to help them persevere through the difficulties of CPS. There, there, it will all be over soon. But Ben noted that his father simply could not understand just how significantly the experience had already changed them and how much they must continue to endure. Whatever their changes and experiences, though, Ben simply wanted to *forget*.

Wanting to forget seems an appropriate response for those who came home from the harsh realities of the war. Men and women had seen and experienced the worst that mankind can do to itself, and in that era, posttraumatic stress disorder was not yet an understood psychological diagnosis. Instead, that generation, the Greatest Generation, had a stiff-upper-lip, pull-yourself-up-by-the-bootstraps mentality. Keep calm and carry on, as the Brits would say. The postwar years focused not on remembering or processing horrible experiences but on the future, on getting back to "normal," and on making babies. Ben and Miriam were no different, though they did not face the war itself. They wanted to forget the harsh realities of working in a mental hospital, the troubled minds within the walls, the smell of industrial floor polish, their boredom in the off-hours, the financial strain, and the single, tiny room they had called their own.

Others who had served in CPS wrote memoirs, polished up small histories like *The Seagull* that account for their time and experiences, or wrote large-H histories of the events (many of which have been invaluable in the writing of this book). Some individuals and churches dove further into postwar relief efforts overseas or in efforts at home to change the mental healthcare system. Many of the histories and historians talk of the significant, positive, life-changing impact the CPS experience had on individuals, on the church, and on the world. But Ben or Miriam simply wanted to forget and get on with living, which they did in large part.

Then there is that lumpy cardboard box of letters. If their goal was truly to forget and move on, why save their letters? Sentimentality most likely played a role in that decision. They had shared a lot in those letters, and the conduit and platform they represented was a foundation for their marriage. Saving love letters was and is common practice. Recall that Miriam spoke early in their dating relationship of having stumbled upon her parents' love letters. Similarly, they saved, and I have in my personal archive, love letters between Benjamin Sr. and Lulu from more than one hundred years ago. These letters are elements of a tangible, material past as well as an emotional past. It only makes sense that Miriam saved the letters because they represented their early years of marriage and the new and growing love they had for each other.

Yet, the letters certainly contain information that they would not necessarily want to share with a broader public. My mother has told me to burn her journals after she dies because what is contained within them is for her eyes only. I will certainly honor that request. She wrote her journals in private and the only intended audience was herself. Letters pose a different conundrum because they were shared and meant to be read by another, sometimes several others. One of the biggest challenges of FHW methodology is the skeletons in closets, the buried stories, and the dirty laundry. There are elements of the past that many believe should be left quietly in the past. Sometimes, those elements are stories of abuse, adultery, or illegal or illicit activities. Sometimes, those elements are simply embarrassing or painful memories that folks who experienced them would just rather not remember.

In light of all of this, how does a researcher using FHW methodology proceed when, on the one hand, Ben and Miriam did not talk much about their experiences and even stated that they wanted to forget, but on the other hand, they saved a box that documents those experiences and stories, which have value in being shared with others? Further questions then arise: Where are the lines drawn for what is acceptable or appropriate to share? What are the ramifications on the family if I tell this story? What are the losses if I do not? It is here in that conflicted, gray space that FHW methodology exists. Answering these questions is part and parcel of archival and family history research. Negotiating one's position between private and public, between researcher and family member, between fact and memory, these are the elements I find most fascinating in FHW methodology. What distinguishes it from other qualitative research methodologies, and what distinguishes small histories from larger social histories? Examining letters "remind[s] us of the fragility of human relationships and the way in which historical knowledge is built on fragmentary and scattered sources. . . . Letters can give us a sense of the intimate impact of public events. . . . They encourage us to think about the drama of war as encompassing a greater range of emotions and a bigger cast of characters than the stock romantic picture of the soldier and his sweetheart."[3]

Family history writing, in this case in letters, helps us "examine the process by which individual stories are transformed into history, and history into nationalist myths."[4] Preserving the letters, examining them as conduit and platform, and then sharing the letters through a text such as this one helps us to "hold onto the conviction of those who experienced war that every desk, and every life interrupted, mattered."[5] Every life matters, and every story matters. Through stories, we are able to see the breadth and depth of the changes wrought by the war. And the more stories we have, the more we preserve and share, "the more ammunition we possess to resist simplistic generalizations about what the war did to . . . society and what it meant to those who live through it."[6] Jacqueline Royster writes,

> We all deserve to be taken seriously, which means that critical inquiry and discovery are absolutely necessary. Those of us who love our own communities, we think, most deeply, most uncompromisingly, without reservation for what they are and also are not, just set aside our misgivings about strangers in the interest of the possibility of deeper understanding (and for the more idealistic among us, the possibility of global peace). Those of us who hold these communities close to our hearts, protect them, and embrace them; those who want to preserve the goodness of the minds and souls in them; those who want to preserve consciously, critically, and also lovingly the record of good work within them must take high risk and give over the exclusivity of our rights to know.[7]

We must be vulnerable and share our stories, our communities, with the hope of others learning and then being careful with what we treasure.

As writers and readers of a small history such as Ben and Miriam's, we invest in the lives and experiences of individuals. We come to know them and know the circumstances they lived within. Not only do we protect and cherish those stories, we are connected to them differently from how we were before; we become invested in their story. Might we then also be impacted to change our own behaviors based on their experiences? Are the crafting of family history and archival history a means by which we might learn and grow and do better than our ancestors? I would like to think so.

Family history writing *changes us* as researchers and as people. Having compiled a small history, having written that small history for others to read and learn from, has changed me. I would estimate that most students who have done FHW projects in my classes would say the same. By telling Ben and Miriam's story, I become responsible to it and to them, and responsible for it and for them. Ben and Miriam are no longer "just" my grandparents or parents to my father. I can no longer think of them only as the plump and comfortable, soft hugging grandparents I knew as a child; in my memory they now are also young and hardworking, passionate, opinionated, and strong-willed. My very *memory* of them has been altered, though I did not actually know them at ages seventeen and twenty in 1943. I have invested time and emotional energy into telling their story, and my own story has been impacted by theirs. Further, knowing the history of how we treated the mentally ill has changed my perspective on current conditions in the mental health field. It has allowed me to see those with visible mental illness with newer, kinder eyes. And it has enabled me to view my own mental health with a different, more understanding perspective.

This methodology embraces the mushy gray area between emic and etic, between objectivity and the personal, and uses that gray area as an asset rather than a liability that must be corrected. As researchers, particularly qualitative researchers, we cannot ever be truly neutral. We cannot be distanced and objective outsiders, though we might pretend to be so. FHW methodology does not even pretend. It *expects* that the research will change us, in part because it is about our family or someone we know therefore it is about "us," and in part because all stories matter, particularly those that the large-H historical accounts have previously silenced.

So how does one end a family history text such as this one? One letter saved from 1946 was from their Aunt Roz (I am uncertain whose aunt she actually was). It seems that they were still serving in CPS at that time and that they were considering sending Miriam back home again to have their second child, my Aunt Connie, that April. We know no more beyond that last letter from a family member. Ben and Miriam's story clearly continued, as I am a product of that story, and I am sitting here writing about it, but there seems to be no clean way of ending this small history. To say "they lived happily ever after" would trivialize both the story we do have and the one they went on to live. Instead, let us end by returning to their letters, to that conduit and platform, to see their perseverance and love for one another one more time.

On November 30, 1944, Ben wrote one letter to Miriam that is typical of those from Rhode Island in its descriptions of daily activities and efforts in the workshop. But there is a break in the normalcy of the letter, and it is clear that time passed between writing the first half and the second. When Ben resumed writing, his handwriting was the messiest, by far, of any of his letters in the entire collection. He had just found a special letter that Miriam left for him before she left for Goshen, and they reestablished the conduit and platform of letter writing for their time apart.

> And oh sweetheart you don't know or can't guess how happy I am. I'm crying so now I can hardly write and oh honey I've read your letter this 4 times already twice on my Knees at our Bed side and I Pray God that I can live up to your opinion of me. Oh Mimmie Darling I'm really not so much as you think I am I'm Just Plain Me. And Oh I think back of how many times and how many days I could have expressed my love more in little things and also word and also actions oh Honey I'm so happy and yet I'm Crying as I write and can hardly make my Pen say what I'd like for it too.

Ben repeated himself a lot over the next six pages He practically babbled on paper, reiterating that he was crying and was so in love with her.

> In my feeble way I'll try to explain and tell you How much you really mean to me Honey. Darling you are the sweetest most lovable, adorable woman in the world. I'm sorry I told you to be a "good girl" Honey when I left you as soon as I said it I was sorry because you are the only woman in the whole world as for as I'm Concerned. I've tried to tell you many times how much I loved you but know I couldn't express my innermost thoughts like I'd like to. all the tongues and languages, words and Vocabularies could never express my love for you Only God above can fathom it. I don't even know can't even tell my self of the great depths of our love and the love I have for you. It's something so great that it makes me soooo small in comparison.

Ben finished the lengthy, emotional letter with a poem that he called "a Crude bit of Verse Darling but it helps a little ~~bit~~ to express my deep emotions and The Love You and I share."

> (To the Best wife a man ever had)
> You are the Joy of My Life.
> My sweetheart, My Wife—
> You're all in the whole world to me—
> Oh Honey, I Love You So.
> Much More than you know
> You mean all the whole world to me.
>
> Tho' You're gone a thousand Miles,
> I can still see your smile,
> Your Words of love—linger in my heart—

I Pray the Time will soon be,
When Darling You and Me
Can Meet again-Never More to Part.

You know I love you dear,
And want you ever near
Oh sweetheart I'll always be true
I'll think of you each day,
While you're so far away:
My Darling I Love only you.
------------------------------and I do LOVE YOU

Toward the end of the lengthy letter, Ben wrote something that embodied the reality of these letters between them. He said, "Darling I really should get to bed it's going on 11:00 I hate to stop writing tho' I'm afraid it'll seem as tho' a spell is broken. These ^are our Sacred Moments together even tho' you're there and I'm here." These letters meant so much more to them than keeping abreast of news. Here in their small history we see one last time the depth of their connection and how the letters performed as both a conduit for their love and relationship, and a platform upon which they continued to build and grow that love and relationship. Letters functioned as so much more than *ars dictaminis* that make visible a business or legal transaction. Ben and Miriam's small history was captured, and the moments they shared writing and reading these handwritten letters are, indeed, sacred.

Notes

Introduction

1. Sibley and Jacob, *Conscription of Conscience*, 126.
2. Luke 6:27–36, New American Standard Bible.
3. Sinor, *Extraordinary Work*, 184.
4. Sinor, *Extraordinary Work*, 182.
5. Morris, "Archival Turn in Rhetorical Studies," 113.
6. Sinor, *Extraordinary Work*, 4.
7. Hobbs, *Elements of Autobiography and Life Narratives*, 4.
8. Rumsey, "Family History Writing."
9. Sharer, "Traces of the Familiar," 55.
10. Montgomerie, *Love in Time of War*, 18–19.
11. Montgomerie, *Love in Time of War*, 6.
12. Sinor, *Extraordinary Work*, 10.
13. Montgomerie, *Love in Time of War*, 6.
14. Barton and Hall, *Letter Writing*, 1.
15. Montgomerie, *Love in Time of War*, 6.
16. Montgomerie, *Love in Time of War*, 16–17.

Chapter 1

1. Barton and Hall, *Letter Writing*, 1.
2. Sinor, *Extraordinary Work*, 17.
3. Bazerman, "Letters," 16.
4. Bazerman, "Letters," 16.
5. Barton and Hall, *Letter Writing*, 5 (quoting M. Trolle-Larsen, "What They Wrote on Clay," in *Literacy and Society*, ed. Karen Schousboe and Mogens Trolle-Larsen [Copenhagen: Akademisk Forlag, 1989]).
6. Bazerman, "Letters," 17.
7. Bazerman, "Letters," 18.
8. Fleckenstein, "Decorous Spectacle," 112.
9. Murphy, *Rhetoric in the Middle Ages*, 202.
10. Fleckenstein, "Decorous Spectacle," 113.
11. Fleckenstein, "Decorous Spectacle," 116.
12. Murphy, *Rhetoric in the Middle Ages*, 222.
13. Murphy, *Rhetoric in the Middle Ages*, 222.
14. Murphy, *Rhetoric in the Middle Ages*, 223.
15. Murphy, *Rhetoric in the Middle Ages*, 223.
16. Murphy, *Rhetoric in the Middle Ages*, 223.
17. Murphy, *Rhetoric in the Middle Ages*, 223.
18. Schultz, "Letter-Writing Instruction," 110.

19. Montgomerie, *Love in Time of War*, 3–4.
20. Fleckenstein, "Decorous Spectacle," 114.
21. Montgomerie, *Love in Time of War*, 4.
22. Bazerman, "Letters," 18.
23. Schlereth, *Material Culture*, 3.
24. Montgomerie, *Love in Time of War*, 55–57.
25. Montgomerie, *Love in Time of War*, 3.
26. Montgomerie, *Love in Time of War*, 63.

Chapter 2
1. Sleeter, "Critical Family History," 12.
2. Bailey, *They Counted the Cost.*

Chapter 3
1. *Selective Service Regulations.*
2. Rumsey, "Heritage Literacy," 575–76.
3. *Selective Service Regulations.*
4. Matthews, *Smoke Jumping*, 21.
5. Matthews, *Smoke Jumping*, 23.
6. Bowman, *Brethren at War*, 270.
7. Bush, *Two Kingdoms, Two Loyalties*, 70.
8. Kovac, *Refusing War Affirming Peace*, 14.
9. Sibley and Jacob, *Conscription of Conscience*, 45.
10. Sibley and Jacob, *Conscription of Conscience*, 111.
11. Matthews, *Smoke Jumping*, 25.
12. Sibley and Jacob, *Conscription of Conscience*, 112.
13. Sibley and Jacob, *Conscription of Conscience*, 112.
14. Matthews, *Smoke Jumping*, 30–31.
15. Sibley and Jacob, *Conscription of Conscience*, 110.
16. Matthews, *Smoke Jumping*, 5.
17. *Turnpike Echo*, vol. 1, no. 20, November 28, 1942, personal collection of Pennsylvania Department of Conservation and Natural Resources Ranger Shawn Lynn, also found in Mennonite Central Committee Archives, Akron, PA (hereafter MCC Archives).
18. Matthew 5: 38–39, New American Standard Bible.
19. Sibley and Jacob, *Conscription of Conscience*, 19–20.
20. Luke 6:27–36, New American Standard Bible.
21. Eisan, *Pathways of Peace*, 20–21.
22. Eisan, *Pathways of Peace*, 66.
23. Matthew 5:9, New American Standard Bible.

Chapter 4
1. Montgomerie, *Love in Time of War*, 25.
2. Montgomerie, *Love in Time of War*, 25.
3. Keim, *CPS Story*, 38.

Chapter 5
1. Okawa, "Unbundling," 96.
2. Sinor, *Extraordinary Work*, 13.

3. "Sideling Hill CCC."
4. *Fulton Democrat*, October 26, 1933, quoted in "Sideling Hill CCC," 4.
5. "Sideling Hill CCC," 15.
6. Hershey quoted in Keim, *CPS Story*, 32.
7. Hershey quoted in Keim, *CPS Story*, 38.
8. Camp Commission Memorandum, National Service Board of Religious Objectors (NSBRO), May 5, 1941, MCC Archives.
9. Correspondence from CCC Headquarters to District Commanding General, 1941, MCC Archives.
10. Correspondence from CCC Headquarters, 1941, p. 60, MCC Archives.
11. L. B. Hershey, Correspondence, 1941, p. 14, MCC Archives.
12. "Sideling Hill CCC," 18.
13. *Turnpike Echo*, November 12, 1942, personal collection of Pennsylvania Department of Conservation and Natural Resources Ranger Shawn Lynn, also found in MCC Archives.
14. *Turnpike Echo*, vol. 1, no. 20, 1942, personal collection of Pennsylvania Department of Conservation and Natural Resources Ranger Shawn Lynn, also found in MCC Archives.
15. Sibley and Jacob, *Conscription of Conscience*, 209.
16. *Statement of Policy, Camp Operations Division of the Selective Service System, the "McLean Statement,"* released 1942, quoted in Sibley and Jacob, *Conscription of Conscience*, 511.
17. NSBRO Work Reports, Sideling Hill, November 1942, MCC Archives.
18. *Turnpike Echo*, November 28, 1942, personal collection of Pennsylvania Department of Conservation and Natural Resources Ranger Shawn Lynn, also found in MCC Archives.
19. Work Report to the NSBRO, Sideling Hill, November 1942, MCC Archives.
20. *Turnpike Echo*, vol. 1, no. 20, 1942, personal collection of Pennsylvania Department of Conservation and Natural Resources Ranger Shawn Lynn, also found in MCC Archives, Akron, PA.
21. Montgomerie, *Love in Time of War*, 29, 134.
22. Sibley and Jacob, *Conscription of Conscience*, 130.

Chapter 6
1. Sinor, *Extraordinary Work*, 3.
2. Brock et al., *Beyond Rosie*, xvi.
3. Brock et al., *Beyond Rosie*, xxvii.
4. Bentley, *Eating for Victory*, 3.
5. Brock et al., *Beyond Rosie*, xxviii.
6. Bentley, *Eating for Victory*, 4.
7. Sibley and Jacob, *Conscription of Conscience*, 217.
8. Crespi, "Public Opinion," 289.
9. Roosevelt, "If You Ask Me."
10. Frazer and O'Sullivan, "Forgotten Women," 48.
11. Correspondence between Eleanor Roosevelt and Paul Comly French, Executive Secretary for the National Service Board for Religious Objection, June 14, 1944, Swarthmore College Peace Collection, Swathmore, PA.
12. Roosevelt, "My Day, June 21, 1944," emphasis added.
13. Roosevelt, "My Day, September 5, 1945."
14. Roosevelt, "My Day, March 29, 1947," emphasis added.
15. Sibley and Jacob, *Conscription of Conscience*, 220.
16. Sibley and Jacob, *Conscription of Conscience*, 46.

17. Goossen, *Women against the Good War*, 3, 4.

18. Goossen, *Women against the Good War*, 2.

19. Sibley and Jacob, *Conscription of Conscience*, 220.

20. Gingerich, *Service for Peace*, 87.

21. *Conscientious Objector*, October 1943, p. 6, MCC Archives.

22. US Census Bureau, "Average Population."

23. Frazer and O'Sullivan, "Forgotten Women," 47.

24. Sibley and Jacob, *Conscription of Conscience*, 124.

25. Fox, "Woman Domestic Workers," 338.

26. Fox, "Woman Domestic Workers," 339.

27. Fox, "Woman Domestic Workers," 347.

28. Fox, "Woman Domestic Workers," 338.

Chapter 7

1. US Census Bureau, "Median Home Values."

2. Bazerman, "Letters and Social Grounding," 18.

3. Bazerman, "Letters and Social Grounding," 19.

Chapter 8

1. Including a print of Norman Rockwell's *Freedom from Want* in the book proved to be cost prohibitive. To view this image, simply search the phrase "Freedom from Want" in an internet browser or go to en.wikipedia.org.

2. *Turnpike Echo*, December 8, 1942, personal collection of Pennsylvania Department of Conservation and Natural Resources Ranger Shawn Lynn, also found in MCC Archives.

3. *Turnpike Echo*, January 5, 1943, personal collection of Pennsylvania Department of Conservation and Natural Resources Ranger Shawn Lynn, also found in MCC Archives.

4. *Turnpike Echo*, January 5, 1943, personal collection of Pennsylvania Department of Conservation and Natural Resources Ranger Shawn Lynn, also found in MCC Archives.

Chapter 9

1. *Turnpike Echo*, November 28, 1942, personal collection of Pennsylvania Department of Conservation and Natural Resources Ranger Shawn Lynn, also found in MCC Archives.

2. Sibley and Jacob, *Conscription of Conscience*, 210.

Chapter 10

1. Boym, *Future of Nostalgia*, xii.

2. Rumsey and Nihiser, "Expectation, Reality, and Rectification," 135–51.

3. Kirsch and Rohan, *Beyond the Archives*, 3.

4. Kirsch and Rohan, *Beyond the Archives*, 3.

5. Kirsch and Rohan, *Beyond the Archives*, 4.

6. Kirsch and Rohan, *Beyond the Archives*, 8.

7. Campbell, "Afterword," 305.

8. Sharer, "Traces of the Familiar," 54.

9. Sharer, "Traces of the Familiar," 54.

10. Sharer, "Traces of the Familiar," 54.

11. Rumsey, "Heritage Literacy," 573–86.

12. Hurd et al., *Institutional Care*, 545.

13. Hurd et al., *Institutional Care*, 547.

14. Hurd et al., *Institutional Care*, 549.
15. Hurd et al., *Institutional Care*, 558.
16. Bruce DeSilva, "Are We Not Our Brothers' Keeper?" *Providence Journal, Sunday Magazine*, December 6, 1981, 14.
17. DeSilva, "Brothers' Keeper," 18.
18. Hurd et al., *Institutional Care*, 563.
19. Sareyan, *Turning Point*, 63.
20. DeSilva, "Brothers' Keeper," 18.
21. Hurd et al., *Institutional Care*, 565.
22. DeSilva, "Brothers' Keeper," 18.
23. Rochefort, "Three Centuries of Care," 121.
24. Rochefort, "Three Centuries of Care," 121.
25. Hurd et al., *Institutional Care*, 569.
26. Jones, *Dark Days*, 4.
27. Katherine Burt, *The History and Development of Public Welfare in the State of Rhode Island and Providence Plantation*, report to Public Welfare Administration, 1930, Rhode Island Historical Society Archives, Providence.
28. Jones, *Dark Days*, 7.
29. Jones, *Dark Days*, 8.
30. Jones, *Dark Days*, 32.
31. DeSilva, "Brothers' Keeper," 19.
32. *Specifications for a Kitchen and Service Building for the State Hospital at Howard, R.I.*, Rhode Island Institute of Mental Health (Cranston), Rhode Island Board of Control and Supply State Medical Center (Cranston) (Providence: E. L. Freeman, State Printers, 1914), Rhode Island Historical Society Archives, Providence.
33. *Specifications for a Men's Ward for the State Hospital, Howard, R.I.*, Rhode Island Institute of Mental Health (Cranston), Rhode Island Board of Control and Supply State Medical Center (Cranston) (Providence: E. L. Freeman, State Printers, 1914), 19, Rhode Island Historical Society Archives, Providence.
34. *Specifications for a Men's Ward*, 129–30.
35. Jones, *Dark Days*, 27.
36. Jones, *Dark Days*, 33.
37. Jones, *Dark Days*, 33.
38. Jones, *Dark Days*, 33–34.
39. Burt, *History and Development of Public Welfare*, 49.
40. Taylor, *Acts of Conscience*, 204.
41. Taylor, *Acts of Conscience*, 204.

Chapter 11

1. Eisan, *Pathways of Peace*, 206.
2. Selig Greenberg, "Mennonites Help to Solve Institution Labor Problem: Conscientious Objectors Staff State Hospital. Tribute Paid to Workers," *Providence Evening Bulletin*, November 11, 1943.
3. *The Howard Reservation*, Legislative Commission Study Report to the General Assembly, (1971), 10, Rhode Island Historical Society Archives, Providence.
4. "Enumeration Districts—1940 Census," Department of Commerce, Bureau of the Census 16-3, Rhode Island, Providence County, p. 20, Rhode Island Historical Society Archives, Providence.

5. DeSilva, "Brothers' Keeper," 32.

6. Greenberg, "Mennonites Help."

7. Greenberg, "Mennonites Help."

8. Greenberg, "Mennonites Help."

9. Greenberg, "Mennonites Help."

10. Sareyan, *Turning Point*, 62.

11. Taylor, *Acts of Conscience*, 202.

12. Information on Paul Goering's service is available at civilianpublicservice.org.

13. Taylor, *Acts of Conscience*, 202.

14. Gingerich, *Service for Peace*, 228.

15. *The Seagull*, unpublished manuscript of CPS Camp #85, Howard, RI, folder 14/63, series IX-13-1, A, p. 7, MCC Archives.

16. *Seagull*, 7.

17. *Seagull*, 8.

18. *Seagull*, 8.

19. *Seagull*, 8.

20. *Seagull*, 7.

21. *Seagull*, 8.

22. *Seagull*, 8.

23. Clark and Burgess, "Work of Conscientious Objectors," 130.

24. Gingerich, *Service for Peace*, 214–15.

25. *Seagull*, 9.

26. *Seagull*, 58–59.

27. Correspondence between Mary E. Corcoran and the U.S. Public Health Services, October 29, 1943, MCC Archives.

28. Taylor, *Acts of Conscience*, 202.

29. "Civilian Public Service Official Work Report," December 1943, MCC Archives.

30. Taylor, *Acts of Conscience*, 205.

31. Brown, "Mentally Ill Criminals," 8–9.

32. Brown, "Mentally Ill Criminals," 13.

33. Brown, "Mentally Ill Criminals," 88.

34. Brown, "Mentally Ill Criminals," 7.

35. Brown, "Mentally Ill Criminals," 8.

36. Brown, "Mentally Ill Criminals," 75–76.

37. Brown, "Mentally Ill Criminals," 86.

38. Brown, "Mentally Ill Criminals," 93.

39. *Seagull*, 10.

40. Greenberg, "Mennonites Help."

41. Greenberg, "Mennonites Help."

42. Greenberg, "Mennonites Help."

43. Eisan, *Pathways of Peace*, 207.

44. "Civilian Public Service Official Work Report," December 1943, MCC Archives.

45. Eisan, *Pathways of Peace*, 207.

46. Al Benglan, "Custodial Care," *Viewpoint* 1.3 (December 1, 1943).

47. Sareyan, *Turning Point*, 62.

48. Sareyan, *Turning Point*, 90.

49. *Seagull*, 13.

50. Benglan, "Custodial Care."

51. *Seagull*, 7.
52. Sareyan, *Turning Point*, 53.
53. Eisan, *Pathways of Peace*, 214.
54. Eisan, *Pathways of Peace*, 214.
55. *Seagull*, 9.
56. Eisan, *Pathways of Peace*, 234–35.
57. Eisan, *Pathways of Peace*, 236.
58. Sareyan, *Turning Point*, 51.
59. Eisan, *Pathways of Peace*, 236–37.
60. *Handbook of Restraint*, CPS orientation handbook, quoted in Eisan, *Pathways of Peace*, 236.
61. Golden and Schneider, "Custody and Control," 121.
62. Golden and Schneider, "Custody and Control," 121.
63. Golden and Schneider, "Custody and Control," 121.
64. Information on Leonard E. Gerber is available at civilianpublicservice.org.
65. Information on Springfield State Hospital is available at civilianpublicservice.org.

Chapter 12
1. Huey, "Problems of Timber Products Procurement."
2. *Newsette*, October 27, 1944, Rhode Island Historical Society Archives, Providence.

Chapter 13
1. US Department of Labor, "History of Federal Minimum Wage Rates."
2. Campbell, "Women as Workers," 86.
3. US Department of Labor, *Occupational Outlook Handbook*, 161.
4. US Census Bureau, "Historical Census of Housing Tables Gross Rent."
5. Sibley and Jacob, *Conscription of Conscience*, 120.
6. *Statement of Policy*, Mennonite Civilian Public Service, September 16, 1943, quoted in Sibley and Jacob, *Conscription of Conscience*, 309.
7. Sibley and Jacob, *Conscription of Conscience*, 309.
8. Matthew 5:38–48, New American Standard Bible.
9. Sibley and Jacob, *Conscription of Conscience*, 154.
10. Sibley and Jacob, *Conscription of Conscience*, 326.

Conclusion
1. Matthew 25:40, New American Standard Bible.
2. Okawa, "Unbundling," 94.
3. Montgomerie, *Love in Time of War*, 5.
4. Montgomerie, *Love in Time of War*, 135.
5. Montgomerie, *Love in Time of War*, 135.
6. Montgomerie, *Love in Time of War*, 132.
7. Royster, "First Voice You Hear," 33.

Bibliography

Ackerman, John, and David Coogan. *The Public Work of Rhetoric: Citizen-Scholars and Civic Engagement*. Columbia: University of South Carolina Press, 2013.

Bailey, Keith. *They Counted the Cost: The History of the Dunkard Brethren Church from 1926 to 2008*. Nappanee, IN: Evangel Press, 2009.

Barton, David, and Nigel Hall. *Letter Writing as a Social Practice*. Philadelphia: John Benjamins Publishing, 2000.

Bazerman, Charles. "Letters and the Social Grounding of Differentiated Genres." In *Letter Writing as a Social Practice*, edited by David Barton and Nigel Hall, 15–29. Philadelphia: John Benjamins Publishing, 2000.

Bennett, Scott H. "American Pacifism, the 'Greatest Generation,' and World War II." In *The United States and the Second World War*, edited by G. Kurt Piehler and Sidney Pash, 258–92. New York: Fordham University Press, 2010.

Bentley, Amy. *Eating for Victory: Food Rationing and the Politics of Domesticity*. Urbana: University of Illinois Press, 1998.

Boym, Svetlana. *The Future of Nostalgia*. New York: Basic Books, 2001.

Brock, Julia, Jennifer Dickey, Richard Harker, and Catherine Lewis. *Beyond Rosie: A Documentary History of Women and World War II*. Fayetteville: University of Arkansas Press, 2015.

Brown, Phyllis. "A Study of Mentally Ill Criminals at the State Hospital for Mental Diseases, Howard, Rhode Island, October 1941." Master's thesis, Brown University, 1942.

Bush, Perry. *Two Kingdoms, Two Loyalties: Mennonite Pacifism in Modern America*. Baltimore: Johns Hopkins University Press, 1998.

Campbell, Jean. "Women as Workers: A Statistical Guide." US Women's Bureau, Washington, DC, 1953.

Campbell, JoAnn. "Afterword: Revealing the Ties That Bind." In *Nineteenth-Century Women Learn to Write*, edited by Catherine Hobbs, 303–12. Charlottesville: University Press of Virginia, 1995.

Clark, Robert, and Alex Burgess. "The Work of Conscientious Objectors in State Mental Hospitals during the Second World War." *Psychiatric Quarterly Supplement* 22, no. 1 (1948): 128–40.

Crespi, Leo P. "Public Opinion toward Conscientious Objectors: IV. Opinions on Significant Conscientious Objector Issues." *Journal of Psychology* 19 (1945): 277–310.

Dierks, Konstantin. "The Familiar Letter and Social Refinement in America, 1750–1800." In *Letter Writing as a Social Practice*, edited by David Barton and Nigel Hall, 31–41. Philadelphia: John Benjamins Publishing, 2000.

Eisan, Leslie. *Pathways of Peace, a History of the Civilian Public Service Program, Administered by the Brethren*. Elgin, IL: Brethren Publishing House, 1948.

Enoch, Jessica. "Changing Research Methods, Changing History: A Reflection on Language, Location, and Archive." *Composition Studies* 38, no. 2 (2010): 47–73.

Fleckenstein, Kristie. "Decorous Spectacle: Mirrors, Manners, and *Ars Dictaminis* in Late Medieval Civic Engagement." *Rhetoric Review* 28, no. 2 (2009): 111–27.

———. "Once Again with Feeling: Empathy in Deliberative Discourse." *JAC: Rhetoric, Writing, Culture, Politics* 27, nos. 3/4 (2007): 701–16.

Fox, Grace. "Woman Domestic Workers in Washington, D.C." *Monthly Labor Review* 54 (1942): 338–59.

Frazer, Heather T., and John O'Sullivan. "Forgotten Women of World War II: Wives of Conscientious Objectors in Civilian Public Service." *Peace and Change* 5, nos. 2/3 (1978): 46–51.

Gingerich, Melvin. *Service for Peace.* Scottsdale, PA: Herald Press, 1949.

Gold, David. "Remapping Revisionist Historiography." *College Composition and Communication* 64, no. 1 (2012): 15–34.

Golden, Janet, and Eric C. Schneider. "Custody and Control: The Rhode Island State Hospital for Mental Diseases, 1870–1970." *Rhode Island Historical Society* 41, no. 4 (1982): 121.

Goossen, Rachel Waltner. *Women against the Good War: Conscientious Objection and Gender on the American Home Front, 1941–1947.* Chapel Hill: University of North Carolina Press, 1997.

Hall, Nigel. "The Materiality of Letter Writing: A Nineteenth Century Perspective." In *Letter Writing as a Social Practice*, edited by David Barton and Nigel Hall, 83–108. Philadelphia: John Benjamins Publishing, 2000.

Hamilton, Robin, and Nicolas Soames, eds. *Intimate Letters.* London: Marginalia Press, 1994.

Huey, Ben Meyer. "Problems of Timber Products Procurement during World War II, 1941–1945." Master's thesis, University of Montana, 1951.

Hurd, Henry M., William F. Dewey, Richard Dewey, Charles W. Pilgrim, G. Alder Blumer, and T. J. W. Burgess. *The Institutional Care of the Insane in the United States and Canada.* Vol. 3. Baltimore: Johns Hopkins University Press, 1916.

Jones, Henry A. *The Dark Days of Social Welfare at the State Institutions at Howard, Rhode Island.* Providence: Rhode Island Department of Social Welfare, 1943.

Keim, Albert N. *The CPS Story: An Illustrated History of Civilian Public Service.* Intercourse, PA: Good Books, 1990.

Kirsch, Gesa, and Liz Rohan, eds. *Beyond the Archives: Research as Lived Process.* Carbondale: Southern Illinois University Press, 2008.

Kirsch, Gesa E., and Jacqueline Jones Royster. *Feminist Rhetorical Practices: New Horizons for Rhetoric, Composition, and Literacy Studies.* Carbondale: Southern Illinois University Press, 2012.

Kovac, Jeffrey. *Refusing War Affirming Peace: A History of Civilian Public Service Camp No. 21 at Cascade Locks.* Corvallis: Oregon State University Press, 2009.

Kraybill, Donald B., and Carl F. Bowman. *On the Backroad to Heaven: Old Order Hutterites, Mennonites, Amish, and Brethren.* Baltimore: Johns Hopkins University Press, 2001.

Matthews, Mark. *Smoke Jumping on the Western Fire Line: Conscientious Objectors during World War II.* Norman: University of Oklahoma Press, 2006.

Montgomerie, Debora. *Love in Time of War: Letter Writing in the Second World War.* Auckland, New Zealand: Auckland University Press, 2005.

Morris, Charles, III. "The Archival Turn in Rhetorical Studies; or, The Archive's Rhetorical (Re)turn." *Rhetoric and Public Affairs* 9, no. 1 (2006): 113–15.

Murphy, James J. *Rhetoric in the Middle Ages: A History of Rhetorical Theory from Saint Augustine to the Renaissance.* Berkeley: University of California Press, 1974.

Okawa, Gail Y. "Unbundling: Archival Research and Japanese American Communal Memory of U.S. Justice Department Internment, 1941–45." In *Beyond the Archives: Research as Lived*

Process, edited by Gesa Kirsh and Liz Rohan, 93–106. Carbondale: Southern Illinois University Press, 2008.

Ratcliffe, Krista. "Rhetorical Listening: A Trope for Interpretive Invention and a 'Code of Cross-Cultural Conduct.'" *College Composition and Communication* 51, no. 2 (1999): 195–224.

Rochefort, David. "Three Centuries of Care of the Mentally Disabled in Rhode Island and the Nation, 1650–1950." *Rhode Island History* 40, no. 4 (1981): 111–32.

Rohan, Rebecca. *"You Write, He'll Fight": An Analysis of World War II Letters from American Women 1941–1945*. Bachelor's thesis, University of Wisconsin, Eau Claire, 2011.

Roosevelt, Eleanor. "If You Ask Me." *Ladies Home Journal* 61 (June 1944): 38. Accessed July 5, 2017. http://www2.gwu.edu.

———. "My Day, March 29, 1944." *The Eleanor Roosevelt Papers Digital Edition*. Accessed July 5, 2017. https://www2.gwu.edu.

———. "My Day, June 21, 1944." *The Eleanor Roosevelt Papers Digital Edition*. Accessed July 5, 2017. https://www2.gwu.edu.

———. "My Day, September 5, 1945." *The Eleanor Roosevelt Papers Digital Edition*. Accessed July 5, 2017. https://www2.gwu.edu.

Royster, Jacqueline. "When the First Voice You Hear Is Not Your Own." *College Composition and Communication* 47, no. 1 (1996): 29–40.

Rumsey, Suzanne Kesler. "Cooking, Recipes, and Work Ethic: Passage of a Heritage Literacy Practice." *Journal of Literacy and Technology* 10, no. 1 (2009): 69–95.

———. "Heritage Literacy: Adoption, Adaptation, and Alienation of Multimodal Literacy Tools." *College Composition and Communication* 60, no. 3 (2009): 573–86.

Rumsey, Suzanne Kesler, and Tanja Nihiser. "Expectation, Reality, and Rectification: The Merits of Failed Service Learning." *Community Literacy Journal* 5, no. 2 (2011): 135–51.

Sareyan, Alex. *The Turning Point: How Men of Conscience Brought about Major Change in the Care of America's Mentally Ill*. Washington, DC: American Psychiatric Press, 1994.

Schlereth, Thomas J., ed. *Material Culture: A Research Guide*. Lawrence: University Press of Kansas, 1985.

Schultz, Lucille M. "Letter-Writing Instruction in 19th Century Schools in the United States." In *Letter Writing as a Social Practice*, edited by David Barton and Nigel Hall, 109–30. Philadelphia: John Benjamins Publishing, 2000.

Selective Service Regulations. Vol. 3, *Classification & Selection, 1940*. Swarthmore College, Military Classifications for Draftees. Accessed June 10, 2015. https://www.swarthmore.edu.

Sharer, Wendy. "Traces of the Familiar: Family Archives as Primary Source Material." In *Beyond the Archives: Research as Lived Process*, edited by Gesa Kirsh and Liz Rohan, 47–55. Carbondale: Southern Illinois University Press, 2008.

Sibley, Mulford Q., and Philip E. Jacob. *Conscription of Conscience: The American State and the Conscientious Objector, 1940–1947*. Ithaca, NY: Cornell University Press, 1952.

"Sideling Hill CCC, CPS, POW Camps of Fulton County, Pennsylvania." *Fulton County Historical Society* 25, no. 2 (2004): 1–56.

Sinor, Jennifer. *The Extraordinary Work of Ordinary Writing: Annie Ray's Diary*. Iowa City: University of Iowa Press, 2002.

Sleeter, Christine. "Critical Family History: Situating Family within Contexts of Power Relationships." *Journal of Multidisciplinary Research* 8, no. 1 (2016): 11–23.

Stewart-Winter, Timothy. "Not a Soldier, Not a Slacker: Conscientious Objectors and Male Citizenship in the United States during the Second World War." *Gender and History* 19, no. 3 (2007): 519–42.

Taylor, Steven J. *Acts of Conscience: World War II, Mental Institutions, and Religious Objectors.* Syracuse, NY: Syracuse University Press, 2009.

US Census Bureau. "Average Population Per Household and Family: 1940 to Present." Accessed May 17, 2019. www.census.gov.

———. "Historical Census of Housing Tables Gross Rent." Accessed May 17, 2019. www.census.gov.

———. "Historical Census of Housing Tables Home Values." Accessed May 15, 2019. www.census.gov.

———. "Median Home Values: Unadjusted." Accessed May 15, 2019. www.census.gov.

US Department of Labor. "History of Federal Minimum Wage Rates under the Fair Labor Standards Act, 1938–2009." Accessed May 13, 2019. www.dol.gov.

———. *Occupational Outlook Handbook: Employment Information on Major Occupations for Use in Guidance.* Bulletin No. 940. Washington, DC: Bureau of Labor Statistics, 1949. Accessed May 13, 2019. babel.hathitrust.org.

Witt, Ronald. "Medieval 'Ars Dictaminis' and the Beginning of Humanism: A New Construction of the Problem." *Renaissance Quarterly* 35, no. 1 (1982): 1–35.

Index

Page numbers in italics refer to figures. Benjamin Elias Kesler Jr. is abbreviated below as B; Miriam Elizabeth Kesler, M; Ben and Miriam, B&M. There are some individuals mentioned in the book for whom a first name or surname is unknown; they are indexed under the name provided in the text and with additional parenthetical identification.